# THE SEA
# TAKES NO
# PRISONERS

# THE SEA TAKES NO PRISONERS

### The Men and Ships of the Royal Navy in the Second World War

Edmund S. Wong

UNIFORM

UNIFORM

Published by Uniform
An imprint of Unicorn Publishing Group
5 Newburgh Street
London W1F 7RG

www.unicornpublishing.org

A catalogue record for this book is available from the British Library

5 4 3 2 1

ISBN 978-1-911604-28-0

Cover design Unicorn Publishing Group
Typeset by Vivian@Bookscribe

Printed and bound in Spain

PICTURE CREDITS

Peter Swarbrick pp.8, 10, 15, 87; Alamy pp.17, 31, 106, 157, 168, 205, 210, 224, 234, 246, 323; HMS Ramillies Assoc. p.70; Wikimedia Common pp.24, 25, 37, 48, 51, 61, 66, 71, 94, 96, 97, 123, 128, 130, 136, 141, 148, 163, 166, 185, 187, 190, 198, 205, 232, 251, 252, 253, 259, 271, 274, 289, 295, 297, 302, 310, 316, 320, 327, 329, 332, 342, 344, 351; naval-history.net p.249; Library of Congress p.218; pp.71, 153, 167, 200, 278 Model ships built and photographed by author. The entire collection can be viewed at https://www.worldwar2navies.wordpress.com

# CONTENTS

# ONE
# BEFORE THE WAR

By 1930, the Royal Navy was planning for a fleet that would include a total of 70 cruisers. Cruisers, well-armed and capable of high speeds and long ranges, were designed to operate independently and far from home to either protect friendly seaborne commerce or to disrupt or destroy that of enemy nations. In peacetime they would often visit far flung ports and 'show the flag'. The Navy's cruisers could quickly reach ports overseas to render assistance in times of disaster and thus exhibit Britain's friendship and good will. At other times, the mere presence of a Royal Navy warship in a foreign port or offshore would serve notice that Britain was keeping a keen eye on her national interests and that she possessed sufficient power to protect them. As 1939 approached, the Royal Navy could count on a total of sixty-three cruisers. Two-thirds of them were twenty years or less in age. Nineteen additional cruisers were under construction.[1]

### 'We Were Sent ... to Stop Illegal Immigrants'
### HMS *Galatea* in the Middle East

HMS *Galatea* was one of the four light cruisers of the *Arethusa* class built between 1934 and 1936. These cruisers were at times criticized for carrying only six 6-inch guns. Their advocates reasoned that enemy commerce raiders were generally converted merchant ships that would not be heavily armed, but would be slow and unarmoured. The heavier shells and quick firing guns carried by the *Arethusa* class cruisers were deemed more than adequate for maintaining security in the shipping lanes.

The Royal Navy maintained a heavy presence in the Mediterranean even well before the outbreak of war. The Mediterranean Fleet was stationed at

HMS *Galatea*

Malta which, with its ample natural harbour and well developed shipyard infrastructure, was well suited for its role as a naval base. The importance of the Suez Canal meant the Royal Navy was always busy showing the flag to all and any who might consider challenging British control of the seas from Gibraltar to Suez. Turmoil was as prevalent in the late 1930s as it is today in the eastern end of the Mediterranean.

When HMS *Galatea* made a port call at Haifa in 1938, London's promise of independence to the British Mandated Territory of Palestine was yet to be fulfilled. Matters were complicated by a different British promise: support of a Jewish homeland in that very territory. The Arabs were in revolt against British rule. Petty Officer Ronald Palmer remembered the times and a shore excursion while *Galatea* was anchored at Haifa.

*We were sent to the eastern end of the Mediterranean to stop illegal (Jewish) immigrants from entering (the British Mandated Territory) ... This meant stopping innumerable ships and searching them, also scouring the sea for small craft, no easy job and lots of sea time. (We went) to Haifa for a rest on one occasion and we could not roam the town freely because of the troubles ... Throughout Palestine were outposts of the Palestinian Police, a body of very tough British men who daily took their lives in their own hands. On average one of them was killed each day.*

*Galatea was the flagship of the destroyers and therefore carried an Admiral and his staff. This Admiral was a great friend of the man in charge of the Palestine Police and through him arranged a wonderful excursion for some 200 of the ship's company. When notice of this journey was posted on the notice board, we realised that there might be some danger. A Palestine Policeman would be in each of the coaches (buses). Also one in ten of the sailors had to be fully armed with rifle and ammunition. Reaching and embarking the coaches we found we would have an escort of three armoured cars, two in front and one in the rear. The first of these kept several hundred yards in front of the convoy, searching for any signs of land mines or other dangers. We did pass the shot riddled remains of a motor car at one place.*[2]

The tour went off without incident as the men were taken to the village of Nain where Jesus performed the miracle of raising the widow's son, and then to Nazareth for a visit to the Churches of the Annunciation and St. Joseph. The sailors also enjoyed stops at Cana where Jesus turned water to wine, the Mount of the Beatitudes, and the Sea of Galilee.

## 'Showing the Flag'
## HMS *Ajax* in the Americas

The *Leander* class light cruiser HMS *Ajax* displaced about 7,000 tons and was armed with a main battery of eight 6-inch guns in four twin turrets, four 4-inch guns, a number of small caliber automatic weapons for air defense, and two sets torpedo tubes. The ship's original antiaircraft battery would have been woefully inadequate during the war and was to be repeatedly updated as time and resources permitted throughout the years of conflict.

*Ajax* was assigned to the 8th Cruiser Squadron stationed at *Royal Naval Dockyard*, Bermuda.[3] The pre-war years provided the crew with an interesting variety of experiences that included a call to Kingston, Jamaica in 1938 to assist with riot control. The global depression had contributed to the discontentment of the local labour force. The workers were mostly unskilled agriculture labourers and as the economic crisis deepened so did their frustrations. Civil unrest was

HMS *Ajax*

brewing when crewmen from the cruiser were sent ashore to lend support to the police at Kingston and at Montego Bay.

Seaman Eric Smith had just turned eighteen in 1938 when *Ajax* received the urgent call from the governor of Jamaica for assistance in containing unruly mobs that were too large for local law enforcement to handle. There was looting and property damage in Kingston. A platoon of marines armed with rifles and another of sailors from *Ajax* were landed in the city to confront one particularly large and vociferous crowd. Seaman Smith remembered that, except for one entrenching tool handle per man, the platoon of sailors was unarmed. He was very nervous as he faced a crowd of about 2,000 locals who were overturning trams and wrecking nearby property. Smith did not think that he or his fellow sailors, with their sticks in hand, would be much of a match for the rampaging mob. Of the contingent of sailors, only the platoon leader was armed. He fired a round or two from his revolver into the air. Much to the relief of Smith and his fellow *Ajax* sailors, the crowd suddenly and quietly dispersed.

Smith was sympathetic with the locals. He had watched from the ship as labourers lined up at the docks to load banana boats. The need for work was such that the line of men regularly extended beyond the waterfront and into the town. Each man would be given a tally sheet that was marked for every stalk of bananas he carried into a ship's hold. After dropping his load, a labourer would trudge back to the end of the line. Smith calculated that at a penny per stalk, a man spending twelve hours waiting in line to load bananas could earn about a shilling a day. His own comfort, while in Jamaica was not lacking however. He was assigned to protect the ship's locally hired refuse scow operator from assault or theft by the host of begrudging boat owners clustered nearby. In appreciation, the scow's owner would give Smith fresh fruit that included coconuts, bananas, and mangoes. All were welcomed supplements to his shipboard diet.[4]

January 1939 found the cruiser on a port call at Valparaiso, Chile when an earthquake measuring over 8.0 on the Richter scale struck. The number of fatalities was estimated to exceed 30,000. The ship's crew turned out to assist as best they could.

At the moment the earthquake struck, Stoker Charles Maggs was ashore having dinner with friends. He noticed that the wine in his glass was sloshing around. He was thinking that Chilean wine must be a very strong variety when one of his dinner companions shouted, *terremoto!* – Spanish for earthquake. He hurried back to his ship. The crew was organised into work and rescue parties. Maggs remembered that after working for several days in the summer heat of the Southern Hemisphere he had to wear a respirator to staunch the odor of decaying corpses as he helped dig them from ruined buildings. Afterwards, as a sign of appreciation, the Chilean Navy commissioned a commemorative plaque for the ship, but *Ajax* sailed before it could be presented. *Ajax* never returned again to Chile. Years later, however, Maggs attended a British veteran's reunion to which he had invited the Chilean ambassador. The story of the ship's assistance and the lost plaque was told and the ambassador promised to look into it. Shortly afterward, the plaque was delivered and it has since been placed aboard each successive Royal Navy ship to be named *Ajax*. The Municipality of Concepción also issued commemorative medals to the crews of *Ajax* and the heavy cruiser *Exeter* for their earthquake assistance. The two ships were further honoured when a city street was named for each of them.[5]

After a brief return to Bermuda, *Ajax* was sent to join the Navy's South American Division based in the Falkland Islands. Among the cruiser's crew was Samuel Shale who had left school at fourteen to work as a butcher's boy before joining the Royal Marines at age seventeen. He felt that, by entering the service, he would be able to contribute financially to his family. He was soon able to send two shillings per week home to his mother. He eventually made, as planned from the outset, a full career of the service in order to earn a pension and enjoy long-term financial security.

In late August 1939, *Ajax* had a port call to Rio de Janeiro cut short as war grew imminent. The ship landed all non-essential equipment and accoutrements and the crew worked extensively to reach full operational readiness. The 6-inch gun crews drilled long and often. Shale remembered the keen competition between the four turrets to earn bragging rights for being the fastest in a 10-shell rapid fire competition. Ammunition and powder charges were sent up to each turret from first, the magazine, and then the handling room. The gun breech would be opened and the loader would pick up a shell that weighed about 112 pounds to place in position for the rammer to push into the gun by hand. The powder bag that weighed about 13½ to 14½ pounds was hand placed behind the projectile, a firing tube was inserted, the breech was closed, and a warning bell sounded, 'ding-ding'. Both guns of a turret fired simultaneously and the process was repeated. Fingers got smashed, toes and ankles got broken, and arms and legs were mangled but, according to Shale, 'it was all a part of the business'. Shale started out as the rammer in Marine manned X turret, but was disappointed that his gun was not the ship's fastest. Shale convinced a fellow Marine on the gun, the loader, to trade places in order to take advantage of Shale's greater physical strength. Within a week X turret had become the fastest.[6]

*Ajax* was operating in a trade defense role in the South Atlantic when war was officially declared between England and Germany in September 1939. The cruiser immediately intercepted two German merchant ships in the waters around the River Plate region. The German vessels were scuttled.

### 'I Was Too Young and Green to Have Charge of Much of Anything' HMS *Renown* and HMS *Hood* collide

The Royal Navy of the 1930s had three battlecruisers in its fleet: HMS *Hood*, *Repulse* and *Renown*. *Renown* commissioned in late 1916 but, was regularly updated through the years. She was completely reconstructed from 1936–1939. Frequent trips to the yard by both *Renown* and sister *Repulse* in the interwar years led to them being derisively referred to as, 'Refit' and 'Repair', respectively. *Renown* was almost 800 feet long, could steam at over 32 knots, and carried six 15-inch guns in three well protected turrets. Along with the Navy's other battlecruisers, *Renown* was built to chase down and destroy enemy cruisers and commerce raiders.

John Lang, the son of a retired civil servant, entered the Royal Navy as a teen aged midshipman by way of Britannia Royal Naval College, Dartmouth. He studied a heavy curriculum of math and science designed to prepare young men for careers as naval officers. In addition to general studies, the college provided instruction in seamanship. Lang 'absolutely loved' his time as a student there. During 1934 he was aboard the training cruiser *Frobisher* for two training cruises; the first of which took him to Northern Europe and Scandinavia, and the second of which brought him to the Mediterranean.

Lang described his time aboard the cruiser as 'absolute bliss' as he felt that, even when spending a lot of time scrubbing decks, he was a 'real sailor'. His studies of navigation, seamanship, and engineering continued during his eight months aboard the training cruiser. He went to *Renown* in 1935 as a midshipman. He recalled an incident between his ship and battlecruiser *Hood* that took place shortly after he reported aboard *Renown*.

*… very soon after sailing for the spring cruise we joined up with the 'Mighty Hood'. There were always two ships at sea from the battlecruiser squadron, the third one which was the* Repulse *was refitting. On the way out to Gib for our part of the exercises we joined up with* Hood *off Portsmouth and we were going down the Portuguese coast for an exercise with the two ships some ten to twelve miles apart … and at the end of the exercise, about lunchtime, the two ships were instructed to close … and we proceeded to close … I was Assistant Midshipman of the Watch (and on the bridge)… too young and green to have the charge of (much of anything) by myself, and I remember that the two ships got closer and closer and closer. And as we were forming up the captain was on the bridge with the navigating officer and his anxiety was very clear, in his voice, saying, 'Navigating*

*Officer, we're getting very close,' and the Navigating Officer said, 'Oh, yes.*
*It's quite alright. The* Hood *will turn to the course and we will form up*
*astern of her.' Well, what didn't happen was the* Hood *didn't turn to the*
*course … but carried on and the two ships bumped our bow into her stern.*
*I remember … watching and first of all, feeling the effect of the engines*
*of* Renown *… going emergency full speed astern … and the whole mast*
*absolutely shaking and the vibration. On the foc'sl below, as it was the*
*lunch hour, a lot of the sailors had been to the head, the toilets, which were*
*always in the fore part of the ship as they had been in Nelson's time, and*
*you could see them all piling up the ladder of the foc'sl hatch and pulling*
*their trousers up.*[7]

When war began, *Renown* was sent to patrol the south Atlantic for German
raiders – especially the large armoured cruiser *Graf Spee*. The German ship was
more powerful than any other ship type of the day except for a battlecruiser or
a battleship. Ships such as *Graf Spee* were especially feared by the Admiralty
who believed them fully capable of singlehandedly destroying British shipping.

### 'Training … Made a Man of Me'
### HMS *Warspite* in Barcelona

Designed in 1912 and completed in 1915, HMS *Warspite*, a battleship of the
*Queen Elizabeth* class earned her first battle honour for her role in one of
history's most memorable fleet actions: the Battle of Jutland in 1916. *Warspite*
received thirteen major calibre shell hits from ships of the German High Seas
Fleet at Jutland and suffered enough damage to have to be ordered out of the
battle line for her own safety. She was extensively modernised from 1935 to1937
and, despite her age, she would see extensive World War II service in the Arctic,
Mediterranean, Indian Ocean and English Channel.

George Nye and his family lived and worked in India. The family was back
in England for a visit when it was decided that young George should remain
with an aunt to continue schooling while his parents returned to India. Nye,
16 at the time, did not want to do that, so he hopped on the back of a friend's
motorbike to go to Chatham where he joined the Navy as a boy seaman. He

HMS *Warspite*

trained at HMS *St. Vincent* which took some getting used to for him as, after being accustomed to a 'soft life in India', life as a Royal Navy boy trainee was 'very harsh'. He most clearly recalled suffering the punishment of being hit with the flail-like stonnachie, climbing the very high sailing ship mast, and having to do his own laundry. At the end of his first month he asked, as was allowed, to be released. Although three classmates accepted their releases Nye was dissuaded from doing so. In the end Nye was glad that he persevered because the training, as so many others would attest, 'made a man of me'. He added that it also most likely helped him survive the war. He joined *Warspite* in 1937.

Nye's first duty aboard the battleship occurred while she was docked at Barcelona in the midst of the Spanish Civil War. *Warspite* was in Spain to promote general European neutrality in hopes of limiting the scope of what was an extremely vicious war, and to protect or evacuate British citizens endangered by the fighting. Although Nye did not understand the conflict at the time, it was very evident to him that the civilian population was under great pressure to just get by on a day-to-day basis. He drew guard duty on dockside trash bins filled with the ship's food scraps and, armed with a rifle and bayonet, was supposed to prevent civilians from scavenging through them. He found the task distasteful as visibly suffering women and children, driven by hunger, clambered to the bins and fought against one another over every scrap and morsel. Unable to bear what he was seeing, Nye turned his back.

Numerous shipmates, motivated by political beliefs that made them sympathetic to Spain's liberal Republicans in their fight against the Nationalists who were supporters of fascism, deserted the ship to join in the struggle. Nye, originally apolitical, was only later able to understand the fervor of those caught up in anti-fascist movements at home and even aboard his ship. Later, at Gibraltar, Nye had the opportunity to board and tour the German battlecruisers *Gneisenau* and *Scharnhorst* that were anchored there. The German ships, like *Warspite*, were in the region to encourage neutrality during Spain's war. Despite the fact that they would be deadly enemies barely a year later, Nye found the German sailors to be cordial and congenial hosts with whom he enjoyed conversing and sharing a smoke.

Life aboard a World War I-era battleship was not physically comfortable. With no air conditioning, the crew was, according to Nye, 'jammed together like cattle' in the mess decks where they slept, ate, and tried to relax when off duty. The food was not memorable but, at least, it was plentiful, and Nye recalled that it was generally 'not bad'. Compared to the destroyer on which he would later serve, however, life aboard *Warspite* was actually good. Nye remembered that the movement of the smaller ship at sea often made it difficult or even impossible to eat one's meals or to accomplish routine tasks. Seasickness aboard a small ship like a destroyer often reduced the ship's efficiency drastically. There was at least one case of a destroyer sailor who was so incapacitated by seasickness that he had to be landed after which he transferred to the Army.

In the fall of 1939, *Warspite* was heading to Naples for a port call when she was ordered back to Malta as war approached. The ship then transferred to Alexandria along with the rest of the Mediterranean Fleet when the British decided that Malta, just 50 miles south of Sicily, would be impossible to defend. The day on which war was declared against Germany Nye went ashore as soon as he was off duty and, with more than a few shipmates, got 'thoroughly plastered'. They were nervous and more than a little afraid because they simply did not know what the war would mean for them. Nye was especially concerned by memories of his father's World War I experiences, but he remained confident that the Royal Navy would be able to handle the Germans at sea if only because the British had more ships. Not long following Italy's June 1940 entry into the war, stories like the one that told of Italian battleship sailors jumping overboard at the mere sight of British warships began to circulate among Royal Navy sailors. Whether they were true or not, such accounts gave Nye and many of his shipmates the idea that the Italian fleet bore an unflattering 'big yellow streak'. *Warspite*'s sailors were realistic enough, however, to know that there would be times when the Italians, with their modern and well-built ships, would need to be taken seriously.[8]

## 'Do You Hear There? Prepare for War With All Haste'

If asked to name the most famous naval ship of World War II many would likely say, HMS *Hood* of the Royal Navy. Throughout the inter-war years *Hood* was the symbol of the Royal Navy's power and prestige. Built by John Brown & Company of Clydebank, Scotland, she was affectionately called 'Britain's

HMS *Hood*

Biggest Bullshittingest Bastard Built By Brown'. After her tragic encounter with the German battleship *Bismarck* in 1941 *Hood* would become a world-wide household name.

*Hood* was completed in 1920 with improvements based on lessons learned from the Royal Navy's battle cruiser losses incurred during the 1916 Battle of Jutland. The improvements included the strengthening of internal framing and the addition of heavier armour. At the time of her completion *Hood*'s armour was only slightly lighter than that of the US Navy's USS *Arizona*. Built at approximately the same time as *Hood*, the American battleship would be destroyed at Pearl Harbor when a Japanese bomb penetrated a forward magazine.

*Hood* was a handsome vessel and, given Britain's long tradition of maritime excellence, she inspired many of the young men who saw her to seek seaborne adventures in far off places through enlistment. Among those who also entered service aboard *Hood* at a tender age was Jim Taylor who reported on board in 1939, just three months shy of his seventeenth birthday. He was a boy first class who would gain eligibility for promotion to ordinary seaman when he turned eighteen. He had started as a thirteen-year-old who went to the naval training establishment at Holbrook as a way to help out with his family. His father had died the previous year and left Jim's mother with five children to care for. The school, founded for the orphaned children of seafarers, offered a maritime-based curriculum and required future entry into the sea services. Young Taylor enjoyed the discipline and training that he got at Holbrook. Two years later, as a boy second class, he moved on to the Royal Navy training establishment ashore at Gosport, HMS *St. Vincent*, where he continued to learn, grow, and thrive.

Life aboard *Hood* was challenging but not unpleasant for Taylor who remembered being well looked after. One big difference between life ashore and that aboard ship according to Taylor,

> *…was that we were allowed to smoke – something which had been absolutely forbidden until now. Although I was now in 'man's service', life was not nearly as hectic for me as it had been in the past … days became much more relaxed and easy … A big difference in the daily routine was that every morning first thing – before 7:00 am – we boys* (twenty of whom transferred to *Hood* with Taylor) *had to scrub the decks. The ship's*

*company in charge had sea boots but we boys were barefooted. A hose pipe was basically thrown over the side of the ship and sea water pumped over the decks until it was nearly ankle deep. The water was dark and very cold and as it washed into the scuppers it got colder still. Eventually one was left on a damp deck colder than you could imagine. If your toes were knocked, as they frequently were, they were too cold to bleed. This deck washing was probably my pet hate in the Navy …*

*… We were studying and we had a schoolroom aboard. We had two hour's schooling and about an hour's homework each day. A typical day on board (included activities like) rise and shine at 7:00 am, lash up and stow hammocks, wash, breakfast, and clean the mess decks. Then (it was) hand's to quarters, clean guns, and assemble at one's part of the ship to be detailed off for* (assigned to) *one of 101 jobs. The boys were not allowed to smoke except at specified times, though I think that the regimen was not so strict for the men. On a lot of occasions the whole ship's company performed 'evolutions'* (shipboard tasks or drills) *such as streaming the paravanes* (mine countermeasure devices towed overboard) *or collision mats – this was all very hard work. After dinner we had school, then more jobs and exercises … Whilst I was in* Hood *my action station was in the aloft director.*

*This was right atop the foremast above the spotting top. What a journey it was to get up there. Normally one would have to climb up the ladders on the outside of the mast struts. These could get very hot indeed from the gasses coming from the funnels. On one occasion I remember the hood of my duffel coat blew down off my head and the back of my neck was singed. Of course, when apart from the risk of burning there was the problem of staying on the ladder. Anyone who served in* Hood *will tell you how the ship pitched and rolled. I can testify to how bad it was when you were towards the top of the mast. Sometimes I would make my way up the inside of the mast struts. There were numerous electrical cables, wires, and junction boxes in there as well as the internal structure of the mast to get around. Having arrived at the spotting top I had to get through its roof to finally arrive at my action station.*[9]

Dick Turner was another youngster, although old enough to have been rated above the rank of boy, to serve in *Hood* in the 1930s. Unlike Taylor, his station was not high above *Hood*'s decks, but deep below them, in the engineering spaces. Turner fulfilled his boyhood dream of joining the Navy once he turned 18. After his initial training and a subsequent eight-week program in which he learned what he would need to know about the ship's propulsive machinery, he arrived aboard *Hood* in September 1936. His descriptions provide a detailed view of his duties, the nature of *Hood*'s engineering spaces, and certain aspects of an enlisted sailor's shipboard life in general.

*Normally my day station was in* Hood*'s middle engine room. She had three engine rooms in all. As a junior stoker my duties usually involved tending various machines and making sure that they were working correctly. The machines included: dynamos that were used to generate electricity throughout the ship, carbon dioxide machinery which was used for making ice and cooling the ship's (ammunition) magazines, evaporators which were used for making fresh water from sea water …  (and) many hydraulic systems …* Hood *had 24 boilers arranged in four groups of six boilers each. The boilers were normally cleaned in a 21-day cycle. There was a special team for this work. One set of six boilers would be closed down for maintenance and the ship would operate on the other three sets if we were at sea. The normal 'economical cruising speed' (for preservation of fuel) was 12 knots and* Hood *would make this speed on three sets of boilers without any difficulty. Progression from stoker 2 to stoker 1 came through training and familiarity with the various machines. Your divisional officer would occasionally grade you in a book that formed part of your records. The grades ran 'Superior', 'Very Good', 'Good', 'Satisfactory' and 'Unsatisfactory'. I was fortunate enough to be graded 'Superior' throughout my time in the Navy. To progress to stoker 1 you had to take a test although I cannot recall anyone ever failing it … Being such a large ship it was impossible to mix socially with many of the crew so you found yourself with a small group of close friends … In the quieter off duty moments in* Hood *I used to try my hand at swinging Indian clubs on the boat deck. I also remember many swimming races taking place alongside* *the ship. I was fortunate enough to get myself on the crew of one of the cutters, and we used to compete in the three-mile races. The less formal races were arranged between groups within* Hood. *A crew of stokers would take on a crew of seamen or marines. More serious races were between* Hood *and other ships. I never managed to get myself onto an inter-ship team, though.*[10]

Albert Pitman was born in Portsmouth. His father died when he was just one year old so he, his two brothers, and a sister were raised by his mother alone. The family was given 15 shillings per week in parish relief. Continued assistance was contingent upon the widow's good behavior. She earned some extra money through charring, or taking in laundry. Pitman enrolled in the Portsmouth Junior Technical School when he was twelve where he studied math, mechanics, chemistry, and physics. He learned mechanical drawing and worked in metal and woodworking shops as well. A good student, he used what he had learned to pass the Navy's Artificer Apprentice exam at just fifteen. His keen intellect allowed him to become an Ordnance Artificer by the time he reported aboard *Hood* in January 1939.

Pleased to be aboard *Hood* as a member of the ship's gunnery department, Pitman recalled that she was a 'marvellous looking ship', and he felt a great sense of pride in being a member of her crew. Only seventeen, Pitman was appreciative that the chief ordnance artificer (OA) to whom he was responsible took some care in his personal welfare. He was grateful for the chief's subtle way of discouraging him from visiting brothels by instructing him and another young and new crewman to go to one on an evening when the ship was anchored at Gibraltar. Pitman was surprised, but complied and carefully followed the chief's instructions to pick a brothel that had a bar, select the girl that he thought he would most enjoy being with, but to refrain from meeting her until he had taken several drinks and observed her for a while. Before long, Pitman watched the very pretty and charming girl he had selected go about her business of going up the stairs and coming back down again with sailor after sailor. The longer she did so, the less appealing she became. He left the place with a much deeper sense of appreciation and respect for his chief and without having done any worse than to buy a few drinks.

Pitman's chief OA was considerably more lax when it came to alcohol. The first drink served to Pitman aboard *Hood* was something that the youngster later remembered as a 'jolly good gin' that he assumed had been somehow snatched from the ward room. It turned out to be a concoction of spirits commonly found in the workshops and equipment of the gunnery department. Many of the men in his department enjoyed the tasty, if unhealthy, beverage that served as a good supplement to the allocated rum ration. This daily tot took place at about 11 o'clock each day on *Hood* when a large kettle filled with rum would be brought to a sailor's mess where the sailor appointed as mess president would measure and pour out an eighth of a pint per man. Lower ratings had their ration cut with water, but chiefs and petty officers were allowed to take theirs neat. It was, according to Pitman, about 120 proof. He added that he thought it was 'a quite a lot of rum' and that 'about a half of us (would be) plastered by lunch time'. Pitman also recalled that there was a general acceptance and tolerance of drinking on the part of the crew whenever the ship was in port. He and his shipmates particularly enjoyed the bars in Spain just across the border from Gibraltar because, for a mere four pence, they could get a schooner of Sherry and all the bread and meat they could care to eat. However inebriated a man might be, if he were able to walk up the gangway and properly salute the quarter deck and walk aft, he was allowed back aboard without question. If a man needed to be carried aboard, he would be placed into one of the cells in the ship's brig 'for his own safety' until the following morning and nothing further would be said about it.[11]

On 2 September 1939, Pitman was dressed in his best whites as he stood on deck waiting for a liberty boat to take him and some friends ashore to Invergordon, Scotland. There was a sudden interruption over the loud speaker:

> ... *Do you hear, there? ... All leave is cancelled ... the following signal has been received from the Admiralty ... Prepare for war with all haste. The ship will proceed to Scapa Flow.*

*Hood* steamed all night towards Scapa, and Pitman spent the time fusing shells stored in the ready room. There were AP, or armour piercing, fuses that delayed detonation until the shell had time to penetrate into a target's interior and instant fuses which allowed for immediate detonation and the creation of shrapnel. Pitman and his fellow ordnance ratings also got the explosive charges ready to be lifted to the turrets from the magazines. They carefully checked and rechecked the readiness of the guns.[12]

ENDNOTES

1.  Roskill, Capt. S. W. *White Ensign: The British Navy at War, 1939–1945*. Naval Institute Press. 1966. p. 25.

2.  Palmer, Ronald. 'Peddler's *Galatea* Service' in Strange, Jean, 'The Tragic Loss of HMS *Galatea*', yourtotalevent.com. Web. Accessed June 2014.

3.  _____ 'The Royal Navy Dockyard – Bermuda'. Thewestend.bm. Web. Accessed May 2014. Over the years the base contributed greatly to the economy of Bermuda by providing employment and training in skilled professions to the local population. Although closed by the Royal Navy in the 1960s, the facility continues to support Bermuda economically as a leading tourist attraction.

4.  Imperial War Museum. Sound recording archive. 9792. Smith, Eric. 1987.

5.  Imperial War Museum. Sound recording archive. 9377. Maggs, Charles. 1986.

6.  Imperial War Museum. Sound recording archive. 9410. Shale, Samuel. 1986.

7.  Imperial War Museum. Sound recording archive. 12503. Lang, John Robert. 1992.

8.  Imperial War Museum. Sound recording archive. 10764. Nye, George Thomas. 1989.

9.  Bevand, Paul (contributor). 'Jim Taylor – Wartime service in HMS *Hood*'. BBC WW2 *People's War*. Article ID A 8243372.

10. Bevand, Paul (contributor). 'Dick Turner's Wartime Memories – Part I: Joining Up and HMS *Hood*'. BBC WW2 *People's War*. Article ID A 8923124. 2006.

11. Imperial War Museum. Sound recording archive. 22147. Pitman, Albert. 2001

12. Imperial War Museum. 22147.

# TWO
# AJAX'S FIRST WAR PATROL

### 'We Made Contact With Our First Enemy Ship'

HMS *Ajax*

During the war's first year, German surface raiders were the principal worry for Britain's naval forces. The Royal Navy celebrated its first victory of the war when a force of its cruisers trapped and sank the powerful German raider *Graf Spee* in December 1939.

German pocket
battleship
*Graf Spee*

Light cruiser *Ajax* had been out to sea for two weeks when the war began. Marine Gunner Samuel Shale remembered that,

> *...on the day war was declared we made contact with our first enemy ship ... a German ship called the* Karl Fritzen *... and we took the crew on board Ajax and we sank her there and then as she stood. She was a merchant ship (and) we was in shipping lanes. And the second day we got another ship called* Ussukuma *and we did exactly the same thing to her, and they were all Germans and we took them aboard ... and they became our prisoners of war ... and we had to look after them and feed them ... there was plenty of room for them and they were fed and they had cigarettes and they seemed quite happy ... (we) used to see them (and) talk to them and (we) got to know them ... they were quite alright ... they knew the war was over for them; they'd been caught and that was it. They didn't hold anything against us; they knew we had a job to do... I had no axe to grind with them; they were just like me doing a job.*[1]

The third ship encountered by *Ajax* was the actual *Ussukuma* that stopped after receiving a shot across her bow from one of the cruiser's 4-inch guns. The German crew immediately took to lifeboats and headed over to *Ajax*. In the meantime, a boarding party of armed marines and stokers who would work the German ship's engines and take the vessel as a prize went over to *Ussukuma*. When they got there, they saw that the ship's sea cocks had been opened to prevent any salvage. She was allowed to sink. The German sailors were confined in *Ajax's* recreation space along with those of *Karl Franken* (called 'Fritzen' by Marine Gunner Shale) and those from another previously interdicted ship, *Olinda*. Several of the German mariners pointed out an SS officer among them who was then quickly separated from the rest. The prisoners were kept below decks except when allowed to get air and exercise on the foc's'l. *Ajax* eventually landed some on the Falklands and the rest were placed aboard a Royal Navy oiler for transport back to Europe.[2]

The British sailors aboard *Ajax* had little, if anything, against their Kriegsmarine counterparts. They had even gotten to know some German naval personnel in the pre-war period as recalled by Seaman John Henry Gates:

> *During the early part of our commission on the* Ajax *(1935–1936)* we had *been on Bermuda with a German sailing ship which had German cadets on it called the* Horst Wessel *and we had a fairly happy time with these cadets and these young chaps were about our own age … there was an island in Bermuda called Ports Island* (which) *was a part of the Naval Dockyard complex on which the various ships on station used to send their ships' companies to have a relaxing week or fortnight … and we met these German cadets off the* Horst Wessel *and we* (competed with them in) *rowing and sailing and swimming and as far as I was concerned they were just seamen.*[3]

The specific concern for *Ajax* and her division companions in those first days of war were the activities of the Kriegsmarine's three panzerschiffe surface raiders: *Graf Spee*, *Deutschland* (later renamed *Lützow*) and *Scheer*. *Graf Spee* had left port in late August and was instructed, a month later, to commence raiding operations. The British tracked her relentlessly. British intelligence as well as the ship's trail of activities alerted the Royal Navy that she was stopping and sinking shipping in the South Atlantic. Over the next two and one half months, *Graf Spee* sank or captured nine merchant ships. In early December, the *panzerschiff* stopped the merchant vessel *Doric Star* which got off a radio signal before being sunk. The next day, she attacked another merchant ship, the *Tairoa*, which also transmitted a distress message by radio. The signals gave the British force patrolling the area a good idea of *Graf Spee's* speed, heading, and destination. *Ajax*, heavy cruiser *Exeter,* and light cruiser HMNZS *Achilles,* under command of Commodore Sir Henry Harwood, made visual contact with the German raider on 13 December. She was not far from the River Plate which lies between Uruguay and Argentina in the area of Buenos Aires and Montevideo.

## 'Suddenly a Lookout Sighted Smoke on the Horizon'
### The Battle of the River Plate

*Graf Spee's* captain assumed that the warship masts her lookouts had sighted belonged to the escorts of an enemy convoy. He turned towards them and, as the tactical situation unfolded, maneuvered in attempts to keep out of range of what he soon realised would be 8-inch and 6-inch British guns. He stayed close enough, however, to allow his own 11-inch guns to be effective. The British divided their force in order to avoid concentrated fire from a ship that clearly outgunned theirs. *Ajax* and *Achilles* steamed together to the east of the German ship while Exeter steamed to her west. In a running gun battle that lasted a bit over an hour, *Exeter* was heavily damaged. Smoke screens and gunfire from the two light cruisers helped protect the heavy cruiser from even greater damage. The Germans later admitted that the *panzerschiff* did not close *Exeter* to finish her off for fear of the torpedoes that practically all British cruisers were known to carry. The British managed a number of gunfire hits on *Graf Spee* but, from their vantage point, they did not appear significant. Despite launching several such attacks, the British made no torpedo hits on *Graf Spee*. *Exeter* was forced to haul off to save herself, *Ajax* suffered gunfire damage which made her two aft turrets inoperable, and, although just lightly damaged, *Achilles* was low on ammunition. *Graf Spee's* captain was apparently concerned with the damage his ship had taken and continued to fret about the possibility of having more torpedoes launched against him. He surprised the British as much as some of his own officers when he broke off the action. *Graf Spee* entered Montevideo harbor for repairs. She also placed her wounded ashore for medical care and buried her dead.

*Ajax, Achilles,* and the recently arrived heavy cruiser *Cumberland* waited outside the mouth of the River Plate. Uruguay, mindful of the laws governing neutrality, could not allow the German ship to remain for a period longer than three days. *Graf Spee*, deliberately deceived by British news broadcasts on BBC into believing that an overwhelming force that included the battlecruiser *Renown* and the aircraft carrier *Ark Royal* was waiting for her nearby, slipped anchor on the 17th. Unwilling to expose his crew to what he thought was certain doom, the German captain, on advice from Berlin, sailed with just a skeleton crew. The Germans set timed scuttling charges aboard the ship which exploded and wrecked her. The *Graf Spee's* sailors then escaped by boat back to Montevideo. Shortly afterwards, the captain, perhaps second guessing his sudden breaking off of the battle, committed suicide by gunshot. He has been remembered kindly by his former adversaries as a gentleman of honour at whose hands not a single captured sailor died.

### 'Our Guns Were Getting So Hot'
### A View of the Battle From Gun Turret B [4]

Leslie T. Denis, a former petty officer aboard *Ajax* wrote the following about the battle with *Graf Spee*,

> *The morning of 13 December dawned fine and clear with a clear horizon. Three parts of the ship's company went to breakfast, and (the) Admiral to his cabin. Suddenly a lookout sighted smoke on the horizon and the alarm bells rang out. Most of the sailors were having a wash or were at breakfast following a night cooped up in the gun turrets on action stations. Mostly the hands arrived back at action stations clad only in shorts. It must have been the first time that a ship had gone into action with a half-naked crew! The Admiral was better dressed – with uniform jacket and pyjama trousers ... HMS* Exeter *attacked* Graf Spee *alone while* Ajax *and* Achilles

*attacked in company. My action station was director layer in B turret. The cabinet was a steel box, six feet by three feet and contained, besides myself, my sight setter and turret trainer. When the door was shut we were penned in. My job was to take over firing the turret if the Director up the mast was shot away. It was rather unnerving sitting there doing nothing while all hell was let loose outside. We were firing a salvo of 8X6-inch guns every 15 seconds at a range of 18,000 yards (nine miles). The* Exeter *was getting a hammering and was in a bad way and had to haul off with many fires on board … By this time our guns were getting so hot that they were expanding in their jackets, and more seriously we were running out of ammunition as we still had only a peacetime allowance. The two light cruisers closed the range and hammered the upper deck of the German pocket battleship until it was a shambles.* Graf Spee *then drew off and headed for Montevideo … By this time HMS* Cumberland *had arrived from the Falklands and was a valuable addition to our force … We withdrew out to sea and buried our dead.*

*On 17 December the* Graf Spee *slipped her moorings and proceeded out to sea … Shortly afterwards huge explosions were heard from her – she was on fire. All ships closed in as far as was safe and the order to cheer ship was given. The ships' companies cheered each other like mad.*[5]

### 'I'm Hit! I'm Hit!'
### The Battle As Seen From Turret X

Gunner Shale of the *Ajax's* Marine X turret offered his version of the battle between the three British cruisers and *Graf Spee* off Montevideo,

*Just after 6:15 am on the 13th of December, Action Stations was sounded … all we could see was a bit of smoke on the horizon … I was dressed in a pair of shorts and gym shoes and I started running to my gun position and as I reached the top of the ladder leading to X turret there was a massive explosion of 16-inch shells* (these were in fact 11-inch which Shale consistently misidentifies as 16-inch. *Ajax* was also hit by 5.9-inch shells from *Graf Spee*'s secondary battery guns) ... *within seconds I was at the rear door of X turret and went inside. Quickly we were loading and firing our six-inch guns. We were now in line ahead and the Exeter was in the rear ... all we saw at the moment was shells landing and the smoke on the horizon.* Exeter *was sent to investigate ... and as she broke off on a different course she was seen to be hit repeatedly by 16-inch shells but all three* (British) *ships carried on firing ... we altered course then to draw fire from* (Exeter) *... and it was then while we was carrying out this maneuver that we hit the control tower of the* Graf Spee *... and some of her ... guns were put out of action and we could see fires burning on her upper deck ... and in the meantime, the* Exeter *... had been hit again and again ... The next thing that happened, a smoke screen was laid across the* Exeter *to allow her to withdraw from the battle and to return to the Falkland Islands. ... the period that* Exeter *was in action lasted about 15 to 18 minutes ... she was in a terrible state. We started then a zig-zag move – the* Achilles *and the* Ajax *– and it was during one of these zig-zag moves that we were carrying out at increased speed some of the 16-inch shells hit the* Ajax *just above the waterline and came through the ship's side exploding underneath X turret ... they killed all the crew in the handling room that was just below us and at the same time that put X turret out of action. Corporal Bashford* (the rammer with whom Shale had traded places during the ship's gunnery competitions) *was hit and he just said to me, 'I'm hit; I'm hit' ... and his stomach just lay at my feet. The temperature inside that turret now was extremely hot; there was smoke and steam; bodies were covered in sweat and Corporal Buckley, during this period, had the presence of mind to flood the cordite* (explosive charge) *hoist to save the turret from blowing up ... we made certain that everything was safe in the turret, then we were given instructions to leave (it) ... as we came out ... we were to discover then that the shrapnel not only killed all the people beneath X turret ... in the handling room ... it had also carried on to another part of the ship and come out in a different area and put Y turret out as well ... We were then ordered to go down below to help with the dead and when we got down there, when you saw the carnage, it was a miracle that we hadn't been blown to pieces.*[6]

The British were as surprised as they were relieved to see *Graf Spee* suddenly break off the action. She did not immediately make for port, but lingered out of British gun range to fire an occasional shell in their general direction. By evening, however, she had gone. *Ajax* took the time to make what repairs she could and to bury her dead at sea. Shale spoke tearfully of his friend, Corporal Bashford,

> *We were mustered quietly on the quarterdeck to say farewell to our mates and friends and they were buried at sea in the traditional way... one my old friend, Corporal Bashford, who died in my place ... someone you can't ever forget after all these years.*[7]

The British sailors on their ships offshore followed events by normal radio broadcasts from Rio de Janeiro or Montevideo. They were even alerted by civilian radio to the fact that *Graf Spee* had slipped her berth on the 17th and was headed their way. At action stations, the men were aware that there were curious crowds all along the waterfront. Some local people had even taken to boats in order to follow whatever events would unfold. The crew of *Ajax* heard several loud explosions which they assumed was the *Graf Spee* opening fire.

Parade in London honouring the crew of HMS *Ajax* and HMS *Exeter* after the Battle of the River Plate

Still listening to the on-going local radio narrations, they soon realised that the *panzerschiff* had been scuttled and, satisfied that they had done their jobs, cheered in relief and in joy.[8]

### 'Frightened to Death'
### Other Views of *Ajax*'s Encounter With *Graf Spee*

Colin Mason left school at fourteen and worked as paper boy. He realised that the poor economy would offer him few prospects better than standing on street corners hawking papers. He joined the Navy as a boy seaman. He recalled that information aboard *Ajax* was not generally plentiful and the younger ratings did not often know what was happening outside of their routine and duties. In December 1939 he did understand, however vaguely, that *Ajax* had put to sea to 'look for something' that the talk in the lower deck suggested to him was 'an enemy ship'.

When action stations was called on the 13th, Mason went into the 6-inch gun director forward and above the bridge where he worked on an instrument called the inclinometer. His job was specific and simple. He had to look through the slit in the turret-like director, visually line up a set of pointers on a selected target, and allow another sailor to make note of its speed and heading. This information was relayed to a station below where it would be used to work out firing solutions on a mechanical computing device. Mason did not know what was happening until he heard voice reports from the bridge stating that *Exeter* had been hit. He continued with his duty of lining up his data collecting pointers and followed the action by listening to voice commands and messages from the bridge. He stated that he was 'frightened to death' but kept himself under control by remaining busy with his job. He had no sensation of the ship being hit and was unaware of any damage to *Ajax* until later. The firing of *Ajax's* guns and the concussion of their blasts masked all his other senses. Between gun discharges, he could hear the ship's spotter plane's radio reports of 'over', 'under', or 'straddle' that told the gunnery department how and where its shells were landing. As the ship began to close on the *panzerschiff* to launch a torpedo attack, Mason watched as they went closer and closer and wondered, 'Oh, God … how much closer are we going to get?' Only then did he realise, as he heard a report from the spotter plane, that the name of their adversary was *Graf Spee*. Unlike Marine Gunner Shale, Mason did not attend or even see the burial service held on the quarterdeck. Not for some time after the action did he even know that there had been casualties aboard *Ajax*, and he never actually saw any of those who had been killed or wounded.[9]

Frederick Cadby, a torpedoman, had an interesting, almost amusing, experience during the battle. He was assigned to a damage control party and merely stood by during action to await any call to make emergency repairs as they might be needed. When one of the gun turrets was hit, he made his way to it, but found that it had already been abandoned and sealed off. He stopped by an empty compartment on his way back to his duty station and picked up a magazine. He idly flipped through its even as *Ajax* continued to fight. He came to a story entitled, 'Five Minutes To Live', was immediately offended, so flung the journal across the deck and left.[10]

After *Graf Spee* had retreated to Montevideo the men on *Ajax* listened to BBC's deliberately false news reports about the force gathering outside the River Plate to await the *panzerschiff's* next appearance. Torpedoman Cadby and his shipmates did not know any better so they spent some anxious hours scouring the horizon and wondering just where the likes of *Ark Royal* and *Renown* could possibly be. All aboard *Ajax* understood that, even supported by *Achilles* and *Cumberland,* their ship would have little chance against *Graf Spee*. A plan for a special mission was devised. *Ajax* was the force flagship and, therefore, carried a sturdy and fast craft in the form of the Admiral's barge. A decision was made to place several depth charges aboard the barge, run it up close to the German ship when she sortied, and set the charges to detonate at a depth of 10 feet. Through great good fortune, they might just manage to sink the panzerschiff. Volunteers were requested and Cadby, 'like an idiot' who was by his own later admission, '... too young and foolish to know better' volunteered even though he knew that he would not likely make it back. In the end, the plan was not needed.[11]

## 'We Had a Whale of a Time'
## Celebrating the Navy's First Victory

After the action against *Graf Spee*, *Ajax* returned to Port Stanley in the Falklands to refuel. She then remained in the area on trade defense duty. She stopped for a port visit to Montevideo on New Year's Day, 1940 and a number of the crewmen were given bus tours of the city. There were crowds out and about to celebrate the New Year with singing and dancing, but many stopped to greet or cheer the British sailors and place offerings of flowers onto the tour buses. *Ajax* then weighed anchor to slowly make her way across the Atlantic. She arrived home at Plymouth at the end of January. The nation was more than ready to celebrate its first victory of the war.

Many of the crew made their way to London where Boy Seaman Mason recalled,

> *When we got back they had a march through London (and we) went to the Mansion House for tea with the Lord Mayor ... we had a whale of a time. We still had our cap bands on then ... with the name 'Ajax' on it (and) of course everywhere you went you got stopped by people wanting to shake your hand and one thing or another ... it certainly boosted us up and being the first naval action of the war it sort of boosted everybody's feelings up a bit.*[12]

Other crewmen reported that, once home, they were granted celebrity status by many whom they had only just met. Round after round of drinks were bought for them whenever they would find themselves in a pub. Leslie Bradley, who had hoisted signal flags aboard *Ajax* during the action with *Graf Spee*, also remembered the march in London and the days that immediately followed:

> *... we marched for two and a half hours and it was so loud the cheering (that) you couldn't even hear the band. Then we had dinner with Churchill at Guildhall and he gave a speech. Then when I went back to my hometown (in Lancashire), eventually (on leave) and I had to go round to all the schools. (At) the first one I didn't mention the River Plate but that's what they wanted ...there was 500 of these kids all asking me questions, 'how long was the ship?' 'how many crew?' -- you know ... and I had to stand at attention and salute while this girl sang (a patriotic song).*[13]

*Ajax* departed Plymouth for Chatham where she was paid off and put into the yard for refit that began in February. She had her damage repaired, guns updated, and received a reinforced mast onto which an air search radar set was installed. She also received the rather novel Mountbatten pink paint scheme. The color, promoted by Lord Mountbatten after he had observed ships of a similar color while at sea, was supposed to render a ship difficult to see in the low light of early morning or at dusk. While suitable in low light, the color had an opposite and highlighting effect in brighter light which resulted in a rather clear and sharp view of the ship during the hours around noon.[14]

ENDNOTES

1.  Imperial War Museum. Sound recording archive. 9410. Shale, Samuel. 1986.

2.  Imperial War Museum. Sound recording archive. 9742. Barrett, George William. 1987.

3.  Imperial War Museum. Sound recording archive. 9335. Gates, John Henry Bishop. 1986.

4.  The two forward gun turrets were designated A and B and the two turrets aft were X and Y.

5.  Denis, Leslie Thomas. 'Battle of the River Plate, December 1939.' BBC WW2 People's War. Article ID A 5954547. 2005.

6.  Imperial War Museum. 9410 (Shale).

7.  Imperial War Museum. 9410.

8.  Imperial War Museum. 9410.

9.  Imperial War Museum. Sound recording archive. 9336. Mason, Colin Edgar. 1986.

10. Imperial War Museum. Sound recording archive. 10205. Cadby, Fredercik. 1988.

11. Imperial War Museum. 10205.

12. Imperial War Museum. 9336 (Mason).

13. Imperial War Museum. Sound recording archive. 10205. Bradley, Leslie Cecil. 1987.

14. Raven, Alan. *Warship Perspectives: Camouflage Volume One: Royal Navy 1939–1941*. WR Press, Inc. 2000. pp. 19–21.

# THREE
# THE ROYAL NAVY'S BOY SEAMEN OF WORLD WAR II

Throughout Britain's history, the size and reach of the Royal Navy levied heavy demands for secure and easy access to legions of healthy young men. The infamous press gangs of sailing ship days that roamed the streets of England's ports or preyed upon poorly defended ships at sea helped fill the ranks to some extent. Reluctant men or boys, however, were not always willing or able to perform to the standards of service called for aboard His Majesty's ships.

The Marine Society, founded in 1756, was one of the very the first organisations that sought to support the Royal Navy's manpower needs with sailors who were not coerced into service, but who had freely undergone training to become professional seamen. The Society recruited youngsters whom it felt could benefit from learning skills that could help them to escape unemployment, poverty, homelessness or other less than desirable circumstances so often found ashore. Many of the day's disadvantaged youth, teenagers and even pre-teens, could be found in the seedier areas of town where they often fell into a culture of thievery, cheating, drunkenness, depravity, and lawlessness. The Society combed such districts for candidates to whom it could offer training for work aboard the nation's merchant or naval ships and the opportunity for a better life.[1]

In the early decades of the twentieth century a boy became eligible to enter naval service as a trainee at the age of fifteen years and three months. The typical volunteer of that era would go to a recruiter and present signed parental consent for him to join the Navy. The youngster would then sit for an initial interview that was to be followed by a general written exam and a physical exam. If deemed qualified, he would be accepted and sent home to await further instructions. Shortly afterwards he would be mailed a rail ticket along with specific instructions on where to report for the commencement of his naval career. In the years leading up to World War II the Navy maintained two shore establishments for the training of boys: HMS *Ganges* located near Shotley on the Suffolk coast, and HMS *St Vincent* in Gosport. During the war itself the boys were all relocated to the Isle of Man for their training as a measure of safety from Nazi air raids.[2]

A parade at HMS *St Vincent* training establishment in Gosport, Hampshire

Every trainee was expected to yield to strict discipline and to master sailing, navigation, small boat handling, knots and splices, rowing, rifle drill, signals, gunnery, nautical rules of the road, sewing and mending, and any other skill deemed appropriate for life in the Navy. The youngsters trained for about a year as second class boy seamen. At the end of their training they were assigned to the fleet as first class boy seamen. Upon continued satisfactory service, they would be promoted to ordinary seaman when they turned eighteen, at which time their obligatory twelve-year term of enlistment would begin. Any time served prior to reaching eighteen did not count towards the twelve-year enlistment, nor did it count towards any future pension.

On parade at HMS *Gangees* training establishment on the Suffolk coast

### 'You're In the Navy Now'
### The First Weeks

During the wartime era many boy volunteers such as Trevor Tipping found themselves under-employed if employed at all, bored, and eager for adventure. Back when the school leaving age was fourteen, Tipping went straight to work after his elementary schooling. His father had suffered a work-related disability and Tipping wanted to help provide for his family. He started as an apprentice to a painter and decorator. Living in a mining area he saw that most of his friends had gone to the mines where they were making more than double what his own wages were. He applied to a mine where he worked for a year. During a period of heavy layoffs Tipping persuaded his parents to consent to his joining up. He was sixteen.

Tipping recalled that his initial interview was not particularly demanding. The recruiters simply wanted to know about his background, why he was interested in the Navy, and if there was any particular branch in which he was interested. Since he had been a boy scout and had learned a little about signaling, he indicated that he would like to be in signals. The teenager recalled that the written exam which included arithmetic, reading and spelling was not difficult. His basic schooling had more than adequately prepared him to pass it. He thought that it might have been just the Navy's way of ensuring that 'you weren't stupid before putting you any further'.[3]

Tipping did not go to *Ganges* or *St Vincent,* but was enlisted as a special service boy in a seven and five program. After training and turning eighteen, he would be obliged to seven years of active service followed by five years in reserve status. A month after passing his exams, Tipping was sent by rail to Sheerness where he would train at one of the smaller and lesser known establishments, HMS *Wildfire*.[4] His first meal was a plentiful serving of sheep's heart which he enjoyed. He thought of it as a good omen for the days ahead.

9 January 1939 began for fifteen-year-old Bill Cotton at home when he was shaken awake at 5:00 am. It would be just the first of many an early wakeup call to come. Cotton recalled his route to Shotley and HMS *Ganges*.

> *'Come on Bill, time to wake up. Uncle Fred will be here soon.' Uncle Fred was taking me to the station to catch the 6:00 am to Derby. It was there that we had to muster en route to Shotley in Suffolk. Train to London, trains to Harwich, ferry to Shotley. HMS* Ganges *was … a harsh place to be when you're only 15 and have never been away from home before. It seemed to be alive with RPOs* (Crushers, as Regulating Petty Officers were called). *Everyone seemed to be shouting at once. 'You're in the Navy now, and don't forget it. And don't ever let me catch any of you smoking.'*[5]

Roland Clark, who would serve aboard small combatant craft during the war, remembered being delivered to the Navy by a train that stopped at every station along the route. The December night was a cold one. As he and the boys who had travelled with him stepped off the train at Shotley, young Clark realised by the shouts hurled his way that things had forever changed.

> *'You're late. The bus has been waiting here an hour,' was the welcome from the Draft Petty Officer. 'Fall in outside the station in some semblance of order with your baggage, and in the future, don't forget … The Royal Navy always keeps to time … (now) Get a move on, it's the 28th December … our duty people have had to forego their Christmas leave to pull you lot in!'*[6]

The new arrivals were loaded aboard Royal Navy trucks and driven through empty nighttime streets and then along darkened country roads. They sat on wooden slats and used arms and legs to brace themselves against the jostle and bump as they wound their way towards *Ganges*. Once the trucks passed through the gates and stopped, the boys were ordered off and hustled, 'chop chop,' into a barracks room. 'Chop chop,' the demand to hurry, would be the only way in which they were expected to get things done in the Navy. Or else. The barracks room into which they were half marched and half herded was unfurnished except for two rows of iron beds. Each bed bore a thin canvas covered mattress, a pillow and three folded blankets. Once they had dropped the possessions with which they had arrived onto a bunk, they were shouted at to, 'Get fell in outside! Chop chop!'[7]

The next order of business would be the issue of their kit as described by David Phillopson, a post-war trainee at HMS *Ganges*. The trainees were taken to the Clothing Store by a man who had introduced himself as, 'Mr. Barnes, Gunner, Royal Navy'.

> *'Come along, you lucky lads,' he cajoled us, 'don't hang back, it's all free! Right. When I sing out an item of kit, make sure you get it. One kitbag …'*

Lined up along a narrow wooden counter that ran the length of the room, the boys began to receive their kit. Following Gunner Barnes' call for 'one kitbag,' each boy had a large tube of heavy white canvas dumped before him. This was rapidly followed by the contents destined for the bag:

> *'Handkerchiefs, blue bundle, two … Square, black silk, two … Collars, blue jean, two … Hatbox, black japanned, one … Jumper, blue serge, number three, men dressed as seamen, one … Trousers, ditto, pair, one.'*[8]

Once issued with all they were to receive, the boys were marched back to the dormitory where they were instructed to dump their kit by their beds and to turn in. They seemingly had only just shut their eyes before lights glared and a harsh, loud voice bellowed, 'Now, wakey, wakey; up you get! Ten minutes to wash and fall in outside!'[9]

So it would go for the next five weeks as the boys were oriented and indoctrinated to the ways of the Royal Navy. After these five weeks, they would be promoted to the instructional class in which they would train for another eight months in preparation for their ultimate destiny of sea duty with the fleet.

## 'Nozzers' – Trainees

One of the earliest lessons and chores assigned to the new trainees, or 'nozzers,' involved the issue of a 'housewife'. The word was roughly pronounced as 'ussiff' and it was a sewing kit. Every piece of gear and clothing issued was to be sewn with the owner's name. The boys would be shown just once how to care for, stow, and dress in each of the items of clothing contained in their kit. They would get the standard close-shaven haircut, be deloused, and have all their personal belongings boxed up and sent home. They would then be examined by the dentist and the doctor, take the swimming test, and begin to master the arts of marching and drill. Non-swimmers, which included anyone who could not manage four lengths of the pool and five minutes of treading water all while clothed, would receive extra instruction early each morning and sometimes in lieu of leave until they could properly swim.

The nozzers were issued with a list of rules titled, *'Rules for the Guidance of Boys'*. Several examples of the many rules were:

> *Rule 7: Should a boy receive any Money, Stamps or a Money Order from his friends or wish to save his Pocket Money, he is at once to take it to the Regulating Office. He is never to retain more than Two Shillings and Sixpence in his possession.*

> *Rule 15: Fighting, Quarrelling, Gambling, Tattooing, and the use of Bad Language are strictly forbidden; and as nearly all the punishments in a Man-of-War arise from Drinking, Boys are strongly advised to avoid the use of Intoxicating Liquors.*[10]

Smoking, against which the boys were well warned from the very beginning, was severely punished, but practiced nonetheless. Those who could not resist were liable to pay a stiff price in more ways than one. According to former nozzer Bill Cotton, a boy who did not smoke could purchase a packet of cigarettes for 11½ pence and then turn around and sell them singly to his fellow trainees for 2 pence each. The toilets were among the favourite places for the boys to sneak a smoke. Lookouts posted at the windows would sing out, 'Lobs a jock' whenever a sentry came near.[11] There were other favoured places in which to smoke. Ernest Kerridge, who trained at *Ganges* from 1933–1934 and would go on to serve in battlecruiser *Renown* and aircraft carriers *Glorious* and *Ark Royal,* remembered a few of them,

> *The only recreation you had, on a Sunday afternoon, you were allowed out of the camp just to go for a long walk around the country lanes. I think that's when these lads who needed a smoke were able to get their tobacco … probably from some friend outside … and anyone caught them, of course, they were in trouble … and I think during the cinema shows … and it was (in) a terrific great gymnasium … it could hold 2,000 (people) … and while the film was on you could look around and see children, or kids, puffing away for a quiet smoke; but if they were caught, they were really in for it.[12]*

Frederick Jewett who was at *Ganges* from 1939 – 1940 remembered the penalties for being caught smoking,

> *Smoking in the Navy, as a boy, was ABSOLUTELY taboo. The first time you were caught you got seven day's jankers, which meant running around the parade ground and all the rest of it. Second time you were caught, you got fourteen days. And the third time, you got six cuts over your buttocks with the cane; and it was done very formally. You've got a duck suit (light canvas uniform trousers) on and you go down to the gym and you're stretched over the vaulting horse and there's this great big 'crusher,' he's got the stick, and the doctor's standing there and he whacks it down there. Now six doesn't sound much, but when they're in the same place, oh, boy![13]*

Jewett claimed that any boy caught smoking a fourth time would be dishonourably discharged. Ernest Kerridge, who trained at *HMS Ganges* some five years before Jewett, remembered things slightly differently. Kerridge stated that the first offense, even if it were being caught with just a grain of tobacco anywhere on his person, earned a boy lashes, or cuts, with a cane. A boy got six cuts for the first offense, the second offense resulted in twelve cuts, while the third would mean twenty-four cuts and immediate discharge. Both veterans stated that they witnessed canings as well as dismissals.

### 'It Would Have Been Unthinkable to Complain to Your Parents' Drill and Discipline

On the grounds of *Ganges,* and easily within sight from within or outside the establishment, was the towering ship's mast. The boys, introduced to it during their first five weeks at *Ganges,* were initially allowed to acclimate themselves by just gradually climbing to increasingly higher levels. Before finishing their training, however, all were required to climb it to the height of the top gallant mast some 130 feet above ground. Some of the more intrepid boys would climb to the button, a wooden disc 18 inches in diameter at the very top, and sit or stand on it. There were some who would boldly invert themselves to stand on their heads. Frederick Jewett described going over the mast,

> *There's six ratlines; places to go up the mast and you line up in front of the mast in sixes ... and they would have six of you standing there and the (instructors) there (would) say, 'close up to the rigging! ... man the rigging!' and you would man the rigging and go (up) four or five ratlines, the things – the bits of rope -- that go across, and you stayed there ... and you'd wait for the order, 'way aloft!' ... and when you got the order 'way aloft' it was a race to get up there ... and you couldn't go through* (the 'lubber's hole;' a safer way to the top yard which was the second of the three yards of the mast) *to the devil's elbow where the platform goes out about six or seven feet at least – probably more – so you've got to use your arms and hang mid-air and go hand over hand with your arms to get to the next set of rigging and then you go right over the mast. You didn't, at that time, have to go over the button – the top of the mast proper – you had to go right to the top gallant mast* (just below the highest of the three yards), *go over and down the other side. Now, what they always used to do, which was a bit rough, the last man used to get a whack – it didn't hurt very much – with what they called a stonnachie ... it was a piece of a rope's end and they used to belt you across the backside with it.*[14] *It didn't*

*worry you very much … you didn't (send) any letters home (about it) … it would have been (unthinkable) to complain to your parents, good God!* [15]

In general, a day began with the call of, 'heave ho, heave ho; lash up and stow,' at a quarter past six (forty-five minutes later on Sundays).The call referred to hammocks, which the boys would not use until they were assigned to a ship in the fleet. The trainees would wash up, have a quick snack of biscuit and cocoa, turn to and 'clean ship' (their quarters), before dressing in the rig (uniform) of the day after breakfast. They would then stand inspection and march to morning assembly that was called Divisions. Any faults found during inspection would be punished with extra duty. The faults needed to be fully corrected by stand easy, the morning break. Once Divisions, which included prayer and hymns was complete, the boys would march off to the Marine Band playing 'Heart of Oak,' the official march of the Royal Navy. Classwork followed. Dinner came at about noon. Afternoon sports were next. A tiny meal of bread and jam was provided at four o'clock for tea. The actual tea was served in a tiny metal cup. The boys changed into night clothing a half hour later. They then proceeded to Evening Quarters which was a muster similar to the earlier Divisions. Evening Quarters was followed by a march to the mast for the daily lowering of the colors. Next was an hour and a half of classes, supper, free time, and the call of 'Boys clean teeth and turn in' at a quarter past nine. The day would end with the call of 'Pipe down, Lights out' fifteen minutes afterwards. [16]

Tommy Cockram, whose father died when he was twelve, left school at fourteen. He went to work to help support his mother and siblings. Influenced by an uncle's seemingly adventuresome and colorful life as a seaman with the Cunard Line, he joined the Navy. Cockram would serve aboard the battlecruiser *Renown* in the Atlantic and Mediterranean. He would also serve in the Pacific aboard a light cruiser. He spoke about some of the instruction he received as a boy second class trainee at *Ganges* in 1939.

*I took to foot drill alright, (but) the first thing that got me on the parade ground was fixing bayonets. It took me a session or two before I got the hang of that. All the other drill was alright… at first you don't see the point but you do it because (it) gives you discipline.*

*Seamanship classes (included) bends and hitches; knots and splices …
being a seaman … that's a part of your job … you learned to splice the wire
and the rope … with the wire splicing, the main thing about it was, the
preparation. Before you start a splice, you put a whipping around each end
of the wire to keep it from fraying … Nowadays you don't have to splice wire;
I've seen it on these modern ships. Once you got the hang of it … at first it
was tricky … your hands as a boy; you're not as strong as later on in life.*

*You learned the compass and how to steer the ship; the telegraph* (for
communication to and from the engine room) *and all. Also the rules of
the road … it was like poetry they taught you:*

'When both lights you see ahead, starboard wheel and show your red.'

*What that means is, if there's two ships coming together towards each
other and you're on the wheel, if you turn your wheel to starboard, which
is right, and he does the same on the other ship. You'll both miss each
other.*

'If in danger, no room to turn, ease her; stop her; go astern.'

*What that means is you ease the ship down, then you stop her, and to
bring her to a stop properly go astern with both engines; that brings a ship
to a stop.*

'If in danger or in doubt; always keep a good look out.'[17]

The boys generally enjoyed gunnery as it usually involved a good amount of
hands on learning. At the time of the war and immediately after it, they would
train on a four-inch gun mount of the type that was ubiquitous aboard Royal
Navy ships. Each student would take a turn at practicing as gun captain, layer,
trainer, and ammunition handlers. When manually operated, as it often was, the
gun and its ammunition – even when it consisted only of practice rounds – were
quite heavy and cumbersome for boys of fifteen and sixteen. The instructors,

apparently ever eager to test the boys' mettle, would complicate matters by kicking as well as tossing shells and shell casings all around while screaming and yelling at their charges to hurry and to not make any mistakes.[18]

Besides serving its designed practical purpose, small arms training was geared to instill a martial spirit in the boys. If nothing else though, it provided them with an outlet for some of their excess energy. Cockram described his time with hand held weapons,

*(There was also) rifle shooting, bayonets, etcetera. We used to do bayonet fighting … that was very good, that. You'd have dummies and you'd have trenches and you'd jump down in the trench and they used to teach you to put your foot on it* (the dummy, or the bayonet victim) *to pull it* (the bayonet) *out … (then) when you done revolver firing it's different than you see now, you see them holding the revolver with two hands … the way we were taught, you'd have the revolver in (one) hand and you'd bring it down … (and) the reason we brought it down was that when you fired it, it used to jump up … and we also done hand grenades. You'd have the pin in and they used to tell you 'bring it to the back of your head and throw it overhand,' just like bowling with a cricket ball.*[19]

The still growing and hard-working trainees were a perpetually ravenous lot and the character of some of the food at *Ganges* is described by Frederick Jewett,

*For breakfast (it was) usually an egg – a hard-boiled egg and bread (and) porridge; always porridge … sometimes (we would get) a fried egg; it usually depended on who the cook was. Sometimes there was a bit of bacon – I say 'bacon' – but you ate it because you were so damned hungry … (for dinner) sometimes you'd get soup … a soup of the day sort of thing … and there was an awful lot of mince; we got a tremendous amount of mince … apples … potatoes … greens … things like that. It was pretty healthy stuff … The best thing they ever made – I've never experienced anything to beat it since I've left Shotley – was their steamed pudding; it was absolutely fantastic! You used to get figgy duff; it was plum duff and custard; it was out of this world!*[20]

### 'It Was Agony on Your Feet'
### Getting Ready for Sea Duty

Being yelled at, marching or running, hard work, strict rules and harsh discipline were relieved, if just briefly, on Wednesdays. Frederick Jewett remembered Wednesday as payday during his time at Shotley. The boys received a shilling each and had the remainder of the afternoon off for 'make and mend' which generally meant free time.

> *To collect your wages in the Navy you go in front of a table and the officers there and you 'off cap' and you put your cap (on the table) and they put a shilling on your cap and you turned right, you'd take the money and 'on cap' ... (and) if you hadn't had a haircut, which you had to pay for yourself, by the way ... there's the Master-at-Arms waiting there (and he'd point you out), 'haircut! ... haircut! ... haircut!' and anybody who hadn't had a haircut ... would be just about shaved ... you know.*

> *Now what do you do? We got a shilling. Postage home was three ha'pence ... and you had to write home to Mum and Dad, so you had to (spend that). A bar of Cadbury's Dairy Milk was tuppence, one of these two ounce bars, you know ... a 'Charlie' which you could get at the canteen ... a sort of a duff between two pieces of pastry ... in a square, they used to cost a penny. The other thing that cost a penny ... was a toffee bar that (came) in eight slabs ... as soon as you got anything, you'd put it in your jumper and the kids used to go up on the mast and sit up there to eat their stuff so nobody would bother them ... you had a lovely view.*[21]

At the end of slightly less than a full year at their training establishments, all the boys who scored well enough on their examinations, and most did, would pass on. They would then go on to a ship aboard which they would finish their training. Charles Embury, who saw wartime service aboard the cruiser HMS *Despatch*, recalled some of his shipboard experiences when he trained as a boy seaman first class aboard the aged World War I era cruiser HMS *Dunedin* in 1938.

*Boys were not permitted to wear their boots between 6.30 am and 9.00 am in the morning. After lashing and stowing your hammock, a hot cup of Kye,*

HMS *Dunedin*

*very strong greasy cocoa, then to the Upper Deck to scrub decks. Seamen wearing sea boots hosed down the decks with sea water, then scattered sand, then we boys scrubbed the deck with 'Holy Stone'. This was followed by drying down by the use of squeegees. During the winter months it was sure agony on your feet.*

*Pay day, six shillings per fortnight. The balance of your pay was kept for you until you reached the age of 18. Any requirement for clothes from the 'Slop Chest' was deducted from this money ... With all the exercise and fresh air, boys were always hungry. Payday for me was a tin of pineapple chunks, 4½d (pence), and (a) tin of cream (for) 1½d. You still had so many hours of schooling (there was a ... school master) ... (that) I actually passed for a school certificate on the Dunedin and was confirmed by the Bishop of Portsmouth. Schooling continued until you became an ordinary seaman.*

*Vendors were permitted on the mess decks during the dog watches[22] (and) two (that) I remember were (the) one selling boot laces and the other selling Paragolic Lozenges, flat (and) gray in color, sold in paper twists, for coughs and colds.*

*Once a fortnight boys of the Duty Watch were marched through Portsmouth to 'Aggie Weston's', a Temperance Society (Royal Sailors' Rests).[23] On arrival you were given a cup of cocoa and rock cakes, then to the cinema to watch a film; usually a Western. This was followed by a rather long lecture on the sins of 'Drinking Alcohol,' given by men in suits, wearing three or four medals, all for abstinence. At the end of the lecture you were asked to sign a pledge (a small price to pay for the cakes and film!).*

*(One) responsibility of the boys was to recover the torpedoes fired in practice by the Fleet Air Arm Swordfish (torpedo planes) at HMS Dunedin. (We had) to man the whaler; a 27 foot clinker (of a) five-oared sea boat. The torpedo floated upright at the end of its run, a calcium flare showed its presence, we hooked it to the whaler and towed it back to the ship under the ship's Torpedo Hoist (which) hoisted it aboard.*

*Once in a while we were taught gun drill, the four-inch anti-aircraft gun … we boys had to stand and watch as the seamen gunners manned the gun and fired it for real, no anti-flash gear in those days, or even cotton wool for your ears. I still remember the Gunner's Mate warning us when we heard the fire bell ring … (because) this is when the Captain of the Gun actually fired … to open your mouth wide to absorb the shock. This four-inch gun was one of the loudest in the Royal Navy (and) quite a shock to us novices.[24]*

With their training done, the boys were soon drafted to a ship, usually larger than a destroyer, and sent to sea. They would be quartered in a mess deck separate from those of the general crew and would be assigned a senior petty officer to watch over them. The main responsibilities of the seasoned sailors, or 'sea daddies,' were to counsel and advise their young charges, as well as to protect boys from any undue bad influence of the older crewmen. In order to provide them with the broadest spectrum of experience and skills, boys would be moved around from department to department and duty to duty aboard their ships.

As the years passed, some boys would be killed and others would leave the service. A good many would stay on to become senior petty officers and chiefs – the very type of men that make a navy a navy. Some would even go on to careers with commissions. A few would rise to admiral's rank. Through the years, some former boy seamen would swear that their days at *Ganges*, *St Vincent* or other training establishments were times of unnecessary harshness, abuse, or barbarism. Some who believed this would remain forever bitter towards the Navy and the types of men who ran it or served in it. There were, however, those who blessed the day, although they would never have thought to do so as 'nozzers', on which they elected to take the King's shilling. Being punched in the face for missing a stitch, while sewing one's name on a piece of kit or being given hours of extra duty, while being denied a week's worth of suppers for leaving a fingerprint on an otherwise immaculately polished piece of equipment seemed unjust or cruel at the time. Those who bore through such treatment, however, would later testify that it ultimately helped them become better men. In more than a few cases they claimed that it helped save their lives during the war. Learning how to tolerate and overcome screaming instructors viciously lashing out with stonnachies was what got a boy to overcome fire, flood, pain, and gore aboard fighting ships at war as a man.

### 'Life on Board for a Boy Was Pretty Hard'
### Growing Up on a Battleship

Bert Ward finished training as a boy seaman in December 1939. He joined his first ship, HMS *Revenge*, after his Christmas leave. The battleship was assigned to convoy escort duty in the North Atlantic.

> *U-boats in those early days did not get far out into the Atlantic. The danger was (from) surface raiders as the sinking of the* (British) *armed merchant cruisers* Rawalpindi *and* Jervis Bay *illustrate. Those ships were armed with six-inch guns and stood no chance against the 11-inch and 8-inch guns of German warships. The routine* (for *Revenge*) *was to escort a convoy from*

HMS *Revenge*

*Halifax* (headed east) *which was met by destroyers off Northern Ireland escorting an outward bound (headed west) convoy. Revenge then turned round and escorted that convoy to Halifax, tied alongside the jetty, and took on provisions and oiled. We would be in harbour forty-eight hours, maybe a bit longer, then off again. Usually two to three weeks at sea.*

*Revenge was one of the ships carrying Britain's gold reserves to Halifax from Greenock. Security was tight. The boxes either contained four gold bars or bags of coins. Guess how (we) found that out! The gold arrived in Greenock harbour in railway box wagons. Marines were the guards. One officer checked the boxes, which were numbered, out of the wagon. An officer checked them going into a boat. An officer checked them going on board* Revenge, *another checked them being lowered into the bomb room, and another checked them arriving in the bomb room. The procedure was reversed in Halifax.*[25]

The British gold shipment aboard *Revenge* was part of a £40 million payment to the United States for armaments, materials and resources. *Revenge* took on 148 boxes that each held 130 pounds of gold. The trans-Atlantic voyage took about a week, with the ship and gold arriving safely in mid-October 1939. *Revenge* repeated the process in January 1940 when she carried £10 million worth of gold from Plymouth to Halifax. In May, as the war continued to go badly for Britain and as fears of a German invasion mounted, another £40 million in gold was sent with the ship to Montreal, Canada for safe keeping.[26]

*My cruising station and defence station as a boy was lookout on the ADP (Air Defence Position). The R Class had tripod foremasts on which, as in the case of Revenge, there was an open bridge. Above and abaft that was the ADP which was an open platform ... If my memory serves me right there were eight lookouts on the ADP, port and starboard, sweeping all sectors with glasses. An officer and a petty officer were in charge. The view from the ADP was quite dramatic, especially in bad weather. With seas running high it was like mountains and valleys. For a boy, just turned seventeen, first ship, to be up there when* Revenge *seemed to hang on a mountain top, then start to run down the side of the mountain heading for the bottom of the Atlantic, and looking down at the skipper in his captain's cap and duffel coat and other officers, not a bit concerned, and then the ship digging her bows into the wall of water on the other side of the valley, picking up and throwing it up over the bridge, was truly inspiring. When we were in the valley there were no other ships in sight. Then back on the top of the mountain with the convoy, or some of it in sight, we would hang for a moment, then hell for leather down the other side.*

*Dhobeying* (laundry) *and bathing on* Revenge *was in buckets or hand basins. Access to the bathrooms, which consisted of a row of hand basins, was down through watertight hatches which were only open for certain times of day. Sometimes the valves, whether through somebody's carelessness or not I don't know, allowed the sea into the bathrooms and flooded them ... (in that case) you raised the hatch ... and what you saw was the Atlantic. So it was move on to the next bathroom. The flooded bathroom would then be pumped out.*

*Another of* Revenge's *idiosyncrasies was the lower deck's heads which were right for'ard. The lavatories were two steps up from the deck, in cubicles with half doors so it was possible to see if they were occupied. They were flushed by pushing a large brass button. Unfortunately, sometimes the valve which allowed the contents of the pan to be sent out into the ocean failed and the Atlantic came in. We could tell by the water surrounding such rogues which ones to avoid. But if a valve had not previously failed there was no way of knowing. In that case the Atlantic came in and the matelot who was sitting there got a right slap in the face, so to speak.*

*The (boys') mess decks were open … not the small compartmentalized messes of modern ships such as the KGV (King George V and 25 years newer) class. When I became an OD (ordinary seaman, next rank up from boy, first class), I moved into the top messdeck.* Revenge *was general messing which meant that we peeled the spuds but apart from that everything was done in the galley. We carried all meals from the galley to the mess. Everybody took a turn at cook of the day which meant collecting the food, dishing it out, and washing up after the meal. The washing up water and gash (food scraps) were carried out to the upper deck and sent down the gash chute. If a piece of cutlery had been left in the water it could be heard hitting the sides of the chute as it went down. That was where I learned the ditty: 'Tinkle, tinkle little spoon; knife and fork will follow soon.'*

*Leading Seaman Telford, a decent man in one of the foc'sle messes had a weakness for rum … (which when issued) was poured into cups. Telford was known for always scrutinizing the cups to see which one he thought had the most in. So one day his mess mates filled one cup with vinegar, and they all waited for Telford to arrive. His eyes flickered over the cups and then he bit. There was an uproar, with everybody laughing their heads off and Telford fuming and threatening all sorts of mayhem. But he was a decent sort and nothing came of it.*[27]

After France surrendered to Germany in June 1940, the Germans and a German controlled French government began to take control in that country and in its overseas colonies. The French Navy became divided as some ships stayed in French ports while others weighed anchor and steamed to British ports. Still others, already being at anchor in England at the time of their country's surrender, stayed put. The British feared that the French ships at Devonport might side with the Axis so, in July, boarding parties from *Revenge* were sent to take them over. Ward remembered the incident.

> *I forget whether we were at Pompey* (Portsmouth) *or Devonport … but the old (French) battleship Paris was tied up astern of Revenge and the submarine* Surcouf *was tied up alongside her. In the early hours of one morning we went to action stations and sent boarding parties to take both ships. The sentries on Paris were taken by surprise. The first man down the ladder on the Surcouf was Leading Seaman Webb. He was shot and killed by a French officer. The British officer following Webb then killed the Frenchman.*[28]

By summer 1941 *Revenge* and a sister ship, *Royal Sovereign*, were sent to the Indian Ocean to serve as convoy escorts. Ward described his action station and some of his ponderings about what might become of him in the war.

> *My action station was in the B shell room* (under B turret) *just below the magazine. Every morning as dusk approached, the ship went to action stations. There we practiced until the order came down the voice pipe (for) second degree of readiness. Then watches would be set, I think we did an hour each in pairs, while the others slept. As dawn approached it was back to action stations and practicing … then cruising stations, breakfast, clean ship and quarters, (and) clean guns. Practice in a fifteen-inch turret meant practicing loading the guns. We could load a … gun in one minute … (which) meant getting a one ton shell and four quarter charges from the shell room and magazine up to the gun house to be rammed into the breech … In the shell room we slept on the shells with our caps or lifebelts for pillows. It was bloody cold … The captain of B shell room was Petty Officer Bing Bingham … the trunk was towards the after end of the shell room and the lights on the bulkheads were in that area. The result was that the farthest end of the shell room was in perpetual gloom.*

*After reverting to second degree, Bing would get his harmonica out and we would have a sing song. As sound carries under water we probably frightened (the Germans) off. The down side of that was when the escorts were dropping depth charges, it sounded like somebody hitting the hull with a giant hammer. We got used to it. Sometimes as I lay on the shells trying to get to sleep I used to wonder what would happen if we were torpedoed. Escape was impossible. Main hatches were clipped down and only escape hatches letting one man at a time through was open. I imagined the ship going down with lights on, and we would be trapped. One night I dreamed we were torpedoed. As the ship sank, she turned over an all the shells came tumbling out of the bins. So that was that problem solved.*[29]

George Aucott was another former boy seaman who remembered many details about his time as a battleship sailor. Aucott was born in 1923 in Birmingham, finished elementary school at fourteen, and had plans to go on with his education. When his family moved, he went to work instead. He became a grocer's assistant. He was paid 8 shillings and 3 pence a week for a sixty-five to seventy-hour week delivering groceries. His pocket money was one of the shillings which he would stretch out and do nicely with. The cinema cost two pence (tuppence) for the cheaper seats and four for the balcony. He once bought a camera at Woolworth's for six pence and a roll of film for tuppence. A large bag of chips sold for one penny in the late 1930s. He, along with two of his friends from school, eventually decided that they wanted to see the world and have something exciting to do. They joined the navy in 1939. They were sent to the boy's establishment at HMS *Ganges* for training. Aucott's two friends would not survive the war.

When his training was done Aucott was drafted to *King George V* (called *KGV* and pronounced 'kay-gee-5') just as she commissioned in October of that year. Aucott was put in the boy's mess with some 200 other boys variously designated as boy seaman, boy signalman, or boy telegraphist. Two leading seamen, or 'sea daddies', were assigned as instructors and guardians to the boys of the mess. Aucott recalled,

*Life on board for a boy was pretty hard. The ship itself, when we were at sea, was what we called a 'wet ship' … The boy's mess was the most*

*forward mess on the ship and the vents on the upper deck were not completely watertight and in a rough sea the water would shower down these vents and we'd … get showered though the ventilation system and … at night when you got out of your hammock you could be standing in several inches of water … My first job on board I was a mess man to the petty officers' mess and you were responsible for keeping the mess clean and you would fetch their meals from the galley, serve them, wash up, and so forth. This carried on for about three months and then I asked for a transfer to somewhere else. I was (put) in the boy's division of the foc'sle in the forward part of the ship … and there you were under the supervision of a petty officer or a chief petty officer for keeping the foc'sle part of the ship clean (which included) painting ship over the side … all the boys were given that job; it was a dirty job … and it wasn't a very good job particularly in the winter time.*[30]

Aucott's action station was in one of the 15-in shell rooms. His job was to attach a shell grab onto a shell so it could be lifted from storage to one of the loading trays before it was sent up the hoist to the turret. When he turned eighteen, Aucott earned his promotion to ordinary seaman and was moved out of the boy's mess to a regular crew's mess. After about 6 months, he passed his able seaman exam and went up to that rank from which he applied to be a torpedoman. In addition to tending to torpedoes, of which there were none on *KGV*, a torpedoman was responsible for shipboard electrical work. Aucott's pay went from six shillings weekly as a boy seaman to 14 shillings as an ordinary seaman, 18 shillings as an able seaman, and 18 shillings and thruppence as a torpedoman.[31]

Among Torpedoman Aucott's several duties was that of topside lookout. There were three lookouts per side of the ship. Each man had a designated zone to scan with his binoculars. They were not fully exposed to the elements on watch, but sat on stools within a tiny 10 foot by 3 foot shelter equipped with a porthole. They were to look for surface ships, aircraft, telltale signs of submarines and, even, mines. In the Arctic waters where *KGV* had been sent in late 1941, wind and spray came through so heavily that the lookouts were constantly wiping their binoculars which they could never really get clean. Spotting anything as small as a floating mine or a periscope poking out of the water was virtually impossible. The bitter cold prevented any of the lookouts from falling asleep, but a chief petty officer of the watch would circulate around to check, anyway. Aucott was once reported for having fallen asleep on watch and, despite his vehement denial of it, he was punished with fourteen days of defaulters. Whenever he was otherwise off duty during those fourteen days, he would be assigned to any of the abundant dirty jobs that constantly needed to be done throughout the ship. Aucott's word, as a mere torpedoman, could never have stood against that of a chief.[32]

During World War II, 534 boy seamen were killed in action, and a further twenty-four died of other causes. A memorial plaque was installed in the Portsmouth Cathedral and was unveiled in March, 2012. The plaque reads as follows:[33]

**1939 – 1945**
**534 Royal Navy Boy Seamen**
**Aged 16 & 17 Years Old**
**Killed by Enemy Action in World War II**
**Serving Their King and Country in 80 Warships**
**'We Will Remember Them'**

ENDNOTES

1.  Pietsch, Roland. *Ship's Boys and Youth Culture in Eighteenth-Century Britain: The Navy Recruits of the London Marine Society.* Unpublished PhD. Thesis. University of London. 2003.

2.  Perkins, David. *'Boy Seaman Training Establishments, Circa 1900.'* Gwpda.org. Web. Accessed July 2014.

3.  Imperial War Museum. Sound recording archive. 10924. Tipping, Trevor. 1989.

4.  HMS *Wildfire* was a former naval gunnery school that reopened in 1937 as a boy's training establishment.

5.  Market Harborough Royal British Legion (contributor) *'HMS Ganges.'* BBC WW2 People's War. Article ID A 4112489. 2005.

6.  Brown, Debbie R. (contributor). *Perlethorp to Portsmouth.* BBC WW2 People's War. Article ID A2945603. 2004.

7.  Phillipson, David. *Band of Brothers: Boy Seamen in the Royal Navy 1800 – 1956.* Sutton Publishing. 1996. P. 51.

8.  Phillipson. pp. 51–53.

9.  Market Harborough Royal British Legion.

10. Phillipson. p. 57.

11. Market Harborough Royal British Legion.

12. Imperial War Museum. Sound recording archive. 18663. Kerridge, Ernest. 1999-01-05.

13. Imperial War Museum. Sound recording archive. 22614. Jewett, Frederick Thomas. 2001-06-11.

14. David Phillipson, in his book, *Band of Brothers,* described stonnachies as, *'flat tubes of canvas a foot in length, filled with sand and jointed in the middle like a flail.'* p. 67.

15. Imperial War Museum. 22614 (Jewett).

16. Phillipson. pp. 65–71.

17. Imperial War Museum. Sound recording archive. 25041. Cockram, Tommy. 2003.

18. Phillipson. pp. 79–80.

19. Imperial War Museum. 25041 (Cockram).

20. Imperial War Museum. 22614 (Jewett).

21. Imperial War Museum. 22614.

22. There were two dog watches during the day. The first was from 4:00 PM until 6:00 PM and the second from 6:00 PM until 8:00 PM.

23. Founded by Aggie Weston, there were establishments at many Royal Navy ports called 'Royal Sailors' Rests' that provided meals, beverages, some opportunities for recreation, baths and lodging to fleet sailors. While the establishments valued sobriety, they did not exist solely to promote temperance.

24. Embury, Charles. *Memories of a Boy Seaman Serving in HMS Dunedin, 1938–1939.* hmsdunedin. co.uk. Web. Accessed July 2014.

25. Ward, Bert. 'The Wartime Memories Project – HMS *Revenge*.' wartimememories.co.uk. Web. Accessed July 2014.

26. Mason, Geoffrey. 'HMS Revenge – Royal Sovereign Class 15-inch Gun Battleship.' naval-history. net. Web. Accessed July 2014.

27. Ward.

28. Ward.

29. Ward.

30. Imperial War Museum. Sound recording archives. 23337. Aucott, George. 2003.

31. Imperial War Museum. 23337. At the United Kingdom's average rate of inflation of 5.9% from 1939 – 2012 , £1 in 1939 would have been the rough equivalent of £64 in 2012. Aucott's six shillings per week as a boy seaman would have represented roughly £19.2 per week, or £76.8 per month in 2012.

32. Imperial War Museum. 23337.

33. Reed, Jim (GI). *RN Boy Seamen WW2 Memorial.* hmsstvincentassoc.com. Web. Accessed July 2014.

# FOUR
# YOUNG MEN, OLD SHIPS

### 'No Match for a Strong Enemy'
### The R-Class Battleships

The Royal Navy began the war with twelve dreadnoughts (Nine Battleships, Three Battlecruisers). Five of the Battleships were *Royal Sovereign* (or 'R') class ships completed in 1916–1917. They were well-armed for the time with eight 15-inch guns each and had good armour protection, but their relatively slow speed, operational wear and material defects would keep them from front-line service during the war. William Crawford, a staff officer of the Admiral 2nd in command of the Eastern Fleet to which these battleships were attached later in the war, viewed the R-class battleships as 'very weak and old'. He criticised them for 'never really (having been) a very good design', whose 'engines were in an appalling state' leaving them 'no match for a strong (enemy) fleet'.[1]

A Nelson-class battleship leads QE and R-class battleships during exercises in the Mediterranean, late 1920s

### 'Thrilled To Be Able to Go to Sea'
### Joining HMS *Royal Oak*

HMS *Royal Oak*

Charles Simpson of Portsmouth skipped three grades in school. By the time he was just 10 years old he had passed the exam to get into a secondary school. The school he attended was divided into two sections: Dockside that would lead students to careers in the military or the trades, and Latin that would lead students to professional careers or to further education at the university level. Simpson eventually wound up in the Dockside section for which he was grateful as it prepared him for the life he really wanted. By the time he reached fifteen, he had already gained a full five years of post-elementary school education, he joined the Navy.

Young Simpson was easily able to pass the required national level exam for entry into the Royal Navy as an artificer apprentice. After signing on to serve for twelve years beginning with his eighteenth birthday, he trained at HMS *Fisgard*, the shore establishment consisting of a series of four training ships anchored at Portsmouth. As apprentice artificers, Simpson and his contemporaries were trained to be experts in naval weapons and electrical or mechanical systems for duty both at sea and ashore. According to Simpson,

> *An artificer is defined in the Bible as a worker in fresh metals. An artificer is a man who … was capable of making the most intricate things out of pure metal. So, a fitter and turner, which I became, was capable of manufacturing replacements for the machines used in Her Majesty's ships from pure metal. If a replacement shaft was required, you manufactured it on board the ship. The apprenticeship was as lengthy as it was – four and a half years – because you progressed from a boy using a hammer and chisel to a fully qualified fitter and turner, or coppersmith, or blacksmith depending on the trade which after six months you were allowed to choose.*[2]

Simpson's very first assignment, as a fifteen-year-old apprentice, was to take just two chisels and a hammer to shape a solid steel cylinder into a hexagon. He used a pair of socks as gloves in order to protect his hands while he worked. By the time he completed his apprenticeship he was capable of manufacturing objects by hand to the nearest 1/1000th of an inch. Unlike his rigorous technical training, his naval or seamanship training was minimal at best since, according to Simpson, his was a technical, rather than a military, branch of the service.

Simpson was assigned to HMS *Royal Oak* in 1930 and was 'thrilled to be able to go to sea'. He thoroughly enjoyed being in the engine room of a real ship where he could dismantle something and then put it back together again. It was not all fun for the young artificer, however, as he was assigned to sling his hammock inside one of the battleship's gun turrets. These were, unbeknownst to Simpson, extremely wet. When he tossed his clothing onto the deck before getting into his hammock one night, he found them floating in six inches of water the next morning.

Aboard *Royal Oak,* Simpson started off by following a senior artificer on large jobs to serve as his assistant. After being given thorough instruction about them, he was required to tend to boilers, engines, dynamos, refrigerators, air compressors, diesel generators and all other manner of engineering equipment, large and small, in every technical detail. After a year, Simpson was rated leading seaman and fifth class engine room artificer; the lowest of artificer ranks. The path of advancement was a long one that could only be made through time, experience and the consistent demonstration of competence and expertise.

The engineering department aboard the pre-war *Royal Oak* was described by Artificer Simpson as being overseen by the chief engineer whose rank was commander (E), where the 'E' was the designation for Engineering. The chief engineer's role was comparable to that of a corporate CEO and the officer under him, the senior engineer, was the 'hands on' head of the department. The remaining officers, all of whom had been selected through the Royal Navy's very demanding system of training and advancement were eight lieutenants (E) and four warrant engineers. The enlisted men of the department, like the officers above them, were men who had been selected through experience, expertise, and exam. From top to bottom were the chief engine room artificer (ERA) followed by all the other artificers from first through fifth classes. During action stations the artificers' primary responsibilities outside of engine room and boiler room duties were in the area of firefighting and damage control.[3]

## 'Keep Calm Boys … Everybody Will Be Alright'
## The Loss of HMS *Royal Oak*

Of the five R-class battleships all but one, *Royal Oak*, would survive the war. The German navy was eager to demonstrate its value to the heavily land-oriented Hitler. Also seeking a morale lifting victory, it sent *U-47* on a raid into Scapa Flow in October 1939. Previous aerial reconnaissance had shown that there were open spots in the otherwise carefully secured anchorage through which a submarine could gain clandestine entry. On arrival, the German submarine's captain, Gunther Prien, was surprised to find most of the British fleet gone. Many ships had lifted anchor and steamed out to sea earlier in the day. Prien's initial disappointment was reversed when, through his periscope, he saw the form of a battleship looming before him. He ordered torpedoes fired. One hit, but caused little damage.

Many of the crew aboard the battleship could not imagine enemy penetration into their base. They assumed that the torpedo's impact was little more than a relatively minor internal explosion. Others of the crew thought that they might have been caught in an air raid. When Prien's boat fired three more torpedoes, all hit. Flames reached a magazine and *Royal Oak* suffered a staggering explosion. The stricken battleship listed heavily and rolled over. Many men were killed by the explosions and fire. Others succumbed to hypothermia when they fell or jumped into icy waters. Still others were caught in and dragged down by the heavy oil that leaked out of the sinking ship. In all, 833 of *Royal Oak's* men died that night. Prien and his crew escaped undetected to become heroes and celebrities in Germany. They were brought to Berlin, awarded medals and introduced to a jubilant Adolf Hitler. As with so many of the German U-boat service, Prien, his boat and the crew that remained with him did not survive the war. *U 47* was sunk by depth charges in March 1941.

According to one of the *Royal Oak's* 386 survivors, the night of 12–13 October 1939 was just an ordinary night on which the expectations of a submarine attack were essentially nil. The disbelief that a submarine could have penetrated British defences was reflected in the surviving sailor's statements about his experiences after the ship was first hit.

> *Well, I was down below when the first explosion took place and nobody knew exactly what had happened. I got dressed and went up to investigate and I finished up on the port side of the upper deck and while I was there I lit up a cigarette, and after about a quarter of an hour; nothing. Everything was still, nothing further had happened, so I thought, 'Well; I'll put my cigarette out and go down below again.' And just as I … threw the cigarette over the side the next three torpedoes hit – on the starboard side, fortunately – away from me and the ship rocked and the showers of water came down and then the ship started to heel over almost immediately and it wasn't long before it was obvious that she was going.*[4]

When the three torpedoes struck home, a chain of frenzied activity started: destroyers went speeding around the harbour, depth charges were being dropped and detonating all around, and all manner of small craft went out looking to assist survivors in the water.

Another crewman who escaped that night remembered being in his hammock below decks when it became clear that a speedy exit would be necessary.

*Almost immediately I felt the ship begin to list and the lights went off, and the public address … had failed, and I knew that we were in very, very deep trouble … I climbed out of my hammock, pulled on my trousers, slipped into my shoes, and headed for the nearest ladder leading to the upper deck in the darkness. And there was a chap showing tremendous courage – he was a petty officer – he was standing at the foot of this ladder … holding a torch … and he was guiding men up the ladder and saying to them quite firmly, 'Keep calm, boys. Keep calm. Everybody will be alright, keep calm, just keep moving. Keep moving.' And it was something of an inspiration to see this man who probably sacrificed his own life to save others.[5]*

Swimming in the water, another crewman remembered,

*I thought to myself, 'This is it. This is the end. I might as well say the Lord's Prayer,' and I did that. I started to recite the Lord's Prayer and I heard the Marine that was with me … he joined in the prayer and halfway through (it) his voice stopped and I looked where he'd been and he had gone and that left me alone. Then I gave a last despairing look over my shoulder – and this is the last thing I recall – was seeing this … the bows of a very small craft coming right towards me, directly towards me and I lost consciousness at that stage and … must have been that someone virtually … run into me and someone (else) leaned over the side and dragged me out of the water.[6]*

Almost immediately after the fact, speculation, theories and rumours about how *Royal Oak* had been sunk became abundant. One of the most popular, but ultimately false, explanations was that a spy had helped by rendezvousing in a small boat with *U 47* to guide it onto its target. A Court of Inquiry eventually determined that there were almost a dozen spots where a gap existed in the harbour's defences and that previous warnings of junior officers about them had been ignored by their superiors. The Court found that the Admiral Commanding the Orkneys and the Shetlands, Wilfred French, was to be held responsible. No allowances were made for the fact that French himself had earlier attempted to correct the defects. The Admiral was forced to retire and was posted to Washington D.C. as an administrative representative.

### 'You Name It, We Did It'
### A Ship's Cook aboard HMS *Ramillies*

As a young man, Victor Stamp, who was born and raised in Plymouth, had no particular interest in military service. He enjoyed his student days, especially sports, but finished school at the leaving age of fourteen. He first went to work in a florist's shop and later became a numbers runner for a local bookie. In September 1938, when he was nineteen, he and a friend decided, purely on a whim, to go to the local naval recruiter and join up. They passed the entrance exam, were told that the Navy needed cooks and, having no cause to object, they became sailors. Following an initial period of basic training that consisted mostly of digging defensive trenches in the face of the looming war, Stamp was sent to cookery school. The young sailor learned to make puddings, roast meats, stew meats, and, 'you name it; we did it'. Years later, he would return to his former training school as a cookery instructor.[7]

In August 1939 and about a year into his enlistment, Stamp was assigned to *Ramillies*. The ship's galley, serving 1,800 men, was coal fired. The galley ran the

HMS *Ramillies*

width of the ship and was located on the upper deck where working conditions were expected to be less hot than if placed below decks. Stamp remembered that the ship's cooks would have to start preparing fish and chips for lunch at midnight the day before. Since breakfast was not taken by many of the men, lunch could usually be ready by the time it was needed. Breakfasts were made up of the usual dishes that included bacon and eggs, sausage and eggs, tomato on toast, and beans and toast. Beef, for dinner or lunch, was always popular. It was roasted, stewed, boiled, and almost always served with dumplings. One of the crew's favourites was Manchester Tart which was a short crust pastry filled with raspberry jam and topped with dried coconut. Another favourite was steamed duff, a flour pudding that could contain almost any type of fruit or nut filling.[8] Stamp found that working as the ship's baker was particularly challenging. There were none of the appliances aboard the old battleship that are common in all kitchens and galleys today. Hundreds of pounds of dough had to be mixed and kneaded by hand. The task was made even more difficult because the coal used to heat the ovens needed to be carefully selected in walnut sized lumps. The water for making the dough also needed to be cooled to specific temperatures that could only be managed through the use of ice that had to be hand chipped from large blocks.

Whenever the ship was sent to the tropics cooks and stokers were given extra pay called 'sweat money'. Given in compensation for the hot conditions in which they had to work, it practically doubled the men's pay. In spite of all his hard work and the constant criticism from the crew, some of it in fun and some serious, Stamp stated that he always enjoyed his time aboard ship. He was particularly proud of being able to bake bread, cakes, and even hot cross buns in the heaviest of seas.

Despite the obvious dangers of working on coal burning stoves in stormy weather, Stamp did not recall any major accidents. Vats of hot soup, he stated, represented the greatest threat, but they would be tightly lashed down and caused no real problems. The worst thing he remembered was the time a galley fire erupted when he went to pour additional oil into a large deep fryer. Unfortunately, the oil drum contained water instead of oil. When the water hit the hot grease, it splattered and set the entire galley ablaze. The fire was readily controlled and there were no injuries. Stamp speculated that the drum, which had been picked up in Malta, had probably been emptied and refilled with water by desperate Maltese dockworkers at the time when the population of the besieged island was subsisting on starvation rations. Stamp would not begrudge them for it, however.

One of the seagoing sailor's staple beverages was a heavy, rich cocoa called Kai (alternate spelling: kye). It was smooth, thick, and not likely to spill even from an almost inverted cup. The chocolate came in big blocks which cooks like Stamp would break into pieces, blend with condensed milk and thicken with what was called the 'secret ingredient' custard. Bridge watches and lookouts in ships large or small, especially at night and in the cold of the northern latitudes, were always grateful for plentiful rations of kai. It was particularly appreciated whenever it was fortified with rum or other spirits. Stamp also always took care to have an abundant supply of sandwiches on hand for watch standers. These included corned beef, pilchers (a type of tinned fish), or salmon. Stamp would also be sure to have gallons and gallons of pea soup, tomato soup, and beef stew soup going all night long; especially in cold weather. Tea, of course, was always available for the men to make for themselves.

Whenever the ship was about to see action Stamp's station, once he had secured the galley, was on one of the ship's six-inch secondary battery guns. Not being trained in gunnery, he and many other ratings assigned to a gun, served as ammunition bearers. If they were not to carry the shells directly to the guns from a ready storage locker, they would work below decks in one of the shell and cordite charge handling spaces. Stamp often found himself in a shell room deep inside the ship. He would take shells one by one out of cases of eight to load onto slings which would convey them upwards to the guns.[9]

### 'This Ship Will Have No Hurt, Provided That the Captain Wears This Ma'ori Skirt'

*Ramillies* was unique for the traditional New Zealand Maori skirt that was kept aboard for the captain to wear. Called a piupiu in the native Maori language, it was presented as a gift to the ship on the occasion of her visit to New Zealand in 1940. *Ramillies* had docked at Wellington in preparation of escorting a convoy bearing the first contingent of New Zealand Army troops to the Suez. Members of the native Ngati'poneke Maori Club were invited to visit the ship. The group performed traditional dances, spoke of Maori culture and, as tokens of both friendship and good fortune, presented the ship with a sacred and specially blessed piupiu. A verse was coined to accompany the skirt:

> *In Wellington this ship is blessed in full Ma'ori tradition,*
> *Skirt of grass was given to her to guard her on her mission.*
> *In action and in battle sway, this ship will have no hurt*
> *Provided that the Captain wears this Ma'ori skirt.*

When the ship pulled away from the dock at Wellington , a military band played the traditional Maori farewell, *Po Ata Rau*, rendered in English as 'Now is the Hour'. The song, well known and beloved throughout New Zealand, left very few dry eyes as the battleship and the transports carrying their young men slowly headed out to sea and the war.[10]

According to Ship's Cook Stamp,

> *The famous Maori skirt ... When we were in New Zealand ... a load of Maoris come aboard and they did the Maori chanting dance with Maori girls with their baubles and all that and they presented the skipper ... with a Maori skirt ... and he was told that whenever the ship went into action, the captain had to wear that skirt. He wore it when we done Fort Capuzzo[11] and all that ... but the major part was, on D-Day ... the captain, on the way out, said, 'I'm just going down below. I won't be five minutes.' And he come back up wearing the Maori skirt. Of course, they all started snickering ... because the ship's company that was on there when (it) was presented wasn't on there then. (The captain) said, 'Take that snickering off your face,' he said, 'Look. We been through five years of war and we haven't lost one man in this ship, so there must be something in it,' and he said, 'I don't intend to lose any.'[12]*

The piupiu was somehow misplaced after the war. A replacement, worn by an original member of the Maori dance group that performed on *Ramilles* in 1940,

Members of the Ngati
Poneke party at the time
HMS *Ramillies* visited
New Zealand

MEMBERS OF THE NGATI PONEKE CONCERT PARTY AT THE TIME THAT HMS RAMILLIES
VISITED NEW ZEALAND IN JANUARY 1940.

```
BACK ROW   - J.Forrester,S.Tahiwl,F.Brown,S.Ihaka,D.Sinclair,Mrs.P Heketa.
L/R        - T.Riwaka, B.Tomuri, N.Tomuri, Rangi Utiku.
THIRD ROW  - W.Watson,E.Wickham,Riria Utiku,Lady Pomare,M.Heketa,A.Wallace.
L/R        - M. Edwards.
SEC ROW    - L.Gunson,J.Stevenson,T.McDonell,L.Metekingi,M.Black,V.Morgan.
L/R        -
FRONT      - T.Brooking, R.Kuru, M.Black, F.Watson, L. Sinclair.
ROW
```

was located. The skirt is now held in trust by the Royal Marines Museum at
Eastney, Portsmouth.[13]

### 'There Were Bullets Flying Everywhere'
### A Midshipman Aboard HMS *Resolution*

One of HMS *Resolution's* crewmen, Midshipman John Stedman, recorded some
of his wartime exploits aboard the old battleship. Encouraged by his father to
pursue a naval life, Midshipman Stedman was 18 years old when he first arrived
aboard. He had spent the previous three years as a cadet aboard the training

HMS *Resolution*

R-Class Battleship
HMS *Royal Sovereign*:
sister of *Revenge,
Resolution, Royal
Oak*, and *Ramillies.
Royal Sovereign* was
transferred to the Soviet
Navy and returned to
Britain after the war.

ship HMS *Conway*. As a cadet, Stedman studied a general education curriculum coupled with a naval one that included seamanship and navigation. In 1939 he found himself to be excited and looking forward to the war. He characterized the old R-class battleship as 'out of date completely' with an 'old fashioned' captain. According to Stedman, the captain followed the naval tradition of inviting newly arrived officers to dine with him. The captain, however, apparently deemed midshipmen as only worthy of his time at a breakfast rather than at a formal dinner. Stedman remembered that the breakfast to which he and his fellow midshipmen were invited was a painfully awkward affair. The midshipmen dared not speak before the captain did. The captain, for his part, said little except to curtly ask the most general of questions about the young men's hometowns, schooling and places of training.

In the early days of the war, when a German invasion could not be ruled out, *Resolution* was one of the Royal Navy's ships used to carry British gold to safety in Canada. Midshipman Stedman thought that the loading process for the gold in England was lackadaisical. He remembered that only a few bored looking police officers stood around as several Bank of England employees casually watched while the ship's sailors carried the boxes of gold bars up the gangway. When they arrived in Canada, however, Stedman noted that security for the gold was much more stringent. He saw large numbers of red-coated Mounties waiting on the dock to escort the boxes to wherever they were destined to go. Once the gold had been taken off in a convoy of stout looking trucks, Stedman took the opportunity to enjoy his time at Halifax. He was granted leave on which he ventured to try his hand at ice skating. He spent an afternoon under the tutelage of what he fondly remembered as a nicely shaped Canadian instructress. He quickly learned that it was more fun to remain unsteady on his feet, as this led to her holding and guiding him around the rink!

The reality of war soon reached Stedman in early 1940 when *Resolution* was assigned to the relief of HMS *Warspite* in the Norwegian theatre. The ship patrolled around the fjords, some of which still remained littered with the hulks of the German destroyers that had been wrecked by *Warspite* and her destroyer companions in the second Battle of Narvik. *Resolution's* general mission while in Norway was to act as a base ship from which troops would be sent ashore to attempt to regain control of Narvik from the Germans. A secondary mission called for the battleship to provide anti-aircraft cover for British forces in the area.

The young midshipman remembered that *Resolution* used her heavy guns to engage in several duels against a heavy calibre German gun that was positioned ashore. The German artillery piece was concealed in a cliff-side excavation from which it would be moved back and forth on rails. The gun would be run out from its hiding place to fire at *Resolution* which would fire back. The trading of gunfire was not considered too dangerous by the ship's captain who was a stickler for cleanliness and the smart appearance of his ship. He ordered painters over the side even as *Resolution's* 15-inch guns were firing at the Germans. Neither German nor British gunners could manage a hit against one another.

Stedman's most notable military action aboard *Resolution* came during the ship's April 1940 foray into one of the fjords. The midshipman was assigned to take a party of French troops ashore from the battleship for an attack against some of the occupying Germans troops.

*It was in our final days in Narvik that we were given one more task. That was to embark a number of French troops and take them … to a fjord where they would be landed … to (try to) drive the Germans further east and away from the coast … but we didn't have any proper landing craft; we had to use the ship's boats. I was put in charge of the ship's 32 foot cutter. I came alongside the (Resolution's) ladder and embarked far too many French troops … they tumbled into the boat in an excited way … with their guns … and there were far too many of them for safety but nobody was going to force them out again. I then made fast to the boom (extending from the ship's side) and the idea was that I would be towed by the boom … until we reached a point as close to the beach as we could go. I would then order the troops to go. The tow to the beach was fairly hairy because the Res was going way too fast for this boat overloaded with soldiers … the boat almost went under … as we got to the beach and there appeared to be no activity … it was not quite daylight … we proceeded as best we could under oars another 100 yards or so. I thought (to) take a sounding to see if the soldiers would sink or swim as they jumped in … the water was about one fathom which was too much for a soldier with all his equipment. So we went on for another few yards and it appeared they would be to the tops of their knees so I gave the order to go,*

*'Allez,' and out they jumped, not one by one but practically all at the same time and this had the awful effect of rocking the boat until we shipped quite a lot of water ... the soldiers by some miracle or other managed to scramble up to the beach. And then all hell let loose. The Germans had been holding their fire and they were there and bullets started flying everywhere and I got as low as possible in the boat as I could and so did everybody else. There was a nasty noise in the bows and a bullet had come straight through the bows and it made a very neat hole above the water. I turned as quickly as I could and made for the ship ... I secured the boat to the boom ... scrambled aboard ... somebody had the nice manners to say,' Well done' and I scrambled along to the gun room and had a nice glass of whiskey ... I was still shivering, not from cold as much as fear, I think.*

*A midshipman has little part in running the ship. We were invariably under instruction, learning subjects ... so as a midshipman of the watch you were mainly there to try to be helpful and trying to be helpful you just got in the way. The most useful thing a midshipman did on the bridge was to make the ship's cocoa which was so thick you could almost stand the spoon in it. If you didn't do it properly you got ticked off for it. It was only this final operation of landing troops in Norway that I felt I was doing something useful ... I think I did (it) quite well ... it gave me a certain amount of self-satisfaction and I was happy about that.*[14]

Around the time of Stedman's amphibious landing adventure, *Resolution* was attacked by German aircraft and hit by a bomb. The bomb penetrated the quarterdeck to detonate in the Royal Marine mess. Stedman watched as a Marine Sergeant mustered the injured troops and marched them in orderly fashion to the sickbay where the three ship's doctors began to tend to them. Witnesses who were in or near the sickbay were suddenly horrified to see the injured men fall to the deck one by one. Unknown at the time, they were suffering from unseen brain damage caused by the concussion of the bomb blast. All of them, 38 Royal Marines, as Stedman recalled, died. The midshipman cried as his deceased and shrouded shipmates were slipped over the side for an at-sea burial.[15]

## 'A Sad Situation'
## The British Attack on the French Fleet at Mers-el-Kebir

After her bomb damage was patched up, *Resolution* was sent to join other Royal Navy ships offshore at the Algerian port of Mers-el-Kebir. She was under orders to assist in the July 1940 attack on the French Navy ships based there. The French fleet included the two pre-World War I battleships *Bretagne* and *Provence,* new battlecruisers *Dunkerque* and *Strasbourg,* six destroyers, and a seaplane carrier. The French battlecruisers had commissioned only in 1937 and 1938 respectively. Among the Royal Navy's greatest worries about the French ships were that they were faster than practically all of Britain's capital ships and that they were even more powerful than Germany's new battlecruisers.

Operation Catapult, as the action was called, had been reluctantly devised. Britain was fervently hoping to keep the French naval units in North Africa from falling under Axis control. The wording of France's surrender document to Germany had stated that the French fleet was to be assembled at German and/or Italian ports for demilitarization. The British could not assume that the French ships would not instead be taken over to be rearmed as units of the German or Italian navies. Attempts to convince the French navy to join with the Royal Navy continued even as *Resolution* and other British warships steamed outside the French base. The crew of *Resolution* was kept apprised through regular announcements over the tannoy of how the tense and bitter negotiations were unfolding. If British terms could not be met, the French fleet would have to be destroyed. The local French naval commander ultimately refused British requests to either sail to a French port in Canada or the Caribbean, surrender his ships to the British, or to scuttle them. As it became increasingly clear that the British would have to open fire against their French ally, *Resolution's* captain informed the ship's company that he would forgive any of them who did not feel that they could participate in the pending action. The captain described the situation as 'sad'. Some accepted their captain's offer. The ship was ordered to commence fire on the afternoon of 3 July.

Midshipman Stedman was on the bridge throughout the action that, by his estimation, lasted two hours. *Resolution* made at least one hit on the battleship *Bretagne* which, also hit by shells from other British ships, exploded and sank.

The French returned fire and, using different coloured dyes in their shells for spotting purposes, made several close misses on *Resolution*. The dye splashed onto the battleship and the captain, ever concerned with his ship's appearance, turned to the navigator to ask, 'Do you think the stuff will stain, Pilot?' He was assured that it would not and, satisfied, returned to directing his ship's actions. The French made smoke screens and some of their ships slipped their moorings to make a dash for Toulon. The British force turned to pursue but, hampered by *Resolution's* slow speed of just 18 knots, could not get into gunfire range. Stedman remained at his post on the bridge and, when not making and serving tea to the bridge personnel, tried to stay quietly out of the way. The British force turned back to Gibraltar on the following day.[16]

### 'We Gave the French an Ultimatum'
### The Action as Seen From HMS *Hood*

Along with *Resolution*, the British force at Mers-el-Kebir included battlecruiser *Hood*, battleship *Valiant*, aircraft carrier *Ark Royal*, cruisers *Enterprise* and *Arethusa*, and 11 destroyers. Aboard *Hood*, Artificer Albert Pitman was at his action station in B turret. Although he did not get to see much, except when he would look through the gun mount's periscope, he offered the following perspective of the action:

> *We gave the French an ultimatum to either (surrender) their ships or come out and join us. And they refused … they said that if there was any chance of the Germans trying to take them over they would proceed to their American Station (Martinique in the Caribbean) … Admiral Somerville didn't want to open fire on them nor did we for they were the* Strasbourg *and* Dunkerque *and* Strasbourg *had been our 'chummy ship' … we'd often been on patrol with her … and often under the command of her admiral who was senior to our admiral. But anyway, eventually, Winston Churchill ordered us to open fire and we killed a lot of Frenchmen that day.*
>
> *I remember that the* Strasbourg *and* Dunkerque *got out and run for it … and I was looking out the periscope of the turret and I could see red splashes*

*and green splashes and I knew the red splashes were from* Dunkerque *and the green from* Strasbourg ... *and you have to remember that they were 13.5-inch shells that were falling ... eventually we went after the* Strasbourg *and we turned and stripped a turbine blade and we had to stop chasing her and I think we were rather relieved that she got away ... she'd been our 'chummy ship'.*[17]

Pitman added that his station during the action was, 'in the working chamber in case anything went wrong'. He recalled that the 15-inch guns did not make much noise, but gave off a 'sort of concussion as they made a forceful 'WHOOMPH!'' The greatest amount of noise was not from the guns going off, but from the shouted orders and the sounds of the machinery raising shells up from the magazines and from the gun breeches opening and closing. In any event, crewmen had little time to dwell on things other than their specific responsibilities. Pitman's job was to remain out of the way of the actual operations of the turret until any part of it might malfunction or become damaged. He was then to step forward, inspect the damage, and make any needed repairs as quickly as possible. Little went wrong, although Pitman recalled that something would 'get stuck' or 'you might spring a leak' from time to time. B turret suffered no mishaps on the day of the attack on the French fleet.[18]

### 'It Was Murder'
### France's Sailors Remember

Andre Jaffre, was a French sailor aboard the hardest hit of the French ships: battleship *Bretagne*. Jaffre remembered that ...

> ... (A) *shell exploded underneath where there were munitions and a fuel store. I saw a friend who had his head blown off. His blood dripped on me. I wanted to be sick ... (as the ship capsized) the water was black with oil that was smoking and bubbling, like a chip pan, and men were struggling and screaming in it. But I had to jump in. I fell into that oil and I let myself sink, sink, sink. I was so burned ... (I) saw bodies all around me, stomachs blown open and severed heads. And the shells kept on falling and guys*

*were shouting, 'Finish me off! Kill me, kill me, please,' because they were so badly burned, had lost limbs, everything. They were asking for the coup de grace. I swam underwater as far as possible from the ship and came up to the surface. But every time I came out of the water I came up into this burning oil. So I breathed in smoke and oil and I'd dive in again for as long as I could. At one point I came up in a spot with no oil and from there I saw an abominable spectacle. The* Bretagne *was capsizing.*[19]

Prior to the commencement of fire, Jaffre had experienced a sense of optimism. Of the appearance of the British he said,

*We were happy to see them. We shouted to each other, 'The British have arrived! They have come to get us to continue the fight against the Nazis!'*[20]

A shipmate of Jaffre, Leon Le Roux added,

*Only two weeks before we'd been with the British in Gibraltar, out on the town, and then suddenly they're firing on us. It was unthinkable. Today we're allies, tomorrow we're enemies. The reasons for it? For that, see Sir Winston Churchill.*[21]

Robert Philpott who was aboard *Hood* that day said of his post-action feelings,

*It was shattering to see what we had just done. It was a scene of utter devastation. I don't have any pride being part of it; only great sadness -- Churchill was in control, not our Admiral (Somerville). If it had been our Admiral, we'd never had done it. But he had a direct order to, 'do it now'.*[22]

Throughout the course of the earlier negotiations, many on the British side, from Admiral Somerville on down, did not believe that some sort of agreement would not be ultimately managed. Philpott added,

*We all firmly believed that the French ships would come out and join us.*[23]

Even into the 21st century there is an enduring French resentment about the attack. Le Roux said,

*What do you want the French to think? It's a betrayal yes, but not only a betrayal, it was murder. A crime. Yes, a real crime.*[24]

Jaffre was not as angry or resentful as his shipmate. He said of the incident,

*It's not betrayal. It was war with all that unfolds, and the consequences of a war. Let us say I was deeply saddened to know that our English friends had sunk us, but what can you do? I speak as an equal, from a French sailor to a British sailor. And let us be honest, have you ever seen an intelligent war?*[25]

In all, 1,297 French were killed and over 300 wounded. Over the course of the war Britain's fears that French naval ships would fight against the Royal Navy were not realised.

### 'The British Sailor With the Eye Patch' Further Adventures for Midshipman Stedman

In September 1940, *Resolution* was on hand for Operation Menace, the invasion of Vichy French Dakar, West Africa (Senegal). The operation was undertaken by combined British and Free French forces led by General Charles DeGaulle. The hope was to quickly oust the Vichy by persuasion rather than by force and to replace them with the Free French. A less publicized justification for the operation on the British side was the long-term security of the 1,500 tons of French, Belgian, and Polish gold stored at Dakar. It had been evacuated in front of Germany's invasion of Europe, but before the fall of France.

Midshipman Stedman was temporarily detached from *Resolution* to board a Free Polish transport ship. From there, he was to take the helm of a landing craft filled with Free French troops. He recalled watching DeGaulle make a rousing and reassuring speech to the landing party assembled on the deck of the Polish ship. They were promised by the future president of France that they would be in no harm. He confidently assured them that, rather than resistance, they would be met with open arms. The landing craft were lowered to the water. Stedman formed up not far behind DeGaulle's own landing craft to follow it towards the beach. Near shore, Stedman watched DeGaulle stand up, wave his arms over his head, and shout, 'I am General DeGaulle and I have come to liberate you. Join with us, the Free French.' This was greeted by a hail of bullets. DeGaulle quickly ducked down and called the landing off. He was not willing to have Frenchmen shed the blood of other Frenchmen. The Allied naval forces remained offshore to shell the harbor and its shore defenses. The new French battleship *Richelieu* was in port and contributed counter fire against the Allies. As she patrolled offshore, *Resolution* was torpedoed by a Vichy submarine and had to be towed back to Freetown. None of her men were killed by the attack. Overall, the operation against the Vichy was not successful. Elements of the Vichy air force bombed Gibraltar in retaliation. The bombing did little damage and Dakar remained firmly under Vichy control.

*Resolution* sat at Freetown for about three months as her crew wrestled with the hole in her hull and a 15-degree list to port. Repair experts from Britain failed to arrive when the ship bringing them to Africa was torpedoed and sunk. Midshipman Stedman remembered that the ship's company spent a miserable time in Freetown. The ship's ventilation system was not functioning and all spaces below decks became unbearably hot. When replenishment ships did not appear, food stores ran low, and the men subsisted on local bananas and sweet potatoes. The crew choked on the fumes of oil and fuel that hung in the hot, heavy air. They could only walk about the ship with an uncomfortable lean as her list could not be corrected. Although they were on 'Tropical Routine' which meant having to work only until one o'clock in the afternoon, there was little to do in the area. According to Stedman, the main recreation was to visit a local beach or go into town to drink 'horrible beer and get thoroughly drunk'. They were finally saved by one of the ship's cooks who had been an underwater welder before the war. The cook volunteered his services and was able to make the ship seaworthy. On 08 December 1940, she steamed out to sea, turned into the cooling Trade Winds, and headed on to Gibraltar.

At Gibraltar, the ship took a number of British ex-patriate refugees on board from southern France where they were being harassed by the Vichy. Stedman found their attitudes hard to take as most were under the impression that the Royal Navy was there to cater to their every whim. He characterized them as, 'a horrible lot'. Many were wealthy and several, among them the writer W. Somerset Maugham, were of celebrity status. Midshipman Stedman found his meeting and personal dealings with the renowned writer less than memorable. Maugham turned out to be 'ultra-demanding'. The writer insisted on fresh water showers when there were none available, demanded a private cabin, most difficult of all, he refused to accept the fact that he and his male companion could not always be served tea punctually and regularly. Unable to contain himself, Stedman boldly confronted Maugham one day by stating, 'Sorry sir. We are not a passenger ship. You'll have to take the rough with the smooth.' Maugham was much taken aback, but was more cordial towards the crew from that point on. All the while, Stedman and the other midshipmen continued with required classroom lessons in French, mathematics, and physics.[26]

As *Resolution* remained under repair at Gibraltar in January 1941, Stedman was once again detached to another ship. This time he was to serve for a while aboard a Royal Navy destroyer. The duty was meant to expand his still very limited naval horizons and experiences. Once aboard, he recalled being told, in very polite terms, to stay off the bridge and out of the way. Added to this admonition was the suggestion that he could likely do best to stay aft to make sure that things would go well there. There was little for him to do on the ship except to go along for the ride. When the destroyer steamed off shore at Genoa, Italy to shell it, Stedman remembered thinking that 'it was rather a nasty thing to do'.

*We arrived off Genoa not having been detected by the Italians at about five in the morning. We opened fire and woke up all the poor Italians who were in their beds. What good it did, I can't think … we had targets, but Genoa did not seem to have any tremendous sort of wartime importance; just a few factories that made a lot of silk and things … we were just firing our … guns into an area … as far as I know there were no Italian warships in Genoa. I think we thought afterwards that it was rather a nasty thing to do … just firing into a seaside port … then we returned to Gibraltar. I think it was just to keep the ships busy and to get the ship's company to think they were doing something.[27]*

Back in Gibraltar, the work on *Resolution* was still not quite complete. The midshipmen were taken to a barracks that had been vacated when the British troops once garrisoned there had been recalled home. The soldiers had left their horses behind, however, and these needed to be exercised. Stedman, who had ridden as a boy, thought the job would be a pleasant one. Things changed when the *Resolution's* navigation instructor took it upon himself to keep the young officers-in-training sharp as they worked with the Army's horses. He took them to the local race track where he climbed into the stands. From up high, where he could be clearly seen, he made hand held flag signals to the mounted trainees below. Each midshipman was to manoeuvre on horseback in response to the signals as if he were navigating a ship at sea.

It was ultimately determined that *Resolution* needed far more work than could be provided at Gibraltar, so she was sent to the US Navy Shipyard at Philadelphia. As the ship approached the American coast, it was asked to please discharge all shells and cordite that were still in the ammunition hoists for the 15-inch guns. When this was done, Stedman was hit in the eye by a hot piece of residue that flew out of a gun's breech as it opened. Normally a blast of compressed air was sent through the still closed breech to rush along the length of the gun barrel from which it would vent all residual gasses. Hot bits of cordite such as struck Stedman would also have been vented out. The air pressure must have been insufficient on this occasion and Stedman was unfortunate enough to be in the way. He was led to sick bay where the surgeon took a look. The medic then gave him the gloomy report of, 'Good, God!' The young sailor suffered from great pain and was transferred to the US Naval Hospital at Philadelphia which he described as 'very splendid'. Stedman commented that his room was so nice and the food was so good that he would have really enjoyed himself there if it had not been for his eye. Over a period of about a week, his eye improved and a patch was placed over it. He began to receive many American visitors who made 'the British sailor with the eye patch' something of a celebrity.

When his eye had fully recovered, Stedman was transferred to the lend-lease US Coast Guard cutter HMS *Sennen*. The midshipman helped sail the ship from New York back to England. *Sennen* would go on to participate in two of the three convoy battles that have been considered as turning points in the war against the U-boats in the Atlantic. Stedman eventually completed his

Lieutenant's course and enjoyed a long naval career. He retired from the Royal Navy in 1965.[28]

## 'Load! Load! Load!'
## Gunfire Support Off the Beaches of Normandy

Following a lengthy yard period and several months on trade defence duty in the Indian Ocean, battleship *Ramillies* was ordered back to England in January 1944. She received an additional refit along with system upgrades. She was to be operated by a reduced crew that meant only two of her four 15-inch turrets could be manned at any given time. Nonetheless, the ship was assigned to provide gunfire support along the British landing zones on D-Day. The ship's sector of responsibility lay between the towns of Arromanches and Caen. Seaman Harry Staff described the conditions within one of *Ramillies* main battery turrets as the big guns fired against the shore.

*When Colours were sounded on the morning of the 6th we raised two enormous battle flags; the White Ensign and the Union Jack. (We were) praying that we had not been spotted by the German shore batteries. Suddenly the order was given, 'With AP and HE shells and a full charge; Load! Load! Load!' Instantly the turret was (filled) with the sounds of breeches, cages, and rammers followed by (the sounds of) the training engine. Nobody spoke, the indicator lights glimmered; the only noise now was the gun layers applying the required range … Approximately at 05.30 the standby two bells sounded. Almost immediately our guns erupted and from then on we were loading and firing as fast as possible. The smell of burning residue crept into the gunhouse and it became very warm. The lads tied the top half of their overalls around their waist. Due to the concussion some of them developed nose bleeding. Being the least occupied I went around with a bucket of water, flannel, and towel. As the day went on we all developed nausea and headaches. After 48 rounds a Walking Pipe (hydraulic) Valve burst. The gun crew immediately transferred to 'B' Turret. During the action we were kept informed of some of the events to date; the progress of the landing craft, the landing, and … the positioning and sinking of the block ships in preparation for the Mulberry Harbors* (large structures towed in to serve as docks and wharves).

*At about 1100 hours the Gunners Mate suggested that I go looking for food and drink (and) anything else I could purloin ... at the galley corn beef sandwiches were available ... and tea ... they were hauled up into the gunhouse. I then went exploring ... the shoreline was a mass of smoke and flame, the noise from all the guns around was horrendous, everything seemed to be vibrating, everywhere I looked smoke was coming from guns. The sea was a mass of ships of all shapes and sizes; landing craft with troops, tanks, guns, and all manner of equipment were heading for the beaches. On our port side a landing craft full up with wounded requested our assistance but they were directed to a hospital ship ... My return to the turret was even more welcome than the food. Passing the Regulating Officer I observed that rum was being issued. On being asked which mess I came from, I explained that the 'A' Turret crew were (shut in) and could not get to their messes. Much to my amazement, I was given a liberal supply.*[29]

ENDNOTES

1.  Imperial War Museum. Sound recording archive. 10673. Crawford, William Godfrey. 1989.

2.  Imperial War Museum. Sound recording archive. 24907. Simpson, Charles. 2003.

3.  Imperial War Museum. 24907.

4.  ——— 'Remembering HMS *Royal Oak*.' rememberingscotlandatwar.org.uk. Web. Accessed July 2014. Transcript of oral history excerpts provided by Royal Oak survivors Kenneth Toop, Taffy Davis, and Don Harris together with local eyewitnesses Captain John Gray and Jim Harrison who spoke about their experiences on the night of the sinking. It cannot be determined which survivor provided which quote.

5.  ——— 'Remembering HMS *Royal Oak*.'

6. —— 'Remembering 'HMS *Royal Oak*.'

7. Imperial War Museum. Sound recording archive. 27302. Stamp, Victor. 2004

8. Manchester tart is described at allrecipes.co.uk and steamed duff is described at celtnet.org.uk. Accessed July 2014.

9. Imperial War Museum. 27302 (Stamp).

10. battleshipbuff (contributor). 'HMS *Ramillies* Legend.' BBC WW2 People's War. Article ID A7535892. 2005.

11. The ship bombarded Italian positions near the Libyan and Egyptian border at Bardia and Fort Capuzzo in August, 1940.

12. Imperial War Museum. 27302. (Stamp).

13. battleshipbuff (contributor).

14. Imperial War Museum. Sound recording archive. 26738. Stedman, John Gilbert. 2004.

15. Imperial War Museum. 26738.

16. Imperial War Museum. 26738.

17. Imperial War Museum. Sound recording archive. 22147. Pitman, Albert. 2001.

18. Imperial War Museum 22147.

19. *Daily Mail*. 'Mass Murder or a Stroke of Genius That Saved Britain?' 05 February 2010. Web. Accessed January 2014.

20. *Daily Mail*.

21. *Daily Mail*.

22. *Daily Mail*.

23. *Daily Mail*.

24. *Daily Mail*.

25. *Daily Mail*.

26. Imperial War Museum. 26738. (Stedman)

27. Imperial War Museum. 26738.

28. Imperial War Museum. 26738.

29. Staff, Harry. 'A Bird's Eye View.' hmsramillies.co.uk. Web. Accessed July 2014.

# FIVE
# FOR THE FALLEN

## HMS *Glorious*

The aircraft carrier *Glorious* was originally ordered and laid down as one of Admiral Fisher's Baltic battle cruisers, in 1915. After World War I though, her limited armament of just four large caliber guns, coupled with thin armour, was considered to be unsatisfactory compared against the Royal Navy's other battle cruisers: *Renown, Repulse* and *Hood.* The shortcomings of *Glorious* (and her sister, HMS *Courageous*), meant that faced with the restrictions on capital ships mandated by the 1922 Naval Arms Limitation Treaty, the opportunities of that document were taken and a seven year process of reconstruction and conversion was embarked upon. Therefore, it was in 1930, that HMS *Glorious* was placed back in commission as an aircraft carrier.

An aircraft carrier in 1939, as down to the present day, was manned by two distinct crews: the ship's company and the air wing. The ship's company included all the officers and men, from the captain to the cooks, who were stationed aboard the ship to operate her. The airwing included the planes, pilots, and all support personnel such as air crew and mechanics. An air wing would go aboard any carrier to which official orders assigned them. Along with their flight-related responsibilities, once shipboard, air wing personnel would take on all duties necessary for the ship's operation and safety

Control of the Royal Navy Air Service, RNAS, by the Royal Air Force, RAF, in the inter-war years had placed severe limitations on the growth and development of British naval aviation. Interested Royal Navy officers, despite their appreciation and understanding of ships and naval warfare, were discouraged from applying for pilot training. There was a broad belief that spending time in the realm of the Air Force would be a detriment to advancement in the Navy. Additionally, the inventory of obsolete aircraft allocated to the Navy along with the slow development of newer models suitable for the demands of carrier warfare left one historian to note,

> In September 1939 the FAA's aircraft were clearly inferior … This was the result of twenty years of dual control with the RAF which caused an alarming drift in naval air policy which affected aircraft procurement. The Air Staff gave a very low priority to naval needs such as torpedo bombers and was actively opposed to dive bombers. The first British dive bomber was the Blackburn Skua, 1938, and it was recognized as a failure before it even entered its short-lived service.[1]

RAF control of Royal Navy aviation, later called the Fleet Air Arm, or FAA, would not be fully relinquished until the spring of 1939. Despite any inconvenience created by that situation Royal Navy pilots and aircrews were dedicated to the challenges of their work and the pending war. The rigours and dangers facing them were deadly serious, but the pilots and crews of the Fleet Air Arm and the ships' companies aboard the fleet's aircraft carriers remained well prepared and undaunted for what was soon to come their way.

## 'A Stroll Along the Waterfront to Ogle the Girls'
### *Glorious'* Sailors and Airmen

Ernest Kerridge was born on a farm in Cambridgeshire and left school at 16 to begin his naval career as a boy seaman in 1933. Upon completion of his training, Kerridge was sent to his duty station for the next five years, the battlecruiser *Renown*. When a fleet-wide call for volunteers to the Fleet Air Arm was issued in 1938, he took a backseat flight in *Renown*'s scout plane. He immediately decided, 'This is the life for me'. He was sent to an RAF training base where he learned radio operations and gunnery. He was a seasoned veteran of almost seven years when he joined *Glorious* as a TAG, Telegraphist-Air Gunner, with 812 Squadron in 1939. 812 was a torpedo-bomber squadron equipped with the durable, but slow-flying and obsolescent Fairey Swordfish torpedo plane. Kerridge recalled that the pilots, aircrews, and other personnel of the squadrons got along well with the officers and men of the ship's company. He thought that flying in the open cockpit of the Swordfish during the pre-war summer cruise days in the Mediterranean was a 'wonderful experience'. Whenever a plane landed back aboard a carrier in those days, the crew would go directly to the bridge. They would present themselves smartly to report with a salute and statement to the captain that, 'such-and-such aircraft has landed aboard, sir!' The start of war was piped throughout the ship over the tannoy as *Glorious* lay at anchor in Alexandria harbor. The crew was not overly alarmed, so many went ashore on liberty that night in pursuit of all the things that young men in uniform most enjoy. Kerridge and 812 Squadron were detached from the ship before she was sent to Norway in 1940.[2]

RAF pilot Walter Sutcliffe served aboard *Glorious* from 1933–1939 with the same 812 squadron as TAG Kerridge. Although he believed that the FAA's reputation was good within the RAF, Sutcliffe indicated that the average RAF pilot may have been reluctant to join it. They shared similar misgivings with their Royal Navy colleagues. Air Force personnel believed that flying for the Navy would do a pilot, in pursuit of a solid RAF career, no real good. Nonetheless, he reiterated that he and other RAF pilots that he flew with were proud to serve with the FAA and the Navy.

Sutcliffe recalled that his early training was in the Blackburn Ripon, a naval torpedo bomber of the mid-1920s that was the Swordfish's predecessor. The plane could fly as slowly as 35 miles per hour and had a top speed of 90 miles per hour. Sutcliffe remembered being able to hover the aircraft at low speed in a strong headwind. He laughingly stated that, if the wind were particularly strong, the plane would even fly backwards. His first carrier landing was his most disconcerting. The narrow 'aerodrome,' or the flight deck below him, pitched about on the sea, the ship's exhaust gases created a forceful turbulence as he made his approach, and he could barely see the ship for the bulk of his airplane's nose. In those pre-war days, the ship had no arresting wires and the Ripon had no brakes. Sutcliffe managed to make a safe landing with 'heart in my mouth'. He credited his survival to the strong wind over the deck and the muscles of the crewmen who had rushed out to grab the wings of his plane as soon as it touched down.[3]

The pilots sometimes practiced torpedo attacks on the fleet's surface ships. Torpedoes were fitted with dummy warheads that had a number painted on them. Whenever a pilot hit his target during practice, the nose of the torpedo would be crushed. Once the torpedoes were hauled out of the water, pilots would gather around them to see who among them was lucky that day. A target ship's movement, coupled with that of the attacking aircraft, made it quite difficult to obtain a hit. According to Sutcliffe, the torpedo plane pilot had to rely on dead reckoning and personal judgment to press home a successful attack. There were also questions regarding the reliability of a Fleet Air Arm airplane itself. Sutcliffe clearly recalled an incident in 1934 when he was in formation at 14,000 feet. He was just about to drop to torpedo attack level when his plane began to quickly lose both speed and altitude. Looking ahead, he noticed that his sparkplug wires were flapping around. The plugs had apparently blown themselves out. Sutcliffe desperately scanned the sea below until he spotted a destroyer that was not too far away. He dropped a distress flare. Wrestling with what control he had over his disabled plane, Sutcliffe nervously glided it to a water landing just ahead of the alerted destroyer.

Sutcliffe's time with 812 Squadron, eventually equipped with the Swordfish, was spent in the Mediterranean going back and forth between *Glorious* and Hal Far shore base on Malta. Shuttling between ship and shore was routine for the FAA. Pilots and planes were able to keep flying even when their carrier was docked. Aboard ship, the air squadrons were under the complete command of the captain. Typically, the captain and the air wing's flight commander, called the Wing Commander, Flying, would consult together to determine what and how flight operations were to be conducted. Factors weighed included weather conditions and the state of the sea. In wartime, strategic and tactical planning would also be shared by the ship's captain and the air wing commander. It was always the captain of the ship, however, who would have the absolute final word no matter what disagreement the wing commander might offer.

On Malta, Hal Far, a very comfortable base, was located about seven or eight miles from the capital city of Valletta. The airstrip was lined with hangars on one side and pilots' quarters on the other. Each pilot had his own high-ceilinged room with a veranda to the front. The soft Maltese stone with which the pilots' quarters had been built made them cool in the summer and warm in the winter. For entertainment, the pilots would all congregate at an establishment called 'Beppo's Bar' which was not a bar in the true sense as it served no alcohol. The fliers would sip orange squashes and soft drinks in the midst of many a long and relaxed conversation. Sutcliffe remembered his three years of service with 812 and *Glorious* as 'a pleasant life'. [4]

Richard Griffin spoke about his early days as a Fleet Air Arm enlisted man:

*The Navy at the time* (1939) *was about to start replacing Royal Air Force personnel then serving on HM ships with newly trained naval ratings. I volunteered for this new air branch as an air mechanic ... My official number was S.F.X. 5 which made me the fifth person to join. After new entry training at HMS* Victory *at Portsmouth.* [5] *I ... went ... for technical training to the RAF gunnery school at Sheerness where we learned all about guns, bombs (and) explosives ... Pay for us in those times was seven shillings* (20 of which made a Pound) *per week, so being broke one night, two 'oppos'* (slang for naval personnel trained for and assigned to the same job) *went into (town). I produced my P.O. bank book at the Post Office, drew out the total balance which amounted to one shilling, then with this huge sum* (12 pence to the shilling) *we bought three half pints of beer which came to sixpence, one packet of five cigarettes at tuppence, then around to the fish and chip shop for four pennyworth of fish and chips. We then took a stroll along the waterfront to ogle the girls. A happy evening for one shilling!* [6]

One of *Glorious'* ship's company was Frederick Cooke. Cooke joined the Royal Navy as a boy seaman in 1930 to seek adventure, have something to do and simply, to get away to someplace interesting. His initial physical exam included lining up completely undressed with the other enlistees to jump up and down so that it could be seen if all their parts were in good order. Their teeth, hearing and vision were then closely checked. Cooke went on to enjoy the sense of discipline and direction that military life offered. He was particularly pleased with the education provided him by the Navy.

Cooke's duties as a torpedoman included serving on the three-man crew responsible for preparing and loading torpedoes onto aircraft. The men would push a torpedo by trolley directly under a plane and, with one man to the front and one each to either side, hoist it up. They would do one test drop and then reload the torpedo. There was no real danger of a premature explosion as the detonator, threaded into the nose of the weapon, would not be armed until it had turned a certain number of revolutions after being released by the plane. The greatest danger, according to torpedoman Cooke, was to the hands or fingers from the sharp edges of a torpedo's propellers. There was little contact between the enlisted men, or ratings, of the lower deck and the ship's officers, but Cooke recalled that there were no problems between the two groups and that '*Glorious* was a good ship'.[7]

James O'Neill joined the Navy in 1936 after leaving school at the age of twelve and having worked in construction for nine years. He volunteered to be a stoker, a term which survived from the age when brute manpower was required for the shoveling of coal into the massive burners that powered a ship. By O'Neill's time, however, a stoker's responsibilities had become quite sophisticated. Stokers kept the ship running smoothly by tending to a wide variety of equipment that included the electricity generating dynamos, condensers that converted seawater to fresh, aircraft elevator and arresting gear hydraulic systems, ship's refrigeration, boilers, and engine rooms. Being a stoker appealed to him because it paid six pence more per month than what a seaman earned. There were still hot and sweaty jobs, however, as *Glorious'* eighteen boilers, placed by threes in a total of six boiler rooms, demanded regular service and cleaning. It was especially important that the fuel jets that pumped oil into the boilers be kept clean.

O'Neill was typical of practically all enlisted personnel in that he had very little contact with the ship's captain. He did, however, get to meet Captain D'Oyly-Hughes of *Glorious* on several occasions when he was put up on charges for fighting ashore or for reporting back on board late from leave. On each occasion, O'Neill was brought into the captain's presence. He would be required to stand in silence while the particular charge against him was pronounced. The captain, after a brief pause during which he would glare in an intimidating manner at the offender, would sternly announce the sentence. The punishment was generally commensurate with the relatively benign nature of O'Neill's transgressions. He was usually given little more than extra duty or restriction from future leave. In general, O'Neill later characterised *Glorious* as a well-disciplined and pleasant ship where everyone worked well together. 'It was great,' he said.[8]

### 'What Took You So Long?'
### Leaving Norway

*Glorious* was at Alexandria on the day the war began. She was sent through the Suez Canal to the Indian Ocean where her assignment was to search for German Surface Raiders. Her patrols took her as far eastward as Colombo, Ceylon. Her embarked airwing during this time consisted of thirty-six Swordfish torpedo bombers and, depending on the date, six to twelve Sea Gladiator fighters.[9] The ship and its planes did not encounter German warships, as such the last months of 1939 were relatively quiet ones for *Glorious*. She then transferred back to the Mediterranean for another period of relative quiet through April of 1940.

In late April, *Glorious* and another aircraft carrier, *Ark Royal*, arrived in Norwegian waters in response to that month's German invasion of Norway. The carriers lent support to the British troops who had landed in Norway about a week behind the invading Germans. *Glorious* had also been ordered to help with the delivery of RAF fighter planes to hastily prepared Norwegian airstrips from which they were expected to support the ongoing Norwegian resistance.

The Navy had agreed to transport Squadron Leader Kenneth Cross and his RAF 46 Squadron's eighteen Hurricanes to Norway in May 1940. The planes had been modified with variable pitch propellers so that they would be better able to take off from *Glorious'* short flight deck. Since the planes would not be returning to a carrier, they were not fitted with arresting hooks. The planes were hoisted aboard by the ship's cranes for the trip. Before flying off, Cross, who would ultimately rise in rank to become Air Chief Marshal Sir Kenneth Cross, made his acquaintance with the ship's commanding officer, Captain D'Oyly-Hughes. The captain spoke just a few curt words that left the young RAF officer with the lingering impression that D'Oyly-Hughes was neither very friendly nor particularly welcoming. Just prior to 46 Squadron's takeoff to Norway, Captain D'Oyly-Hughes and Squadron Leader Cross had a disagreement over operational procedures. In a manner that seemed particularly odd to him, the junior officer had to endure an upbraiding from the captain about military manners and how junior officers needed to know their place when in the company of their superiors.[10] The ship launched all of 46 Squadron's aircraft in a routine manner and all reached Norway safely. The next day, however, the German air force found them parked in the open on a makeshift air field and attacked. Ten of the planes were destroyed.

For the remainder of April and all of May, *Glorious'* airwing flew support for ground operations and attacked enemy shipping in and around Norway. Between air operations, the ship shuttled between Scotland and Norway to ferry in replacement aircraft to be used ashore by the RAF. By early June, on the heels of the German invasion of France and the Dunkirk evacuation, the British position back on the European continent had become dire. Mounting fears of a German invasion of England forced the British hand. They needed as many troops and aircraft as possible at home. Norway was to be evacuated.

*Glorious* and *Ark Royal* were ordered to provide air cover for the convoy that would carry British troops and equipment homeward. King Haakon VII of Norway, his government, plus a substantial portion of Norway's gold reserves were embarked aboard the British cruiser *Devonshire* for transport to England. The Norwegian monarch would ultimately establish a Norwegian government in exile in London. British Army troops were loaded aboard troop transports that were accompanied by an escort of several cruisers and a strong contingent of destroyers.

When the British reached the decision to leave Norway just a few weeks after *Glorious'* delivery of 46 Squadron, Squadron Leader Cross was given two drastic alternatives. He was either to destroy his ten remaining planes before leaving, or fly them to a far northern airstrip, dismantle them, and wait for possible transport of both men and planes by freighter should one become available. The former choice was wholly unappealing to Cross and his squadron and the second left too much to chance. Cross requested permission to use sand bags to weight down his planes' tails. He would then attempt to fly them back aboard either *Ark Royal* or *Glorious*. The request was granted, but *Ark Royal,* despite having the longer flight deck of the two carriers, could not accommodate the Hurricanes. The fighters were not equipped with the folding wings typical of naval aircraft. They would not fit onto *Ark Royal*'s elevators for transport from the flight deck to the hangar spaces below. The planes, therefore, flew to *Glorious* where they all landed within the span of just two thirds of her flight deck albeit with the very firm application, by each pilot, of full brakes. Cross, safely aboard *Glorious* for the second time, was rather pleased with his squadron's accomplishment. He reported to Captain D'Oyly-Hughes on the bridge. The captain's response, according to Cross, was a sharp and dismissive, 'What took you so long?'[11] The aircraft, sorely needed at home for defence against the Blitz, would all soon be lost.

Early on 8 June, Captain Guy D'Oyly-Hughes of *Glorious*, requested permission to separate from the well protected primary evacuation force. D'Oyly-Hughes' rationale for sacrificing the safety of numbers for independent steaming was that,

HMS *Ark Royal*

in addition to being low on fuel, his immediate presence was required at Scapa Flow for a court martial proceeding. The captain had instigated the court martial several weeks earlier against Commander (Air) J.B. Heath. Differences between the two men about procedures pertinent to air operations had escalated to the point where Captain D'Oyly-Hughes ordered Commander Heath ashore in late May, just prior to *Glorious'* latest deployment. Commander Heath had allegedly refused orders to plan and execute air strikes against German shore targets in Norway. The conduct of the captain in this matter had been characterized as less than professional by some aboard *Glorious,* but it has also been noted that not all of the ship's airwing was in full support of Commander Heath. [12.] After the war, there were suggestions that Captain D'Oyly-Hughes seemed to be excessively impatient and harsh with his officers. The ship's Master at Arms had also expressed concern that morale had been suffering among the enlisted men, and that there were more of them than usual who were going AWOL.[13] This led some to think that *Glorious* had been a troubled or unhappy ship under Captain D'Oyly-Hughes. This view has been partially refuted by Vice Admiral Donald Cameron Gibson who, at the time, was a junior officer and pilot of the embarked 804 Squadron. After the war, Vice Adm Gibson said he felt that, although aware that there was friction among some of the higher ranking officers on board, his recollection was that *Glorious* 'was a very happy ship, indeed'. When asked about the nature of the morale aboard the carrier, the admiral stated that 'it seemed very good'. He added that, as a flyer serving under Commander Heath, he felt that he 'was a very nice man,' although the commander's preference for not using arresting cables on landing bothered him greatly.[14]

Very early on 8 June, *Glorious* was granted permission by the overall commander of the carriers aboard *Ark Royal*, Vice Admiral L. V. Wells, to detach. The carrier was assigned a pair of destroyers, HMS *Acasta* and *Ardent,* as escort. The three ships steamed along at 17 knots with the destroyers disposed ahead of and off each bow of the carrier. Condition four readiness, the least urgent of conditions numbered from one through four, was set. There were no aircraft spotted on the carrier's deck, and none were aloft on patrol. At about 4:o'clock that afternoon, visual contact with two unknown ships was made by a lookout aboard *Glorious.* As several Swordfish were brought up from the carrier's hangar deck, *Ardent* was sent to investigate. Action stations was sounded aboard *Glorious.*

## German Battlecruisers

The ships sighted were the Kriegsmarine's sister battlecruisers *Gneisenau* and *Scharnhorst* that had originally sortied for a mission designed to support German ground operations in Norway. They were under additional orders to attack any enemy shipping that might cross their path. The two ships were each armed with a main battery of nine 11-inch guns and a secondary battery of twelve 5.9-inch guns. The combined secondary batteries of the two Kriegsmarine warships alone could readily supply the equivalent firepower of as many as four British light cruisers. By this time, the German force commander had sensed that the British were evacuating Norway. He had already sunk a small tanker and a troopship while searching for a possible convoy to attack. Now, he had just met up with the much surprised *Glorious, Ardent,* and *Acasta.* The Germans wasted little time in opening fire. *Ardent* responded by launching torpedoes which did not hit anything. The destroyer turned about and steamed back to

Battlecruiser
*Scharnhorst* In
Wilhelmshaven
when first completed

View of the *Gneisenau*'s forward two triple 283mm (11-in) gun turrets, with forecastle and capstans in the foreground. The battleship *Scharnhorst* can be seen in the distance

rejoin *Glorious*. The two British destroyers began to make smoke screens with which to cover their carrier. Unable to spot a clear target through the smoke, the Germans held fire on *Glorious* for a while. *Ardent,* however, steamed back towards the Germans. She challenged them with her guns and managed to make a hit on *Scharnhorst*. The Germans countered with a barrage of 5.9-inch shells that soon found the destroyer's range. *Ardent* could not survive the heavy hits placed onto her by her enemies. Meanwhile, the smokescreen began to dissipate enough for the Germans to begin shooting at *Glorious* with their main batteries again. The carrier took a hit from just the third German salvo. The shell pierced the flight deck to continue on its way into the hangar deck where it started a fire. *Glorious*, her flight deck holed and hangar deck ablaze, was now incapable of launching any of her hurriedly and belatedly prepared Swordfish. Several of the torpedo planes were destroyed by the German shell hits, anyhow. The smoke screen further dissipated to allow the Germans to pour fire onto the carrier. As she was being pummeled by shell after shell, she took a hit to her engineering spaces that caused her to lose speed. She burned and smoked heavily.

*Glorious* went down less than an hour after absorbing her first hit and no more than 20 minutes after the order to abandon ship was first passed. *Acasta* made a dash towards the Germans and launched torpedoes. One hit *Scharnhorst* aft, below her 11-inch gun turret and caused her to lose speed. *Acasta* also placed a gunfire hit on the German battlecruiser but, as the brave destroyer turned to retire, she was pursued by heavy salvoes of return gunfire which sank her about a half hour after *Ardent* had gone down.[15]

The Germans felt compelled to follow standing orders for instances in which any of their ships were to be damaged in combat. They immediately broke off action and returned to port. They did not stop to search for survivors. The German battlecruisers were later criticized by higher authority for not following orders to attack shipping and for chasing down an old aircraft carrier instead. In the end, only 37 men from *Glorious* survived along with one each from the destroyers for a total of 39.[16]

## 'There Was Absolutely No Sign of Panic'
## The Attack

As it was very early in the morning of 8 June by the time the last of 46 Squadron's planes had landed aboard *Glorious*, the pilots all retired to their bunks for some much needed sleep. Squadron Leader Cross slept until very late, but was in the wardroom having a cup of tea when action stations sounded. He initially thought it was a drill, but nonetheless hurried to his assigned position. Since he was not a member of the ship's company or the attached air wing, his instructions were to report to his abandon ship station. Standing by, Cross soon saw two patches of smoke on the horizon. They were followed by bright flashes. Shortly afterwards, three great plumes of water sprouted upwards just 10 yards from the ship. Cross thought to report to the bridge for instructions in the hope being given something useful to do, but a shell penetrated the flight deck. He decided that it would be best to not get in the way of the ships' officers, so he stayed put. The bridge soon took a hit and the ship's internal communications became inoperable. Commands had to be handled by messengers and runners. It was assumed (correctly) that the hit on the bridge had killed the captain. Over the next thirty to forty minutes *Glorious* continued to absorb damage. Burning and smoking with a sharp list while still making 12 knots, the stricken carrier was ordered abandoned. According to Cross,

(T)he atmosphere aboard *Glorious* during the attack … *was absolutely splendid. There was absolutely no sign of panic from the beginning to the end ... and when the inter-communication system failed which might have led to some disorder it was quickly picked up by the messenger system and I saw no sign of panic or indiscipline of any sort during the whole of the action. I've got the greatest admiration for the naval crew and the way they behaved during the action.*[17]

Torpedoman Cooke, who had the additional duty of running the ship's cinema, recalled that *Glorious* was expected to be in port by the evening of the 8th. He spent a part of his day setting up the projector and film reels for that night's movie. When he was done, he had no other duty, so he went to his quarters. He took a shower and changed clothes, before stopping by the mess decks for a little something to eat. He then went back to check on the projector when he noticed a sudden 'bang – bang,' felt the ship surge forward and heard the call to action stations. He went to his action station below decks in a damage control station where he donned his assigned set of headphones. He job was to monitor reports of damage or calls for repairs. While he was unable to see what was happening, he was able to follow much of *Glorious*' last action over the ship's voice communication circuits. He first heard orders for torpedoes to be taken to the flight deck for loading onto any available or ready Swordfish. He recalled saying aloud to himself, 'Thank goodness for that'. He wished that he were on the flight deck to help with his usual duty of loading the torpedoes. He next heard, 'I don't think they're gonna do it (take torpedoes up) now ... I think they've scrubbed it and they're taking them back down.' At the same time, Cooke could 'hear and feel crashes all over the place'. He did not know that Glorious had taken hits on the flight and hangar decks or that there would no longer be any way to launch aircraft. What he heard next gave him a clear picture of the ship's status, though, '... the hangar's on fire ... they're trying to get the screens down ... the screens are down'. As he fretted about torpedoes and other munitions possibly exploding from the fires, he heard, 'Hands prepare to abandon ship'. That announcement was shortly followed by, 'Hands to abandon ship stations'.[18]

Vernon Day would survive the loss of *Glorious* and go on to endure further terrors in the form of Japanese Kamikaze attacks in the Pacific. He joined the Navy in February 1939 in response to an ad that called for volunteer air mechanics. Day thought that it would provide him with good job training for the future. He also assumed that war was not long in coming, so he decided that he might as well join as wait to be called up. On the day of the attack on *Glorious,* Day had little to do because the plane to which he was assigned had been damaged earlier by a hard landing. He was below decks at tea when action stations sounded. He was sent to the after part of the hangar deck to help prepare one of the ship's five remaining Swordfish for launch. He replaced the plane's engine cowling while armourers swapped out its bomb racks for a torpedo rack. As he was finishing his job, a shell crashed through the flight deck and landed amidships in the hangar deck. This set 46 Squadron's Hurricanes on fire. Day was ordered to help get the sprinkler system going and then to assist with lowering the fire screens. Although he could see many injured and dead shipmates all around him, he had little time to be frightened. When he heard the call to abandon ship, he went to his abandon ship station on the forward portion of the ship's original lower flying off deck. While he waited, he heard the call to return to action stations but, knowing the extent of the damage to the hangar deck, he did not go. Soon afterwards, abandon ship was called again. Day jumped 'a long way down' into the water.[19]

## 'It All Seems Like a Dream to Me' – Survivors

Squadron Leader Cross remembered that, during abandon ship, hundreds of Carley floats were tossed over the side. Men had to jump immediately after them if they did not want the ship's momentum to carry them too far away from a float. Cross was wearing his Mae West when he jumped. In the water, he found a raft just 10 yards away. He did not delay in climbing onto it. There were already about 20 to 30 men, including 46 Squadron's second in command who would also survive, in the raft. They watched as *Glorious* surged on for another quarter mile before stopping. Mere moments later, the carrier disappeared beneath the surface. With the action over, Cross warily watched the two large German ships approach his group of survivors. Worried that he could be picked up by the Germans, he carefully removed the squadron's papers from his pocket, dropped them into the water, and saw them sink away. Both of the German battlecruisers passed very close, but neither so much as slowed down.

It was early evening and the water was rough and cold. Within three hours, men began to die of exposure. There were soon only seven men left alive on Cross' raft. The pilot was amazed to notice that several of the survivors on the raft were older or wounded, while many of those who had died were young and uninjured. The seven men sat there without food or water for hour after hour. They could not get a sense of time as the far northern latitudes remained light twenty-four hours a day during the summer months. By what was probably the next day, there were no other floats within sight of that which held Cross and his remaining six companions. Hundreds of men and floats had simply disappeared. Cross and those with him mostly slept, but they were careful to keep at least one man awake as a lookout at all times. At the end of the second day, they were spotted by a Norwegian tramp steamer that was sailing away from home to escape the German occupation. The ship rescued the seven men.[20]

Torpedoman Cooke had difficulty moving about as the ship, still making way ahead, was listing 45-degrees to starboard. He climbed over a pile of bodies just to make his way over or through even more bodies before reaching a boat. He and several others struggled, but the boat was stuck fast and could not be moved in the least. Cooke decided to blow up his lifebelt, kick off his shoes, and jump into the water. It was very cold as he swam about looking for a boat or raft. He was repeatedly hit in the face by waves and swallowed a good deal of seawater before spotting a raft. Although it was crowded to the point of being submerged, he was helped into it. The men, a good number standing in the raft's center, squeezed together even more closely to make room for Cooke. There were two paddles aboard so the torpedoman took one and used it to row. He was trying to move the raft away from the ship which was continuing to give off large amounts of smoke. Cooke assumed that the smoke was from the hangar deck fires. He did not relish being caught up in an explosion. He watched as a destroyer that he thought was *Acasta* lay quietly behind the burning *Glorious* until the carrier slipped under. Then, according to Cooke, the destroyer …

> … *went straight at them two battleships and started firing, firing, and everything. I thought it was a wonderful sight, that. I never saw the* Acasta *struck.*[21]

Cooke maintained a strong belief that he would be picked up. He even practiced the little bit of German that he had once learned, just in case either *Scharnhorst* or *Gneisenau* were to rescue him. Someone on the raft told him, 'You'll be alright; you can talk to them'. The Germans steamed away but, Cooke still thought that he and the others were bound to be picked up before too long. Then, everyone on the raft spotted a distant plane. They tried to draw the pilot's attention by waving vigorously in its direction, but it flew off. Someone said, 'It's one of ours. They'll be coming back'. Eventually, all the other rafts had drifted away and Cooke and his raft mates were alone.

It was not long before men began to die. For the most part, they would just quietly slip away as if falling asleep. At first, those who were still alive would try to revive or resuscitate those who died, but they soon gave up as weariness set in. The living would lift the dead and drop them into the water. As the raft became lighter, it floated higher. Those remaining could at least prop themselves up to attempt to dry off. Soon, there were only four others besides Cooke. Two were Maltese who passed the time in prayer. The others were an Irishman from Belfast and an Englishman from Liverpool. They sat on the bodies of those that they had been too weak to put over the side. Once the four others had also died, Cooke took some of their clothing, said his prayers every half hour, and continued to paddle just to stay active and warm. He finally saw smoke on the horizon and, shortly after, what he was certain was a ship. He draped some clothing onto the end of his paddle and waved it and waved it. It was, indeed, a ship. The Norwegian trawler *Borgund* was picking up other survivors, but it spotted Cooke and soon pulled him aboard. He figured that he had been adrift for two days and nineteen hours and that originally there had been forty-seven men on his raft. Of his physical condition at the time of his rescue he said, 'I was pretty good, really. I was so pleased to be alive.'[22]

Vernon Day's main recollections of his time in the water were of the cold and the thirst. He recalled that the water temperature was just above freezing. He watched as some drank sea water. He understood the futility and fatal nature of it so did not himself do so. He also saw men drink their own urine and watched as one cut his own finger in order to suck on the blood. Someone suggested that they suck on buttons which Day did just to keep the moisture from his saliva going.[23]

Frederick Thornton had left school at fourteen to work as a grocer's boy and a merchant seaman. He volunteered for the Royal Navy as a seventeen-year-old boy seaman in 1939. The youngster, who had gotten so homesick that he cried on the train back to his training base following Christmas leave, now found himself immersed to the waist in freezing water aboard a Carley float. His main thoughts and hopes were that the ship must have sent distress messages and rescue would not be long in coming. At first, he and his shipmates were certain that the Germans who had sunk them would stop. Then, they were confident that a plane that appeared shortly after the Germans had steamed off would report their plight. They passed a wet, cold, and rough night alone. Thornton recalled that, after the first night, the sea remained calm and the sky was mostly sunny and bright. He remembered that his spirits lifted several times after seeing smoke on the horizon, but he retained enough of his wits to remember that when nothing came of the sightings, they must have been mirages. Thornton still managed to remain hopeful even after one of the men on the raft stood up, quietly announced, 'I'm leaving,' stepped off into the water, and swam away. Finally, he was amazed and grateful to see what turned out to be the *Bogund*. After watching it steam slowly back and forth, it pulled alongside and a line was placed around his waist to haul him aboard. A second man, and the only other survivor in Thornton's raft, James O'Neill, was likewise taken aboard *Bogund*. Speaking about the experience in 1996 Thornton said, 'It all seems like a dream to me.'[24]

Stoker O'Neill's experiences while in the water were similar to those of the other survivors. In the end, he attributed his survival to an old superstition. His mother had been given a baby's caul, a piece of birth membrane that covers a newborn's face. Many years later, she gave it to O'Neill. The popular belief, dating back to ancient times, was that a caul would help save a sailor from drowning at sea.

After being returned to England, O'Neill remembered that all of the survivors were kept separated. O'Neill thought that the Navy was afraid that they would 'cause trouble'. He thought that it had somehow come to the Navy's attention that some of the men had made comments to the effect that they might have been unnecessarily abandoned. For his own part, O'Neill was interviewed by what he remembered was 'a panel of officers' representing the Admiralty. O'Neill remembered the following bits from his interview:

> *... whose fault did I think it was that* Glorious *was sunk ... (I) told them it was their fault, saying, 'we should never have been sunk the way we were; we should have had more protection ... we should have had more planes ... to spot for us at least.'*

O'Neill said that his statement was not taken down and added that he '... was a bit needled about that'. Despite his earlier recollections that things were 'great' aboard *Glorious*, he apparently developed hard feelings against the captain which he admitted came about through what he had read after the war. Of Captain D'Oyly-Hughes he said, '(I) don't care much for him' and that he blamed him for '... what he done to *Glorious*'. He was critical of the captain for being a glory hunter who was seeking a second VC to go with the one he earned as a submarine officer during World War I. O'Neill claimed to have been within earshot and '... (the Captain) was talking one time, and that's what he said'. O'Neill also expressed frustration about how he felt the captain had handled the tactical situation poorly on the day *Glorious* was sunk. O'Neill felt that it was the inappropriate detachment of the ship just for the sake of the captain making it to Scapa Flow to attend Commander Heath's court martial that endangered them all.[25]

After the war, some Kriegsmarine veterans who had been aboard *Gneisenau* when *Glorious, Ardent,* and *Acasta* were sunk were especially generous with their praise for the two destroyers that seemingly have been all but forgotten by history. According to the former Kriegsmarine sailors, the men aboard *Ardent* and *Acasta* fought with ...

> *... real naval skill. It was outstanding, the way they fought for* Glorious. Ardent *was motionless (but) she was firing up to the end. We couldn't help being impressed. Our flags flew at half-mast and the whole bridge stood at attention because of the courage of the English sailors.*[26]

William Smith was one of the *Glorious* survivors picked up by the Norwegians. He stated, in 1996, that he, and the other two men with whom he shared a Carley raft for three days, had originally decided that if it were the Germans that were to find them, they would refuse to be picked up. Their pre-war impressions of the Germans had made them feel that death at sea would have been preferable to wasting away in a German POW camp. Smith recalled that, as a youngster, his uncle, a merchant sailor, had told him stories of the way that Jews were being treated in Germany. Smith, therefore, retained a very unfavourable and fearful impression of the Germans. By 1996, he was suffering from continual pain and discomfort. He had been classified as 80 per cent disabled for the injuries he endured when *Glorious* was sunk but, when asked if he held anything against the Germans, he adamantly denied that he did. He said that he believed that those aboard the ships that had attacked his were just sailors much like himself. He added that, after the war, he worked with a former German army paratrooper who had become a British citizen. The two of them became good friends for which Smith received criticism from certain co-workers. Smith said that he had been offended and angered by such ignorance but, he would be willing to put his arm around any German today, as he sincerely believed them to be a fine people.[27]

### 'Through Fire and Water'
### HMS *Ardent* in 1939

The A-class destroyer *Ardent* commissioned in March 1930. Like her ten sister ships, HMS *Acasta* among them, *Ardent* was capable of a very speedy 35 knots,

HMS *Ardent*, pennant number H41

carried four 4.7 inch guns and a pair of quadruple 21-inch torpedo tubes. *Ardent* spent much of 1937 and a part of 1938 under refit in Sheerness. Once free of the yard, the destroyer remained in Home Waters, mostly at Plymouth, for training and preparation in view of the pending war.

*Ardent* was joined by Able Seaman Roger Hooke in March 1939 as she was employed in the role of training ship for boy sailors and reservists. At the outbreak of war she was tasked to patrol and escort convoys through the English Channel out to the Southwestern Approaches beyond the Lizard Peninsula and back. The ship was transferred to the Western Approaches Command in October where she frequently operated together with *Acasta*. Just fifteen months into the future there would be only one man from each of the two destroyers left alive: Leading Seaman Cyril Carter of *Acasta* and Able Seaman Roger Hooke of *Ardent*.

*Ardent* and her crew were kept busy during the first months of the war. According to a brief memoir written by AB Hooke, *Ardent* witnessed the torpedoing of the merchant vessel *Teakwood* on the destroyer's second convoy. The damaged ship was able to reach port safely with the loss of just one crewman. Soon afterwards the destroyer was assigned to a submarine hunting force that included the aircraft carrier *Courageous*. Although not credited with a U-boat sinking, *Ardent* was present for the destruction of a Nazi submarine by land-based aircraft, and, not long afterwards, the destroyer was a part of a group that managed to sink a submarine near Dover. *Ardent* was also once

HMS *Acasta*

called upon to assist with the towing back to port of a fellow destroyer that had suffered a serious collision. During a brief yard period at the end of 1939 Hooke was granted Christmas leave on which he, '… had an enjoyable week with my wife and baby, who was seven months old'.[28]

### 'And Very Soon Bombs and Guns Started Exploding'
### AB Roger Hooke and HMS *Ardent*

In April the ship was sent to Norway where she was to carry and support ground troops in countering the German invasion of that country. The mission resulted in a mix of calm days and frantic ones. Hooke's memoir describes his ship's activities as she ferried troops ashore and patrolled against possible enemy attacks by sea or by air.

> … (We) *found ourselves with a convoy of five transport ships and quite a few of our warships. The most outstanding were the (battleship)* Valiant *and* Protector *(a net laying ship) … As our journey progressed it began to get colder as our course was nearly due north. We steamed for five days before sighting land, and, believe me, it was cold by then. It was a lovely morning as we all steamed up one of the many fjords for which Norway is so noted. Then the transports separated and went to different berths to anchor. Some of the destroyers began patrolling the fjords while others went alongside the transport ships to disembark the troops. That was our duty and the ship we went alongside was the* Rio del Pacifico *and the moving of the soldiers started immediately. After loading up with about two hundred and fifty soldiers and stores, we steamed for about forty minutes, which brought us to a town called Harstad, where we went alongside the jetty. After unloading, back once more for some more troops. During the first day's operations everything went well, but the following day, I am afraid things were a bit different.*
>
> *The German aircraft made a visit, and very soon bombs and guns started exploding and ships moving about to make it harder for the aircraft to keep a good watch on them. We came in for our share of target practice,*

*but sometimes the bombs dropped too close to be comfortable. One of the bombs that fell into the town started a house on fire and killed a soldier ...*

*Then we did some patrolling of the fjords for likely submarines for some days before being detailed for another duty. This time we embarked on two trips about five hundred Scots Guards for passage to Narvik where, previously, some of our destroyers had done such good work. One thing, even though it was war, one could not help but admire the lovely scenery which one saw on these trips through the fjords. During these trips, on nearing our destination, we went to Action Stations in case of meeting some unexpected enemy ships, but nothing ever showed up to worry us. Once more, we did some patrolling and, believe me, when I say it was cold, but we all remained cheerful, just waiting for our return to England, as we knew it would not be long ...*[29]

The ship returned to Greenock, Scotland during the first week of May for repairs to her underwater sound detecting gear. Seaman Hooke remembered that *Ardent* arrived so low on fuel that she required the assistance of a tug to reach her berth. As several days were needed to complete the repairs, leave was granted. Hooke had neither enough money nor time for the train trip home, so he remained in Scotland. He took a little time off from the ship to enjoy the sights of Glasgow. He was pleased to receive free items from a 'Jock's Box' which was a sort of canteen established for servicemen during the war. The men would typically get free cigarettes, chocolates, as well as small things for personal hygiene. Once repaired, *Ardent* escorted troops to the Faroe Islands. When that duty was done, the destroyer was assigned to accompany the newly built light cruiser *Bonaventure* as she underwent trials.[30]

### 'Then We Knew They Were German Battleships' With HMS *Glorious* in June 1940

On 31 May 1940 *Ardent* was attached to a force of destroyers tasked with protecting the aircraft carriers *Ark Royal* and *Glorious* at Scapa Flow. Seaman Hooke wrote, 'Once more we made for Norway, but what we were to do, we did not know ...'

As Hooke recalled, the force arrived at Hartsad on Monday, 3 June. He then learned that *Ark Royal* and *Glorious* were to provide air cover for the withdrawal of British troops from Norway and that the destroyers were to act as an anti-submarine screen for carriers. From midnight of the day they arrived through to Saturday, 8 June, the carriers launched relays of six planes for air cover every two hours. After the last of the troops had been embarked onto transports, 'very early Saturday morning we (*Ardent*) had orders with the *Acasta* to go as escort for *Glorious* who was returning to England'.[31]

Hooke noted that the crew was excited and pleased to be headed out of the Arctic cold for home. Most of Saturday went well, but in the late afternoon things changed when the German battlecruisers *Gneisenau* and *Scharnhorst* appeared on the horizon.

> (At) about half past four in the afternoon all of us were enjoying a nice cup of tea when Action Stations was sounded. Everyone was quite taken by surprise; some saying it must be a submarine about. When we were at our stations we could see on the horizon, two ships.[32] To whom they belonged, we did not know. The Glorious then told us to go and investigate and ascertain who they were. We, therefore, steamed off in their direction, until we could see them much plainer. (We) then challenged them which they also did to us. Then we knew they were German battleships, and then the fun started.

> They very soon began to open fire on all three of us. The very first salvo at us went into number one boiler room which, naturally, reduced our speed. We endeavored to put them off by zig-zagging and making a smoke screen, but it was of no avail, time after time we were hit, and, considering the range between us, it showed the accuracy of their guns and range finders. Our guns were really of no great hindrance to the German ships, and we got into position for firing torpedoes to see if there was a chance of putting them off, even if only for a little while. We fired four torpedoes at them, but (the Germans) did not seem to make any alteration in course at all.

> We could see the other two ships of ours off to the westward and plenty

*of steam escaping from* Glorious. *What we could not at first make out was why the aircraft carrier did not send up any aeroplanes. It was to be learned afterwards that the first salvo of the enemy's big guns had landed on the flying deck and, therefore made it an impossibility for aircraft to take off. Well, all this time we were being constantly hit, and men were being injured so that it was a case of every man for himself. The ship was listing well over to port and still doing fifteen knots ... there seemed no way of stopping her so that boats could be lowered to pick up men who had already jumped for it. What with the smoke and steam escaping everywhere, it was impossible to do very much or to see anything. After about half an hour of this ordeal the ship began to sink and I had given help to get a raft over the side on which I managed to scramble. From that raft I saw the end of a good ship, officers, and men.*[33]

### 'We Settled Down to Our Fate as Best We Could'
### From Six to Two, Then Just One

Hooke recalled events that followed his departure from his sinking ship,

*Well, (of the) four of us (who) decided to cut a raft from the torpedo tubes and get it in the water ... I am afraid I did not see any of the other three after that. Owing to the ship not being able to stop, she was quite a few hundred yards away from me when she finally sank. Five men and myself eventually got on the raft, but it was impossible to help any of the others as we could not get the paddles from underneath the raft in time to be of any use in helping to rescue some more of our shipmates ... (W)e settled down to our fate as best we could as the raft we were on was very small and, therefore it was a bit crowded with six men on it. Where we were there was no darkness at night, so one had to guess whether it was day or night.*

*After one day on the raft, one man died from the cold and sea. He was a stoker. Then, during the day, another man also passed away – an AB (able seaman) this time ... We were beginning by now to wonder if there was any likelihood of anything coming to our aid, as with no food or water, things were not too good for us. Another man passed away the next day which left three of us. That man was an engine room artificer.*

*Then, during the early hours of the following morning, we saw (some ships coming from the direction of) Norway. With the two paddles that we had, we tried to get toward them, but although the ships were quite plain to us, none was able to spot us. After they had passed us, we got down for a little sleep, as owing to the cold and sea, it was not very nice for getting very comfortable. Then later on in the day … we saw an aircraft flying around … Our hopes began to rise as the flying boat, which it turned out to be, came nearer and nearer … then headed towards us, but then she turned away … Still hoping for the best, we carried on waving and shouting … they failed to see us. So once more we were left to the mercy of the sea and cold weather. Then, the same afternoon, another ship came into view, and with all our waving she did not see us. Things by now were beginning to get a bit agonizing. We had to lie down on the side of the raft to get a bit of sleep as our strength was giving out very fast. Once more, another comrade passed away. He was a leading seaman.*

By what, according to Hooke's accounting, would have been the third day an aircraft flew close by to the raft bearing *Ardent*'s two survivors. It bore German markings but, even so, Hooke was much relieved that the pilot had spotted him. It was a float plane which landed very nearby. As Hooke remembered,

*Coming towards us, the pilot got our raft between the floats and the navigator gave us a hand into the rear of the plane. I had enough left in me to ask where we were being taken, and he said, 'Trondheim' … Our first words, of course, were to ask for a drink and, after five days without food or water, we could not swallow enough. Once we had been given a drink, we both lay down for a sleep as it was much warmer and one could stretch out quite comfortably. Then we were shaken and told that we were at Trondheim. After being lifted from the plane, I saw a German soldier carrying a pot of coffee and I at once asked for some. Straightaway I was given a cup and enjoyed it.*[34]

### 'She Fought With a Dash Which Was Outstanding'
### A German Report

Very shortly after the war Rear Admiral (Konteradmiral) Günther Schubert wrote a memory based report about the action. He had held the rank of captain and was *Scharnhorst*'s executive officer at the time. Of HMS *Ardent*'s initial attack against his ship, Schubert wrote:

> (Ardent) *attacked with torpedoes, and endeavored in an extremely skilled manner to escape the effective defensive fire of the medium guns of the battleships by constant alterations of course. Finally* (Ardent) *also opened fire on the battleships.*[35] *She fought with a dash which was outstanding in a hopeless situation. The destroyer received numerous hits and finally went down.*[36]

Schubert's report continued with his account of the attack made by *Acasta* after *Ardent* and *Glorious* had gone down.

> (Acasta) *closed to attack the battleship force, and at a very close range fired torpedoes at the battleships which took evasive action. At this stage of the battle, at about the time of the carrier capsizing,* Scharnhorst *received a torpedo hit on the starboard side by the heavy for'ard turret … The ship still continued action with the destroyer which was now very heavily damaged. The destroyer, with her greatly inferior armament, fought a hopeless fight against the battleships. As far as I can remember, she scored a minor hit with her guns on the middle of the second heavy turret … When the destroyer, with her guns out of action, ceased fire the battleships did the same … The two battleships, leaving the destroyer which was damaged but still afloat, proceeded southwards at a greatly reduced speed.*[37]

At the conclusion of his report, Schubert noted:

> *Not only the tactical handling, but the audacity and pluck of the destroyers were outstanding. Every* (German) *officer taking part in the action was of*

*the same opinion. The destroyers put their utmost into the task, although in their hopeless position success was impossible from the start.*[38]

Hooke and his companion were given good treatment at a local hospital. After a little over a week they were transferred to a hospital in Oslo. It was there that Hook's fellow survivor from *Ardent* died. Hooke remained in German hands as a prisoner of war until October 1943 when he was repatriated due to ill health. While he was a prisoner Hooke made an intricate and detailed tapestry showing his ship's crest, the Union Jack and the White Ensign crossed, a silhouette of the *Ardent*, and a banner bearing the words 'Royal Navy'. The tapestry is held by the Imperial War Museum.

### 'The Loss of Their Loved Ones Has Not Been Properly Explained' Questions Concerning the Fate of the Crews of *Glorious, Ardent* and *Acasta*

The destruction of the three British ships was, as would be expected, devastating to the Navy and the families and other loved ones of the men who were lost that day. The lack of information from responsible and informed sources, the Admiralty among them, continued to burden the relatives for months after the sinkings. MP Richard Stokes, a veteran of the Royal Artillery in World War I, raised queries in the House of Commons in November 1940 on behalf of his constituents who had lost relatives aboard the ships. His questions, as well as those that would follow in later years, centered largely on why the carrier had been detached with inadequate escort from a relatively powerful force, how German surface units could catch *Glorious, Acasta* and *Ardent* by surprise, and why there were no aircraft aloft or at least on deck ready for immediate launch.

MP Stokes was careful to note that, although he was seeking answers for people who were upset by thoughts that facts about the sinkings were being hidden from them, he would endeavor to say and ask nothing that might be of any possible use or aid to the enemy. Still, the First Lord of the Admiralty responded that he was reluctant to provide answers to any of Stokes' questions for the sake of the public interest. The First Lord went on to offer an analogy by which he explained how happy the Board of the Admiralty would be had it been privileged enough to sit in on a German Kriegsmarine debate about the loss of its pocket battleship *Graf Spee* in 1939. He remained concerned that such open debates were sure to prove helpful to the enemy as they would reveal classified information relevant to naval operations and plans. When the hour had gotten late, the session was adjourned with no clarification for Stokes' questions.[39]

As time passed, the original concerns and doubts were kept alive by certain suggestions or reports by survivors and others familiar with *Glorious*. Questions about possible instability of the Captain, rifts amongst the ship's officers, the illogic of allowing the carrier to detach herself from the safety of a larger force of ships, and MP Stoke's specific query about how over 1,000 men could have been left alone in the water following the sinkings, lingered throughout the war years and beyond. The relatives of the crews of *Glorious, Ardent,* and *Acasta* could derive little comfort from the knowledge that the dutiful and brave actions of the men, with a special note to *Acasta's* valiant torpedo attack on *Scharnhorst*, kept the Germans so occupied that the British evacuation convoy was able to steam on unmolested. All of the troops removed from Norway, the loss of whom would have been a major blow against England, arrived safely home.

In June 1997, Channel 4 aired 'The Tragedy of HMS *Glorious*' as a part of its long running 'Secret History' series. The program included wartime footage made by a German film group aboard *Gneisenau* during the attack. The film showed the German ships firing at the British, hits on *Glorious*, other hits on at least one of the destroyers, and *Glorious* burning and listing prior to sinking. These images, along with the program's interviews with survivors and other persons who had been involved, could not have but reawakened deep emotions among those whose fathers and grandfathers perished when the three ships went down. The grandson of a sailor aboard *Ardent* wrote that he was particularly moved as he watched the German footage. He could not help but imagine the terrible things happening to his grandfather as the Kriegsmarine ships sent round after round of explosives in his direction.[40]

Although the television program addressed numerous issues, among them, Captain D'Oyly-Hughes' personality, psychological state, and disagreements with his air officers, it raised two key questions concerning the fate of the British crews during and after the action of 8 June 1940. The first of these sought clarification as to why the Admiralty chose to ignore intelligence reports that *Scharnhorst* and *Gneisenau* had departed their base at Kiel and were being tracked as they steamed toward the Arctic Circle. Sir Harry Hinsley appeared on the show to say that it was he, while working at the Government Code and Cypher School at Bletchley Park at the age of twenty-one, who had made a number of calls directly to the Admiralty with the information. He stated that his calls were disregarded so that *Glorious, Ardent* and *Acasta* were never warned of the approaching danger. An opportunity to try to avoid the disaster that was soon was to befall them was thus lost. There was no immediate official response to Sir Harry's statements on the programme.

The second key question concerned statements by the Admiralty and later, the Ministry of Defence, maintaining that a possible distress message from *Glorious* received aboard the cruiser *Devonshire* was garbled. The message was in Morse code, but it was said to have been so unclear that it warranted no response by the cruiser. *Devonshire*, furthermore, had been under orders to maintain radio silence as she was responsible for carrying the extremely important cargo of Norway's king, the king's cabinet, and almost 30 tons of Norwegian gold reserves towards Scapa Flow. The telegraphist on duty aboard the cruiser at the time disputed the official contention that the message was garbled. He stated that he had very clearly heard *Glorious'* signal that announced the presence of two enemy warships along with their bearing, speed, course, and position. The telegraphist claimed that he immediately relayed the message to the bridge, but it was never passed on from the *Devonshire*. The telegraphist's contention that the message was not garbled has been corroborated by several other knowledgeable persons. The Naval Historical Branch, fully aware of the veteran telegraphist's statements to Channel 4, responded on that very same program that, after such a long time, it felt that the value of such a report should be disregarded.[41]

MP A. J. Beith was compelled to speak in the House on behalf of some of his constituents whose interest in the event had been rekindled by the Channel 4 programme. In January 1998, Beith opened his comments by declaring that he was merely performing his duty for

> *… those people (who) have been deeply troubled by the belief that the loss of their loved ones has not been properly explained.*

Beith then continued,

> *No one is looking, after all these years, for blame or retribution, but where a supreme sacrifice has been made on such a scale, the record should surely be as accurate as possible. An unconvincing explanation produced in conditions of war should no longer be given unchallenged official approval … The Admiralty, and now the Ministry of Defence, always maintained that the sinkings were merely an unfortunate accident of war. A significant number of naval historians continue to suggest what the few survivors and the relatives have long suspected – that a catalog of errors and misjudgments culminated in the tragic events of that afternoon … We are still asking (Mr. Stokes' original questions) sixty years later. Why was* Glorious *returning independently of the main convoy? Why was she so badly prepared (low readiness condition; insufficient number of lookouts)? Why was her air power not even used for reconnaissance? Was there not sufficient intelligence about German activity in the region to suggest that* Glorious *should have been in a much greater state of readiness? Could* HMS Devonshire *have helped the stricken vessel, or did its commander have no idea of what was happening?*[42]

John Spellar, the Parliamentary Under-Secretary of State for Defence, maintained the previous Admiralty position of 1940 and 1947 (when Mr. Stokes had again raised the matter in the House) that *Glorious* had been allowed to steam away essentially alone because she was low on fuel. Further elabouration was not offered and the matter was deemed by Spellar to be satisfactorily concluded.[43] Knowledgeable relatives of the men lost aboard *Glorious*, *Ardent* and *Acasta* remained, as had none other than Winston Churchill, fully skeptical about the shortage of fuel explanation.

The matter was brought up once again in the House, on 27 January 2000. Three years had passed since '*The Tragedy of HMS Glorious*' had originally aired and Harry Hinsley had since died, Secretary of State for Defence Peter Kilfoyle made a brief statement in the House that, '… the late Sir Harry Hinsley's recollections, broadcast in the Channel 4 programme were in error'. Kilfoyle added that Sir Harry's reports were believed 'by experts at the time' to refer not to powerful surface ships, but to U-boats.[44] In addition to stating that Sir Harry Hinsley had been mistaken, Kilfoyle said that the C-in-C Home Fleet had ordered *Glorious* detached for the purpose of Commander Heath's pending court martial.[45] The persistent refusal by the Admiralty and, more recently, the Ministry of Defence to deviate from the original explanations of 1940, despite reasonable evidence that they have always been insufficient, continues to frustrate and/or anger those whose loved ones perished with *Glorious, Ardent* and *Acasta*. Belief remains that if their plight could have been immediately known, or even avoided altogether, hundreds of men need not have died.

## Remembrance

At a recent memorial service to the men *of Acasta, Ardent* and *Glorious*, relatives laid a wreath in the waters near the spot of the sinkings and held a moment of silence. 'For the Fallen,' Laurence Binyon's enduring tribute to those who died in an earlier war, was solemnly read aloud.

> *They shall not grow old as we that are left grow old;*
> *Age shall not weary them, nor the years condemn.*
> *At the going down of the sun and in the morning*
> *We will remember them.*

The mottos of the ships, lost that faraway June day, make fitting words of parting from each. For *Glorious* they are 'Explicit Nomen' – *The Name Explains Itself*. *Ardent,* so true to her motto, fought her last fight 'Per Ignem et Aquam' – *Through Fire and Water*. *Acasta* leaves us a supplication that we would be honoured to heed: 'Memores Majoris' – *Remember Your Ancestors*.

Special thanks are directed to Mr David Woodcock and Mr Gary Martin of the GLARAC Association for their kind and attentive assistance with the preceding portion of this book.

ENDNOTES

1. Linton, Dan. 'Evolution of the Aircraft Carrier, Part 8: Glorious and Courageous.' Web. Accessed February 2014. Linton cites: Robbins, G. *The Aircraft Carrier Story*. Cassell & Co. 2001.

2. Imperial War Museum. Sound recording archive. 18663. Kerridge, Ernest. 1991.

3. Imperial War Museum. Sound recording archive. 4586. Sutcliffe, Walter. 1980.

4. Imperial War Museum. 4586.

5. This was not Admiral Nelson's famous flagship, but a barracks and training establishment located at Plymouth. The Royal Navy has named shore bases as if they were seagoing ships. These have been nicknamed 'stone frigates.'

6. writerray (contributor). BBC WW2 *People's War*. 'My Fleet Air Arm Experiences.' Article ID A3394109. 2004.

7. Imperial War Museum. Sound recording archive. 12276. Cooke, Frederick. 1991.

8. Imperial War Museum. Sound recording archive. 11443. O'Neill, James. 1990.

9. Fleet Air Arm Archive. 'HMS *Glorious*, Fleet Aircraft Carrier.' Aircraft Carrier Database of the Fleet Air Arm Archive. fleetairarmarchive.net. Web. Accessed February 2014. According to the Fleet Air Arm Archive, the ship's captain landed all of Glorious' fighters at Malta during the carrier's operations east of the Suez Canal. Nine Sea Gladiators were re-embarked when the ship was ordered to leave Malta for operations in Norway in April 1940.

10. Imperial War Museum. Sound recording archive. 10481. Cross, Kenneth. 1988.

11. Imperial War Museum. 10481.

12. Winton, John. *Carrier Glorious: The Life and Death of an Aircraft Carrier*. Cassell Military Paperbacks. 1999. p.145.

13. Winton. p. 133.

14. Imperial War Museum. Sound recording archive. 9696. Gibson, Donald Cameron. 1987.

15. Winton. pp. 147–182.

16. HMS *Glorious, Ardent* and *Acasta* Association. glarac.co.uk Web. Accessed February 2014.

17. Imperial War Museum. 10481 (Cross).

18. Imperial War Museum. 12276 (Cooke).

19. Imperial War Museum. Sound recording archive. 12334. Day, Vernon Henry. 1991.

20. Imperial War Museum. 10481 (Cross).

21. Imperial War Museum. 12276 (Cooke).

22. Imperial War Museum. 12276.

23. Imperial War Museum. 12334 (Day).

24. Imperial War Museum. Sound recording archive. 16701. Thornton, Frederick Ernest. 1996.

25. Imperial War Museum. 11443 (O'Neill).

26. Channel 4. 'Secret History: The Tragedy of HMS *Glorious*.' Originally aired on 30 June 1997. The names of the German veterans who appeared in the film are: Georg Wiens, Gerhard Gramm, and Killian Fries.

27. Imperial War Museum. Sound recording archive. 16700. Smith, William. 1996.

28. Hooke, Roger. 'The Time I Sailed in HMS *Ardent*.' Photocopy of typed document provided by GLARAC (HMS *Glorious, Ardent*, and *Acasta* Association), Undated. p. 4. According to Hooke, his account was written entirely from memory while he was confined to the hospital in order to recover from the ordeal of having been sunk and adrift at sea for several days.

29. Hooke. pp. 4–6.

30. HMS *Bonaventure* would have a short life. She was torpedoed and sunk off Sollum, Egypt on 30 March 1941.

31. Hooke. p. 8.

32. AB Hooke was a member of the X gun crew. The 4.7-inch gun was placed in an open mount that included a front shield for the protection of both the gun and its crew. The men serving the gun were exposed to the sea, weather, and shrapnel from enemy gunfire.

33. Hooke. pp. 8–9.

34. Hooke, Roger. 'How I Was Rescued From The Sea.' This is an un-numbered three page attachment to the nine pages of 'The Time I Sailed in HMS *Ardent*.'

35. Scharnhorst and Gneisenau have been widely recognized as battle cruisers. The original German word used in Schubert's report was probably 'Schlactshiff' which translates into English as 'battleship.'

36. Schubert, Admiral Günther. A Report on the action fought by 'Scharnhorst' and 'Gneisenau' with 'HMS *Glorious*' and her destroyer escort on 8 June 1940, written by Konteradmiral Schubert from memory on 19 July 1945, and submitted to the Flag Officer Schleswig-Holstein. (Translated version).

37. Schubert. The report also states that the Germans believed that the torpedo hit made by *Acasta* on *Scharnhorst* had actually come from a submarine. This belief was used to justify the hasty withdrawal of the German force and its reluctance to stop for British survivors.

38. Schubert.

39. 'Loss of HMS *Glorious*.' House of Commons Debates. 7 November 1940.

40. Personal correspondence to author. March 2014.

41. Channel 4.

42. House of Commons Debates for 28 January 1998.

43. House of Commons Debates for 28 January 1998.

44. Written Answers to Questions, Thursday 27 January 2000. DEFENCE, HMS *Glorious*. Photocopy.

45. Written Answers to Questions, Thursday 27 January 2000.

# SIX
# THE ARCTIC CONVOYS

### 'We Are Fulfilling Our Obligations'
### Supplies to Russia

Britain's Second World War Arctic Convoys delivered four million tonnes of military equipment to the Soviet Union at a cost of hundreds of ships and thousands of lives

Britain's unquestioned dependence upon her sea lanes led the Admiralty and the Air Ministry to agree in 1937 that British merchant shipping should only sail in protective convoys. Pre-war preparations included assigning planning personnel to all major commercial ports, mapping of convoy routes and the Admiralty's taking control of all merchant shipping. By early 1941 the Battle of the Atlantic and the struggle for Malta were both in full rage. Already scant resources were stretched to the limit when Germany invaded Russia in June. With yet another theater of war heavily reliant on sea transport opened, the Royal Navy scrambled to assemble the needed convoys. Hard-pressed escort ships were forced to shuttle between the Mediterranean and the Arctic. Winston Churchill called it the 'worst journey in the world', but he vowed to keep Russia supplied as the fall of that country to the Germans would have left Britain and Western Europe fully exposed to the concentrated force of the Nazi war machine.

The convoys ran from Hvalfjordur in Iceland or Loch Ewe in Scotland to the Soviet ports of Murmansk and Archangel. The battle to get ships from Scotland and Iceland through the treacherously rough and freezing cold waters of the Denmark Strait, Norwegian Sea, Arctic Ocean, and Barents Sea and into Murmansk or Archangel was as deadly as it was frightening. In the far northern latitudes, groups of slow and unarmed merchant ships under the protection of harried, but brave escorts waged countless struggles for survival against determined enemy air, surface, and submarine attacks. An equally cruel enemy of Britain's ships and sailors was the fury of nature's elements.

The voiceover of a wartime British newsreel stated,

> *The help which Britain is giving to the Soviets is no light thing to be brushed aside. As her ally, we are fulfilling our obligations, and will continue to do so, until the Nazis are finally obliterated by the United Nations.*[1]

The Russian convoys bore the designations of 'PQ' (eastbound, full) and 'QP' (westbound, empty) until December, 1942, when they were changed to 'JW'. The first of the numerically sequential PQ convoys sailed in August 1941. For a time, the convoys were fortunate that the Germans were not as yet fully prepared to attempt disrupting them. PQs 1 through 12 and return convoys QP 1 through 9 were able to sail with minimal losses: a total of two merchant ships and one Royal Navy destroyer sunk and one merchant ship damaged against the loss of one U-boat for the Germans. Once the Germans began to mount better organised efforts against the convoys, however, casualties among ships, material, and men rose. PQ 13 lost five out of 19 merchant ships, PQ 14 lost 17 out of 25, it was three out of 22 on PQ 15, and seven out of 35 supply vessels were sunk from PQ 16.[2]

It was July 1942 as PQ 17 was making good headway towards Murmansk. Three of its ships had been sunk by air attacks and several others had been forced to turn back for various reasons. The remaining 30 ships and their escorts had just sailed past Bear Island, directly to the north of Norway. Meanwhile, the Admiralty was busy with intelligence that a powerful force of German surface ships was on its way to attack the convoy. Before realizing that the information was incorrect, the Admiralty ordered PQ 17's escort to withdraw and the merchant ships to scatter. U-boats and aircraft took advantage of the situation to methodically pick off twenty of the fragmented convoy's unprotected ships. The surviving merchant sailors were angry and bitter about what they considered wanton, or even cowardly, abandonment. Since many of the ships were American, the diplomatic relations between Washington and London suffered severe strains.

Many of the officers and men aboard the escorts were frustrated and even ashamed that they had to leave their charges to the slaughter. Although they could not know at the time that there were to be no German ships to fight, the crews aboard the escort ships had been eager for battle. As it turned from the convoy, an officer aboard one of the escort group's cruisers wrote,

> *Our last sight of the merchantmen showed them opening up and separating* (as per orders). *The effect on the ship's company was devastating. Twenty-four hours earlier, there had only been one thought – that, at last, we were going to bring enemy surface ships to action. I have never known the men in such good heart … then … we abandoned the convoy. The ship was in turmoil; everyone was boiling, and the Master at Arms (a senior enlisted man who would closely know the men's attitudes) told me he had never known such strong feelings before … It was the blackest day we ever knew – sheer bloody murder.*[3]

The next convoy, PQ 18 of September, consisted of forty merchant ships that were extremely heavily escorted. A total of seventeen warships were disposed as the close escort and two battleships, three heavy cruisers, and a number of light cruisers and destroyers were formed into the distant escort. Close escorts, as suggested by the name, remained near at hand to the merchant ships. They were usually destroyers, frigates, or corvettes responsible for anti-submarine and anti-air defense. The distant escort was made up of large ships that stayed beyond the horizon. It was there to provide protection in the event of an appearance by enemy cruisers or battleships. PQ 18's close escort included, for the first time on an Arctic convoy, an escort carrier. Small carriers had just begun to become available in late 1941 and early 1942. Eventually many of these small aircraft carriers would be transferred to the Royal Navy via the American Lend-Lease Program. Over the remaining course of the war, they would prove invaluable against all manner of enemy threats. Twenty-seven of PQ 18's forty ships made it to Archangel which lay several dangerous days' additional sailing to the east of Murmansk. The escort carrier's airwing shot down more than 40 aerial attackers and assisted in the sinking of one of the three U-boats destroyed by the near escort.[4]

A convoy escort vessel drops depth charges against a U-boat

Until the final victory in Europe, a total of seventy-eight convoys travelled to or from Russia. Some made the journey relatively unmolested while others, like PQ 17 which was the worst hit of all, endured terrifying struggles and heavy losses of ships and men. Of about 1,400 ships that sailed in the Arctic convoys, eighty-five were lost. Of the escorts that accompanied them, two cruisers, six destroyers, and eight other escorts were sunk.[5]

## 'You Were Attacked From the Time You Left'
## Convoys to Hell

Thousands of men went to sea on the Arctic convoys. No ship, large or small, merchant or naval, was ever immune from sudden destruction. No amount of training or preparation could help prevent the unspeakable injuries and suffering that attack victims endured. Survivors of ships that went down in an Arctic convoy, if they chose to speak about it, were unanimous about the terror of the experience. At one extreme there was fire, such as from an exploding tanker. The fortunate ones were those killed by the blast. At the other extreme, there was water which brought on such a quick state of hypothermia that anyone who fell or jumped into the sea could be frozen dead before he even had a chance to drown.

One former convoy sailor recalled,

> *Well, Winston Churchill called them the convoys to hell, (and) it was terrible; we lost ships there and (if) you went into the water, you were gone ... You were attacked from the time you left until the time you got there and you was attacked even when you got there... I was seventeen when we went to the Arctic, not old enough to have any sense, somebody said.*

Another former merchant sailor described some of the rigors of Arctic convoy duty.

> *We went to Philadelphia to load, with alcohol – industrial alcohol – we were assured it wasn't for Russian Vodka. We then sailed back to Loch Ewe in Scotland, and waited there for the convoy to be assembled. (They)*

*then provisioned us, (and they) even sent some big boxes with corned beef in them. I remember the Captain taking one look at that and saying, 'If anybody thinks I'm going to eat corned beef, they've got another thing coming!'[6] … We never knew what they (the ships) were loaded with … all we knew was to get them loaded and get the bloomin' steam going … we were taking all the goods; aircraft, tanks, motor vehicles, aluminum; all sorts of stuff to support the Russians who were fighting at the front up there … We sailed from Loch Ewe and went up round North Cape (the* northernmost point on the mainland of Norway), *for Archangel. There were about 30 ships and about 40 escorts … We left in a tremendous gale, massive waves and everything; a hurricane. I must tell you now (that) I was always seasick. I never, ever got my sea legs. And the ship was top heavy and she rolled; I couldn't eat; I was sick … When the seas broke over the ship, immediately they hit the cold surfaces (and) they froze. You were always the expert with your little chipping hammers; so we used those and you had to keep getting the ice off, otherwise the ship became top heavy and would go over … you hear them banging and you knew very well they were chipping the ice away, (and) you didn't touch nothing without gloves on, (the cold would) take the skin off your fingers. It was pretty grim … When it got a little bit lighter we were shadowed by a Focke-Wulfe Kondor, the German reconnaissance plane which circled the convoy, and he sent signals to the U-boats about us … you'd see the plane and we'd fire haphazard shots at him … of course, it was just out of range and there was nothing we could do … then you just waited and waited … you had to go about your normal work, you couldn't just wait to see if you got torpedoed or not; just hope that it (would be) somebody else, and not you, that would get it.*

A member of an engine room crew spoke of his constant dread of being sunk. While he was fortunate to have escaped the experience, he could not forget a time when others were not so lucky.

*My job was in the engine room. The oil used to be pumped through sprayers going into the furnace (and) sometimes during action stations*

*I would have to go down to where the steering went to keep checking on temperatures down there to make sure anything didn't overheat in the shafts driving the propellers ... it was warm down there because everything was shut and there wasn't anything open and if you was torpedoed, then you didn't get out -- couldn't really worry, could you? You was hundreds and hundreds of miles away from land so you couldn't worry too much. ... if you did get out* (in case of being sunk) *you wouldn't have lasted very long, because you weren't dressed for that kind of weather. The seamen; they were alright; they had duffel coats on, and masks, and gloves; they weren't too bad. In the call to abandon ship and you had to dive out, all you* (an engine room rating) *was* (dressed) *in was a boiler suit. And you'd be going into a lifeboat or going into the water (it would be) freezing cold without anything on.*

*We were doing this every day (and) week after week. Month after month. We were at sea – we were at sea all the time. You'd hear these big bangs and you wouldn't know if they (Germans) were dropping bombs or if we were dropping depth charges. You would have to shout to your mates, 'What the hell was that, I wonder.' I'd be on the ladder, ready to run up (from below decks) if I felt water coming through ... one of the worst things; we had been equipped with radio telephones because usually the convoy signaled by flag, but due to the darkness this was a bit difficult ... and we could hear the people in the radio office on this destroyer as it was sinking, still talking to us quite calmly ... we had seen people being killed and so on before, but the first time we had heard people dying, I think, in some ways it was worse than seeing it. The last thing they said was, 'The water is now coming in through the door. It's rising higher.'* [7]

The torpedoing of a ship was recounted as follows,

*We left the convoy because of U-boat activity; we jumped from the frying pan into the fire.* [8] *We ran into two U-boats. One of them fired all his torpedoes at us and missed but the other one fired all his torpedoes and two of them hit us. I was having my tea and that's when the torpedo hit the next mess deck down below. There was a huge flash, a red flash and kind of a bang. There was 57 killed there. All of a sudden the ship goes dead quiet because before that you had things like fans, machines going; noise … after that the ship goes deadly quiet and it was heaving over on the starboard side … next thing, I was going up a sloping deck; the ship was going to turn over. All oil and water coming in, in the dark. I couldn't walk. I was on my hands and knees; the only way to the escape hatch was to hang on to the legs of the lockers and pull myself up that way. When I woke up – I was unconscious – I had regained consciousness after being blown unconscious by (another) torpedo (that hit us). Around me was cable, pipes, bits of deck, bulkhead, and what have you. So (I'm) lying there and what have you, and I thought, 'Am I alright? Anything broken?' I started tentatively moving my arms one at a time, then my legs, but for a long time I wouldn't bother to try my body; my spine. I thought, 'I hope that's not gone.' So I lay there for a while (then) I found I was physically fit. I was blown unconscious and I was physically fit. Anyway they said, 'Abandon ship.' So we all left the ship and I went on (another ship from the convoy). I watched the ship go down then; because you get attached to a ship.*[9]

Yet another merchant sailor offered additional memories of the convoys to and from Russia.

*It's very hard to go as far north as you could. Close up to Bear Island. But the ice pack forced you south. Now, they* (the Germans) *had* Tirpitz (sister *of* Bismarck) *in Norway. They had dive bombers on the Norwegian coast, and they had the submarine packs at the exit of the Bering Sea coming into the Kola inlet* (and Murmansk). *And of course, all the skippers were told the same, 'No heroics. If you're hit, drive the ship ashore. You lose the ship; you'll save the crew.' … Cold journey. It was bitterly, bitterly cold. If you sneeze, all the globules of spit froze as they came out of your mouth. It was the same for everybody. And of course, two minutes in the water and you were finished.*[10]

Stanley Shield served in the Arctic aboard the destroyer HMS *Somali*. Shield had worked as a postal clerk for two years before deciding to join the Navy in 1941. After serving as an ordinary seaman for an initial period of six months, he was deemed to have performed well enough to merit an opportunity to seek a commission. He eventually went on for officer training. Shield experienced a total of four PQ convoys. Of life aboard *Somali* he said, '... well, frankly it wouldn't be tolerated in today's (2005) prisons.'[11]

HMS *Somali*

(We would start in) *Iceland; that's where the convoys mustered. Merchant ships came over from America and Canada as well as UK ... and then we* (the escorting warships) *came round ... to the Arctic Circle and into Kola Inlet (and Murmansk). It was about 3,000 miles ... and they used most(ly) ships of the Home Fleet ... on escorting convoys to Russia. The German battleships were always a peril ... every convoy (I was on) was attacked all the way by submarines and aircraft because we were only 300 miles away from the Luftwaffe bases, you see, they were in north(ern) Norway and we were 3,000 miles from home and 300 miles from them! ... the speed of (a) convoy was only 5 knots ... they didn't put the best merchant ships into these convoys, I have to say, some of them were real old tramps because they lost so many ... we communicated with Aldis (signal) lamps ... didn't*

*use radio unless it was urgent because they could pick it up. Not that they needed it; they knew exactly where we were. As soon as we left Iceland, we would be picked up by German reconnaissance aircraft which just (flew) round and round the convoy and we couldn't hit it* (with gunfire)! *They were there every mile of the way! We were there from March to September … 24 hour daylight most of that time. That's why the aircraft were such a damned nuisance because they came around the clock.*[12]

Many years afterwards the thoughts of Arctic convoy veterans reflected ongoing relief that they would need never again experience trips to Murmansk or Archangel.

*I don't think the population, as a whole, was told of the losses that we suffered on the Russian convoys … I never talked about it a lot; very little. It just doesn't seem relevant. It was finished, all over now. Forget it. We're back home safe and that's it. It's not days that you want to remember much, either. It weren't very pleasant, so get it out of your mind. When I came home … I had stress – post-traumatic stress – but I got over it …*

*I think if the Arctic convoys hadn't been going, it would have made a hell of a difference to the war. Russia would have been gone, wouldn't they? They wouldn't have been having any materials from us … I think it was worth it, really … there was a lot of losses and the loss of human life; we just accepted it, did it, and were very glad when it was all over.*

*My wife and I went cruising in our later years, and she sometimes said, 'Let's go to Russia and the Baltic.' I said, 'No, thank you very much. I don't want to go back there again. I've had my trip to Russia and that was good enough for me.'*[13]

There was scant relief for the men assigned to Arctic convoy duty even when they were safely in port and not under attack. At one end of the convoy run was Hvalfjordur near Reykjavik, Iceland where the bleak and empty landscape provided little to see. With only a single wet canteen ashore that served Canadian beer there was just as little to do. At the other end of the convoy runs were Murmansk and the Kola Inlet where there was even less to see and do than in Iceland. Marine musician Gus Guthrie of the cruiser HMS *Cumberland* still managed, on at least one of his days ashore in Russia, to enjoy a little entertainment.

*There was a hill down which a lot of people were skiing so a friend and I made our way to the top and some Russian soldiers were offering their skis to some of the ship's company. And I thought, 'Ooh, I'll have a go at this.' And a Russian chap invited me and I said, 'Oh, yes' and I eventually got my shoes in the skis and then, without handing me the poles, he gave me an almighty shove and down ten feet of this hill I went like clappers, upright. The remaining 200 feet was upside-down, backwards, and forwards … when I eventually stopped and looked back up the hill, they were all laughing … having a tremendous time at my expense.* [14.]

## 'I'll Have Your Balls for a Necktie!'
## A Hostilities Only Sailor and HMS *Edinburgh*

Aerial view of HMS *Edinburgh*, 'Southampton' class (third group) cruiser in Scapa Flow, October 1941

HMS *Edinburgh* was a *Town* class cruiser of the mid- to late-1930s. The lone surviving example of the class is the museum ship HMS *Belfast* which is presently anchored in the Thames. *Edinburgh, Belfast,* and their eight sister ships were designed and built for the protection of British shipping. The cruisers carried twelve six-inch guns in four turrets but, were criticized for being under armed in comparison to the then new Japanese and American light cruisers of the time. The latter ships carried fifteen six-inch guns in five turrets. Britain made no effort to alter its *Town* class ships as it was unwilling to assume the additional costs of equipping them with any more guns.

Raymond Veneables enjoyed academics and athletics at school. In the late 1930s he entered university to study English, German, and French. He had met his wife to be as a student at Leicester University and, as war approached, imagined that he would wind up in the army. His uncles had told him horror stories of their World War I experiences, and Veneables fully expected to become an infantryman charging over the top to his death. Following his Christian beliefs, he considered himself a pacifist but, faced with his personal aversion to Hitler and the persecution of Jews in Germany, he did not really feel that he was a good enough Christian to be excluded from service. He eventually chose what he called 'the lesser of three evils' from among the army, navy, and air force. He enlisted in the Royal Navy as a hostilities only ordinary seaman, or HOOD, in January 1941.[15]

Veneables remembered that there were volunteer ladies at the station to offer hot cocoa, buns, and other refreshments to recruits waiting for the trains that would take them to their training bases. While train travel of the era, according to Veneables, was awful, it was at least interesting because the trips were long enough for passengers to learn about one another through conversation. Once in training, Veneables quickly came to realise that the Navy's way of teaching things to people was to scream and bark at them. He did not enjoy such instructional methodology, but bore it as he knew that he had no choice but to do so. He remembered that there was lots of marching and drill which he did not take seriously. He felt that there would never be any use for any of it in the operation of a ship. He felt that one of the least useful drills he had to endure was bayonet training. He believed that it was conducted simply to instill a sense of martial spirit into the trainees. He found that seamanship, knots, and gunnery made more sense, however. He fondly remembered being accomplished at tying the bowline on the bite because it would be the knot of choice to tie around one's own waist in order to be pulled aboard a rescue vessel in case of having had to abandon ship. Another useful knot that he kept with him his entire life was that which was used in slinging a hammock.

After training and leave, he was given orders to report to a temporary barracks at Plymouth to await assignment to a ship. While he was on a short leave from Plymouth, the city suffered extremely heavy bombing by the Germans that left large portions of it in ruins. When he returned, Veneables could see search parties combing through the rubble to look either for bodies or safes from businesses that had been destroyed. Veneables spent a few days assisting on search and rescue parties in Plymouth until he was sent north to Scapa where he joined *Edinburgh*. The cruiser remained at Scapa for a number of months.

Veneables remembered the base as dull, boring, cold, and bleak. He got only one brief leave on which he and his companions simply went to the nearest drinking establishment. All returned to the ship thoroughly intoxicated. Many sailors who went through Scapa do not recall that there was any difference between being anchored there and steaming out at sea. As an HOOD, Veneables was at the absolute bottom end of the naval social ladder. The inexperienced ordinary seaman would be constantly reminded of his lowly status by the many regular professional sailors who had been aboard the cruiser since the pre-war days. He learned to use expletives and crude language in order to fit in. As a university trained linguist, Veneables rationalized that it was natural for him to adapt to the language of whatever location he should find himself in. As an ordinary seaman, his duties were those of a general deckhand. He did lots of scrubbing, cleaning and painting. Painting was an endless chore as there would always be some part of the ship where old paint would need to be chipped off so that new paint could be applied. One shipboard routine on *Edinburgh* was the daily early morning scrubbing of the wooden decks. Veneables recalled that he and his shipmates did such a good job that the cruiser's decks literally shone white. When the admiral of the force to which *Edinburgh* was attached came aboard one morning, he was incensed to see the ship in such a polished peacetime condition. He demanded that the decks be immediately darkened and camouflaged. The deck crew enthusiastically saw to it right away. From that point onwards, Veneables and his shipmates were happy to have been relieved of their deck scrubbing chores.

Tasks of daily living that are generally simple ashore can be difficult to get done at sea. Sailors must often resort to creative means by which to accomplish them. Veneables recalled how the need to dry a pair of just washed work overalls led to his one and only face to face conversation with an officer aboard *Edinburgh*.

*Ordinary seamen spent a lot of time washing and cleaning the ship …
(and) I hardly ever met an officer in that ship (although) once I did because
I wore overalls all the time and I had to wash them a lot and if I went on
the upper deck a great blast of hot air came out of a funnel. I tied them to
this and they stood out horizontal and would dry in ten minutes. Well, the
young engineer officer came up to me and said, 'Did you put your overalls
by MY funnel?' I said, 'Yes, I did, sir.' (He replied) 'If you do that again, I'll
have your balls for a necktie!'*[16]

Outside of their immediate duties of running the ship, there was essentially
no relationship between enlisted men and officers at all. Ships all had various
sports teams that would compete against those of other ships. One sport, field
hockey, was reserved for play by officers only. *Edinburgh's* team saw fit to add
Ordinary Seaman Veneables and one of the ship's gunners to the team, however,
after word got around that they were highly skilled players. The fraternisation
went no further than that.

*It must have appeared in my papers that I had once played hockey so I
was invited to play hockey for the (ship) and I was the only non-officer
except the gunner's mate who also played. It was in Gibraltar where there
was no grass on the pitch. It was very dusty and very hot. I found that the
midshipmen, in particular, were rather surprised that an ordinary seaman
could play, I may say, a lot better than they could, but they didn't see it like
that. What really horrified me was, at the end of the match, they all took
into an officer's bar and drank beer and failed even to send a glass out to
these two non-officers who had been playing. That was in 1941. Edinburgh
had been in commission since before the war started and the relations
between the officers and the men were not good.*[17]

The crew was quartered in the mess decks which were large open spaces used
for eating or sleeping. The meals would be taken on rows of long tables set up
for that purpose. Several of the hands would go to the galley and bring food
back to dish out for the men. The best food at sea was that which was served
immediately after a period ashore and replenishment because things would be

fresh. After a few days out to sea, the fresh food would have been all consumed. Frozen, tinned, or powdered forms of comestibles would be served until the next run to shore. Among the tinned foods more commonly remembered by the Royal Navy's wartime sailors, were things like corned beef, kippers, and enormous solid puddings. One of the first things a man would do whenever in port would be to go ashore for a meal.

Mess tables would be cleared in the evening and hammocks would be slung from hooks in the overhead (ceiling). There was a minimum of privacy. The space allotted per man, at not more than about 18 inches, was scant. Veneables recalled that he developed a technique of scrunching down and pulling the hammock netting around his head and shoulders in order to read. Reading, for lack of other activities, was popular among sailors at sea. When off watch, men seemed to always be able to find a quiet corner in an otherwise busy and crowded ship to read. Most ships had a lending library on board. There was also the Royal Navy War Library which would send, upon request, books to men out at sea. Books were one of the more popular purchases ashore. Many men would have friends or family send parcels of reading material to them which sometimes included hometown newspapers that, however dated, were always welcome and passed around from man to man. Veneables was fortunate to have discovered that it was alright for him to sling his hammock outside the crowded mess deck in the narrow passageway beside the ship's store. He had a good deal more privacy and quiet there, and the storekeeper would, on closing shop, toss him a nightly bar of chocolate.

The mess deck was also the usual spot from which the daily tot would be issued. At six bells of the forenoon watch, 11:00 am, the call of 'up spirits' would be piped throughout the ship. Each man who was not under aged would receive his daily tot of 1/8 pint of rum. During the war years (but not because of the war) the rum issued to seamen was diluted 1:2 with water. Petty officers and above received their rum 'neat', or undiluted, which made it approximately 2½ times the strength of normal commercially sold rum. Neat rum was sufficiently strong to cause at least mild drunkenness in some crewmembers. Under aged crewmen and those who chose not to drink received extra pay, or 'grog money', in lieu of rum. Some of the teetotalers would sell or trade their ration to others for greater value than provided by grog money. Others, who did drink, would take their daily ration, accumulate it, and drink it in quantity later. Under special circumstances, a ship's captain could order an extra rum ration which was announced by the call to 'splice the main brace'.[18]

A day at sea included watch standing which, depending on the potential for danger, varied in intensity and frequency. If danger were imminent, however, action stations would be called. Short of action stations, a watch usually lasted four hours and could involve being on lookout. One relaxing and enjoyable deck watch might involve keeping a lookout for a friendly ship that could be delivering mail from home. A less relaxing lookout would be keeping alert for telltale signs of an enemy submarine, surface ship, or aircraft. Routine watches also involved working with or maintaining shipboard equipment. Stokers would tend to engines and boilers, gunners would tend to guns, and seamen would perform the tasks of ship's upkeep through cleaning, washing, painting, or chipping paint.

### 'Going to Bat Against a Nasty Fast Bowler on a Bumpy Pitch' HMS *Edinburgh* at War

While *Edinburgh* was attached to the Home Fleet at Scapa, she assisted in the interception of a German weather ship. The significance of the capture was magnified by the recovery of a highly prized 'Enigma' coding machine from the captured vessel. The device was sent to the British Government Code and Cypher School at Bletchley Park; the heart of British intelligence. Many ships and sailors' lives were spared by advanced knowledge of German plans and operations when the mysteries of 'Enigma' were unraveled. *Edinburgh* also helped with the capture of a merchant vessel attempting to sneak war materials into Germany.

Ordinary Seaman Veneables was assigned to guard some of the German sailors from the captured ships. As a former language student, he was pleased that he could converse with the prisoners. He remembered that they were all relieved to be out of the war even though things were going well for Germany at that time. When Veneables asked the Germans about their feelings towards Hitler, they mostly expressed that they were not at all in favour of him or his style of government. Veneables admitted that he felt a certain bond with the Germans

HMS *Edinburgh* underway in the Atlantic Ocean while escorting USS *Wasp*, April 1942

as he felt that he and they shared the common experiences and dangers of a life at sea. He continued to chat with them and they sang folksongs in German until the ship's Master at Arms, the head of shipboard discipline, made him stop. Veneables was sternly warned that he was dealing with enemies who might, at any moment, attempt to kill him. At the time, Veneables had no sense whatsoever that the Germans were even remotely considering such an act.[19]

In late 1940, *Edinburgh* was sent to join Force H at Gibraltar and to escort a convoy to Malta. The ship endured the gauntlet of Axis threats and attacks by submarine, aircraft, and surface ships, but managed to get through, stand by as the merchant ships off loaded their cargoes and make the return to Gibraltar. The crew's spirits were lifted by the sight of cheering Maltese who lined the shore as the convoy and its escorts made their way into Valletta's Grand Harbour. The sailors were not less frightened by the war, but their morale received a boost. They were granted some time ashore when they got back to Gibraltar.

Shore leave was not always plentiful during the war years. Ports like Scapa and those in Iceland or Russia were unpleasant for their barren and extremely cold nature. In contrast, Gibraltar, whose harbor was continuously packed with Royal Navy and merchant ships, was sunny, warm, and not subject to too many air raids. The port offered all manner of recreation and entertainment such as shopping, dining, beaches, cinemas, and, of course, bars. Shipboard sailors often complained, however, that the prices for drinks in Gibraltar establishments seemed to be needlessly high. The residential sections of the town included steep and narrow streets that Veneables recalled lazily wandering through. He enjoyed listening to the Spanish style music that drifted softly through the open windows of people's houses. There were many shore based military personnel who could be readily distinguished from ship based sailors by their well-tanned skin. The men who had been out to sea would have had little time to be out in the sun and were, for the most part, pale and pasty in appearance. Many of the naval personnel on Gibraltar were Wrens, and these, according to Veneables, usually seemed pleased to go dancing or for other recreation with sailors on leave from their ships.

After her first Malta convoy, *Edinburgh* was assigned to meet troop convoys going from the United Kingdom to the Red Sea by way of the Cape of Good Hope. The cruiser, tasked with keeping a watch for German surface raiders, would steam out of Gibraltar to accompany the convoys as far as Freetown before turning about to return to Gibraltar. Since no German raiders appeared and the weather was generally fine, these runs were not particularly dangerous. The duty produced what Veneables characterized as 'mostly lazy journeys' and, on one of them the cruiser was met at sea by a destroyer which was carrying mail for *Edinburgh*. Veneables received 30 letters from his sweetheart. Reading her letters, he found it ironic that she was being strafed and bombed during the Luftwaffe's blitzes on Liverpool while he was leisurely reading his mail under warm sunshine with his feet up on the ship's rails. Letters were always valuable for morale and Veneables found them so precious that, many years after the war, he refused to discard them even when his wife, who had originally written them, asked him to throw them out.

*When Edinburgh* made a weeklong port call to Cape Town, a Royal Navy admiral who had been born in South Africa made arrangements for the ship's crew to be well received and treated kindly by the citizens of that city. Veneables and three of his shipmates were met by the owner of a local luxury hotel and his wife who took them into their home. Later on during their leave, and not having had much opportunity to spend money previously, the four young men decided to treat themselves to the type of lavish meal that every man aboard every Royal Navy ship constantly dreamt about in those wartime days. When they requested the bill after the meal which had included cigars and fine liqueurs, they were told that there would be none. The restaurant had been informed ahead of time by 'some rich old lady' that any Royal Navy sailors who chose to dine there would have their bill paid by her.[20]

Although they enjoyed hitherto unknown kindness, and even luxury while in Cape Town, many of *Edinburgh*'s men were shocked by the behavior of white South Africans towards black people. They found it odd and even horrifying that people who were treating them so kindly, generously and gently, could turn in an instant to talk and act with such degrees of cruelty to the blacks. Veneables and his friends were surprised at the segregation aboard busses and naively elected to sit in the 'black only' seats. They earned an unpleasant, if unspoken, lesson in the nature of racism when they observed the extreme discomfort they were causing the black passengers. The four sailors switched seats.[21]

After South Africa, it was back to Gibraltar for assignment to another Malta convoy for *Edinburgh*. Veneables became very uncomfortable when he heard the news. He thought that after surviving one Malta Convoy, going on any others would simply be tempting fate. The evening before their scheduled departure began with a beautiful sunset. As Veneables gazed at it, the thought crossed his mind that he might be spending his last night alive. He compared his feelings to a cricket match where he was 'waiting to go in to bat against a particularly nasty fast bowler on a bumpy pitch'. Once underway and busy, however, he began to feel better. He and his equally nervous shipmates took great pains to pretend that they were not frightened. Even as they were piped to action stations and reminded to don tin hats and to blow up their life belts, they continued to strike poses of unconcern and bravado. They frequently made jokes or off-color comments to get a laugh. Even the tannoy announcer, seated topside by the central gun director, would try to lighten mood with casual wording and a jovial tone for his reports on the progress of a particular action. Veneables mimicked him from memory: 'Lovely day up here … we have just over 120 Italian planes inbound … but not to worry, some of our ships are going to blow the pants off of (some Italian base) …'[22]

Such announcements were made especially for the hands stationed below decks and, as was the practice throughout the Royal Navy, they were designed to reduce tension as much as to be informative. According to Veneables, air attacks out to sea did not usually last more than a matter of ten or fifteen minutes during which enemy planes would fly low overhead to drop bombs or torpedoes and to sometimes strafe. The ships would twist, turn, and dodge at speed with the helm hard over one way only to be hastily followed by a high speed hard over the opposite way. The ships would fire every possible gun at their attackers. By the action's end their decks would be awash in spent brass shell casings.

Both Veneables and *Edinburgh* survived their second Malta convoy and were deployed back to Scapa with the Home Fleet by late 1941. The ship next served with the distant escort for several convoys to and from Murmansk in the early months of 1942.

### 'There Was This Huge Explosion'
### *Edinburgh*'s Sunken Treasure

After bringing a convoy to Murmansk in late April 1942, *Edinburgh* was tied to a dock when several Russian barges were pulled alongside by a tug. Ninety-one heavy boxes were hoisted aboard by crane and lowered into the ship's empty bomb magazine well below decks. Until one slipped and broke open, hardly any of the ship's company knew that they contained bars of gold that were a part of Russia's payments for Allied war supplies. Once loaded, the convoy, designated QP 11, headed homeward with 5.5 tons of gold aboard *Edinburgh*. According to one of the old crew, likely a former officer,

> The boxes were covered with ice and snow when they arrived alongside the starboard side ... and we started getting it up with (a) derrick ... Because (we were by) the head of the galley there was a full head of steam (that was) red hot ... the ice and snow started to melt away and running like a river of blood ... (it was) the (red coloured) paint coming from the stencilling on the boxes. And Commander Jeffries came and said, 'How are we getting along?' ... I said, 'This is a bad omen, you know ... all this

*Russian gold, running with blood.' And he said, 'Oh, I hope you don't think like that.' Well, as it happened, three days later we were gone and the gold was gone with us.*[23]

*Edinburgh* was well in front of the convoy and on a zig-zag course when she was hit by two submarine launched torpedoes. According to a second crewman,

*I had a cup of tea in my hand, and all of a sudden there was this huge explosion. The table disappeared, my cup of tea disappeared, and the stool (I was sitting on) disappeared. A huge flash penetrated the mess deck ... the lights went out and the ship felt as if someone had it in a giant hand tremblingly turning it over to port ... I saw them dragging the lads covered in fuel oil from the hatch where they had lowered the stuff (gold) down ... I saw them hand to hand, bringing people out from there ... Up until then I thought we'd been hit by just the one torpedo, but going aft, I saw that 50 feet of stern had been completely blown away and the quarter deck had ripped up like a sardine tin ... guns of the Y turret (were) poking through the deck.*[24]

*Edinburgh* was badly damaged, but still seaworthy. While her rudder and one propeller were destroyed by the hit on her stern, she could still make way with her remaining two propellers. Two British destroyers, *Foresight* and *Forester*, and a pair of Russian ones joined her. One of the British ships took the cruiser under tow. Several British minesweepers stationed nearby in the Kola inlet to help keep access to Murmansk clear of mines were ordered out to assist *Edinburgh*. Additional assistance was sent in the form of a Russian tug and the Russian gunboat, *Rubin*. The tow from the British destroyer broke. The Russian tug took over, but lacked sufficient power to make any headway with the damaged cruiser. One of the minesweepers attached herself by cable to what remained of the cruiser's stern to provide steering as the damaged ship pushed herself forward with her propellers. The destroyers, gunboat, and remaining minesweepers circled *Edinburgh* as an antisubmarine screen. [25.]

As she slowly laboured through the water, *Edinburgh* was set upon by a force of three German destroyers. The minesweepers had been ordered to retire under smoke screens in the event that enemy surface ships were to appear, but they either did not get the word or elected to ignore it. They commenced fire, as did *Edinburgh* and her two faithful destroyers. The Germans fired back on the British but, possibly assuming that they were against greater strength than a handful of small combatants

HMS *Edinburgh* taken at the time when she was carrying Russian gold valued at £45 million

and a crippled cruiser, maintained their distance. *Edinburgh*'s gunners were good. They scored hits on one of the German destroyers that so damaged her that she eventually sank. The two remaining German destroyers, however, were able to maneuver into torpedo launching position. As she could only move in a slow circle, *Edinburgh* took a hit amidships. One of her crew recalled,

> *I came up onto the bridge and I saw this firing from these ships and the next thing I saw three torpedoes approaching … the next thing (there was) an explosion on the port side. A huge column of water came over the flag deck … I thought, 'Well, this is my lot now'*[26]

The Germans did not press their attack, but *Edinburgh*'s engineers had determined that she was just a few steel plates shy of breaking in two. She was ordered abandoned and her crew was removed by two of the minesweepers. Lest the Germans realise what her cargo was and manage to get at it, one of the minesweepers was ordered to sink the hulk by gunfire. The little warship fired some twenty rounds into the cruiser with little effect. The minesweeper was then ordered to lie alongside and drop depth charges set to detonate directly beneath *Edinburgh*, but even after that the cruiser still would not sink. There was some thought of re-boarding her with a skeleton crew, but *Foresight* was requested to fire her last remaining torpedo at *Edinburgh*. The torpedo hit and sank the cruiser. About 60 of Edinburgh's men had been killed. The ship and all the gold she was carrying went under in icy water more than 800 feet deep on 2 May 1942.

The British and Soviet governments were well aware of the gold's underwater location but, given the limitations of technology available for the first quarter century after the war, could not hope to recover it. In 1981, however, a privately contracted salvage company did recover most of the gold. By 1986, all but five of the original 465 bars had been raised. Britain claimed 45 per cent of the gold which, at the time of its salvage was estimated to be worth £40 million. The Soviet Union was awarded the other 55 per cent. The whereabouts of the five missing bars remains unknown.[27]

Many Royal Navy veterans of the Arctic convoys along with many historians tend to characterize the Russians at Murmansk and Archangel as stand-offish or even hostile. The Captain of the *Rubin* offered some lie to that belief. Moved by the brave battle put up by the Royal Navy's men and ships in their determination to save *Edinburgh*, he sent the following message to the commander of the British minesweeping flotilla based in the Kola Inlet:

*From Commander of Divisions, USSR Gunboat* Rubin, *4th day of May, 1942*

*Dear Sir, Soviets seamen was witness of heroic Battle of English seamen with predominants powers of enemy. English seamen did observe their sacred duty before Fatherland. We are proud of staunchness and courage of English seamens – our allies. I am very sorry what injured your ship by approach to board for what I must beg pardon. Commander of Division.*[28]

ENDNOTES

1. BBC Radio Wales. 'Arctic Convoys.' Originally broadcast on 27 July 2013. bbc.co.uk. Web. Accessed June 2014.

2. _____ 'Russian Convoys 1941–1945.' naval-history.net. Accessed June 2014.

3. Roskill, Capt. S. W. *White Ensign: The British Navy at War 1939–1945*. Naval Institute Press. 1966. pp. 206 – 208.

4. _____ 'Russian Convoys 1941–1945.'

5. _____ 'Russian Convoys 1941–1945.'

6. While far from inedible, tinned corned beef has a fatty texture and metallic taste that are entirely foreign to all other forms of true corned beef. The type of meat contained in the tin cannot be identified through its flavor.

7. According to 'Russian Convoys 1941–1945,' the destroyer was possibly HMS *Matabele* of convoy PQ 8 and sunk on 17 January 1942.

8. An occasional strategy for convoys under simultaneous attack by multiple U-boats was to break formation. This would force the submarines to chase individual and scattered targets and thus provide opportunities for most of the other ships to steam away from the danger.

9. BBC Radio Wales. The men whose anecdotes were presented in the broadcast were not identified by name.

10. 'Convoys to Murmansk.' BBC WW2 *People's War*. Article ID A 4120011. 2005.

11. Shield, Stanley. 'Memories of a C.W. Candidate Part One – North Atlantic Convoys and Life Aboard HMS Somali.' BBC WW2 *People's War*. Article ID A 5795751. 2005.

12. Shield.

13. BBC Radio Wales. These are the comments of three separate, but unidentified men.

14. Imperial War Museum. Sound recording archive. 31437. Guthrie, Gus. 2008.

15. Imperial War Museum. Sound recording archive. 21552. Veneables, Raymond Briggs. 2001.

16. Imperial War Museum. 21552.

17. Imperial War Museum. 21552.

18. The daily rum ration was abandoned on 31 July 1970 on what was called 'Black Tot Day.' The reasoning for its abandonment was that shipboard equipment and machinery had become so technologically sophisticated and delicate that they should not be hazarded in the hands of an operator who might be less than fully sober.

19. Imperial War Museum. 21552 (Veneables).

20. Imperial War Museum. 21552.

21. Imperial War Museum. 21552.

22. Imperial War Museum. 21552.

23. BBC. 'Gold From the Deep: The Salvage of The Century.' Originally broadcast in the UK in 1981 and first broadcast in the USA in 1983.

24. BBC.

25. Moore, David. 'HMS *Edinburgh*.' BBC WW2 *People's War*. Article ID A 2076518. 2003,

27. BBC.

28. BBC.

29. Moore. The last sentence in the Russian captain's message refers to the accidental bumping of one of the British minesweepers by Rubin during the evacuation of survivors from *Edinburgh*.

# SEVEN
# LITTLE SHIPS WITH
# HEAVY BURDENS

The minesweepers, corvettes, and escort carriers of World War II and their crews often laboured and fought in unknown places and in obscure actions that have been all too easy to forget. Even those that made large and indispensable contributions without which the war could not have been won were frequently overlooked. Nonetheless, the men aboard these small naval combatants proved themselves to be as dedicated, hardworking, and proud of their ships as were those who served on their larger and more popular heavy units such as the battleships, battle cruisers, and aircraft carriers.

## 'They Would Roll on Wet Grass'
### Corvettes

By the early 1920s the German Navy was well on its way to developing new anti-shipping tactics for any future war in Europe. Through trial, error, and dogged practice Germany's sailors learned that large groups of submarines simultaneously firing torpedoes while surfaced were far more effective against enemy shipping than individual and random attacks made by U-Boats lurking beneath the water's surface. By 1941 'wolf packs' of as many as fifty German submarines executing coordinated attacks against British shipping were reaping deadly results.[1]

In response to the U-Boat threat the British revived the concept of the maritime convoy. Convoys had proven successful in the First World War. The British hoped they could once again be effective. The ideal convoy was described as,

*... the supply train and reinforcement column of the sea. A group of merchant vessels or troop transports, highly vulnerable to surface or submarine attack when alone, steam in company escorted by warships of types able to ward off the anticipated attack: battleships, cruisers, and carriers to deal with enemy warships, raiders or aircraft; destroyers and smaller vessels to handle submarines. In 1917–1918 the convoy system was brought to a high state of efficiency. More than any other factor it defeated the German unrestricted submarine warfare ...*[2]

Unfortunately, the Royal Navy's interwar policy of dedicating the bulk of its limited shipbuilding funds to large capital ships caused it to suffer from a shortage of 'smaller vessels to handle submarines' precisely at the time when they were most needed. In order to meet the demand, the Navy adopted the expedient of quickly building, converting, or purchasing large numbers of relatively inexpensive vessels that could be quickly prepared for convoy duty. Among these escorts ships were the more than 200 corvettes of the *Flower* class which were built from a design originally used for whaling vessels. These hastily commissioned ships were manned by equally hastily mobilized crews. The *Flowers* were almost exclusively served by scantily trained 'Hostilities Only' ratings and reservist officers. Commanding officers were often former merchant ship captains or even former yachtsmen. Many of these new corvette captains entered service with little or no naval experience.

The *Flower* class corvettes bore unintimidating names such as *Tulip, Begonia, Lavender,* and *Buttercup.* They measured 205 feet in length and had a shallow draft that made them very uncomfortable in the rough Atlantic seas where they were most often to serve. Their chief weapon was the depth charge of which they carried about 100. Each packing hundreds of pounds of high explosives, depth charges were carried on racks at the corvette's stern from which they could be rolled atop an enemy submarine by hand. The corvettes were also equipped with mechanical throwers which could launch a depth charge away from the sides of the ship.

Conditions aboard *Flower* class corvettes were extreme. Their buoyancy gave them a bounce that gave rise to the sarcastic catchphrase among crews that, 'they would roll on wet grass'. Cramped, noisy, crowded, wet, hot, and stuffy, they were difficult to live in no matter what the weather. They tended to pitch, roll, and swing in the slightest breeze. Seasickness greatly reduced crew morale and effectiveness. Food could not be stored or properly prepared so rations were typically limited to tinned beef, bread dampened or even soaked by seawater, and powdered potatoes. No sooner had their final coating of paint dried at the builder's yard than the corvettes and their men were sent to war.

## 'Convoy Work Was Extremely Wearing on the Nerves'
## U-Boats

Capture of a German U-boat, June 1944

After the war Dick Turner, a former crewman of the Flower class corvette HMS *Vetch* wrote down some of his thoughts about convoy duty.

*The uncertainty of convoy work was extremely wearing on the nerves. During the passage it was impossible to grab more than a couple of hours of doze. There was no opportunity for any restful sleep – the bell that announced 'Action Stations' could, and would ring at any time of the day or night. This was brought home to me when we were at Liverpool following a convoy passage. For the first time in some weeks I thought that I could get a decent night's sleep. However, in the morning, when the alarm bell went off, I leapt out of bed, grabbed my clothes, dressed and headed for the door when I was interrupted by my wife saying, 'What on earth are you doing, Dick?' In my mind I was still on the ship and the Action Stations alarm had just sounded. It had become a completely automatic reaction and was a sign of the high state of nervous tension in which we all lived our lives in those days.*[3]

Turner described a convoy action in which *Vetch*, earned credit for a U-boat kill.

*Two days after sailing* (with convoy HG 82 on 12 April 1942) *we were warned that U-boats had been reported as operating in the area of the*

HMS *Vetch*, Flower
Class Corvette 1:350

*convoy. During the evening of 14 April, Vetch was at the front of the convoy with* (Captain Frederic 'Johnnie') *Walker ... in HMS* Stork, *bringing up the rear. Vetch's radar reported a U-boat off the port side of the convoy and we turned to investigate. Starshell were fired and we sighted the boat – which turned out to be U-252. The U-boat was about a mile from Vetch and closing on the convoy. When they saw Vetch approaching, the enemy fired torpedoes which missed Vetch by a very small margin indeed – a matter of feet. In* Stork, *Walker had seen the starshell and had rushed up to join the action. A chase ensued in which both* Stork *and* Vetch *fired depth charges. Eventually wreckage was sighted on the water confirming that the attack had been successful. It was* Vetch*'s first confirmed kill and there was much excitement on the ship.* Vetch*'s commander signaled* Stork *asking permission to 'splice the main brace (issue an extra ration of rum to the crew)'. Walker agreed. That was to start a custom in the ships that Walker commanded and thereafter 'splice the main brace' was ordered after every U-boat success.*[4]

### 'God Bless You for Stopping'
### Nicholas Monsarrat, RNVR and Rescue at Sea

The novel *The Cruel Sea* and the short story collection *Three Corvettes* provide detailed descriptions of wartime operations aboard several corvette types. Based on his highly unauthorised wartime diary, they were penned by Nicholas Monsarrat, a naval reserve officer who had been a writer before the war. Monsarrat served from 1939–1945 aboard *Flowers* and other small combatants.

One of the corvettes aboard which Monsarrat served as an officer was HMS *Campanula*. Bearing pennant number K-18, *Campanula* commissioned on 6 September 1940 and served as inspiration for the fictional HMS *Compass Rose* of Monsarrat's novel, *The Cruel Sea*.[5] *Campanula*'s first significant activity was the at-sea rescue of crewmen from the merchant vessel SS *Alva* that had been sunk by German submarine *U-559* in August 1941. Several days later *Campanula* picked up survivors of the *Empire Oak*, also a U-boat victim. Among the men recovered from the water were other crewmen of the *Alva* that *Empire Oak* had previously rescued. In an excerpt from *The Cruel Sea*, the fictional HMS *Compass Rose* picked up survivors from a ship sunk while in a convoy headed for Gibraltar from England.

*Three more ships that last night cost, and one of them – yet another loaded tanker to be torpedoed and set on fire – was the special concern of* Compass Rose. *It was she who was nearest when the ship was struck, and she circled round as the oil, cascading and spouting from the tanker's side, took fire and spread over the water like a flaming carpet in a pitch black room. Silhouetted against this roaring backcloth, which soon rose to fifty feet in the air,* Compass Rose *must have been visible for miles around: even in swift movement she made a perfect target and (the captain), trying to decide whether to stop and pick up survivors, or whether the risk would not be justified, could visualize clearly what they would look like when stationary against this wall of flame.* Compass Rose *with her crew … would be a sitting mark from ten miles away … It was a captain's moment; a pure test of nerve … the order when it came was swift and decisive, 'Stop engines! … Stand by to get those survivors inboard. We won't lower a boat – they'll have to swim or row towards us. God knows they can see us easily enough. Use a megaphone to hurry them along … we don't want to waste any time.'*

*All over the ship, a prickling silence fell as* Compass Rose *came to a stop and waited, rolling gently, lit by the glare from the fire. From the bridge every detail of the upper deck could be picked out; there was no flickering in this huge illumination, simply a steady glow that threw a black shadow on the sea behind them, and showed them naked to the enemy … the flames roared and three boats crept towards them, and faint shouting and bobbing lights here and there on the water indicated a valiant swimmer making for safety … (T)he work of rescue (included) … rigging a sling for the wounded men, securing the scrambling nets that hung over the side, by which men could pull themselves up … a boat drew alongside, bumping and scraping … 'Hook on forrard!' there were sounds of scrambling; an anonymous voice, foreign, slightly breathless said: 'God bless you for stopping.'* [6]

## 'Merchant Ships Fitted With Catapults'
## Air Power on a Shoestring

As thoroughly determined on their jobs as they were, the corvettes and their crews could not hope to defeat Germany's U-boats alone. The last war had shown the value of airborne protection for convoys, but the land-based planes and airships sent to fly over the formations of merchant ships and their escorts suffered from limited range. Something more would be needed that could offer full air protection over the vast expanses that encompassed the transoceanic shipping routes. The natural solution would have been to have an aircraft carrier, even if just a small one, attached to each convoy. As with practically everything else, however, there were shortages of both aircraft and of the ships that could carry them.

An interim measure was the creation of the Catapult Aircraft Merchant ship, or CAM. As the name suggests, a catapult and an aircraft were installed onto an ordinary cargo vessel. The idea originated with none other than Winston Churchill himself. Captain Eric Brown, Royal Navy, who would go on to become one of the world's premiere test pilots and live until 2016, described the CAM concept and his demonstration of it for Churchill,

> *...we had in the navy, at that time, merchant ships fitted with catapults and a fighter. These ships were the brainchild of Churchill himself and we suddenly got a message that this great man would like to come down and see this for himself. This Seafire* (the navalised version of the Spitfire) *was on a cradle which had rockets attached, and it was rocketed along the catapult and it was stopped ... when it reached the end ... by two prongs on the cradle penetrating two tubes filled with water ... that arrested this trolley in the astonishing distance of about eight feet. Well, on the great day, the chap who filled the tubes with water – I think, must have got a bit of nerve – because he failed to fill (them) with water, unknown to anybody else, of course. ... I was shot off in front of the great man and, of course, the cradle went clean through the tubes and was still attached to the aircraft. It's a fair bit of iron-mongery* (the Captain chuckles) *to have hanging under your airplane, and, after a bit of a struggle and shaking of the aircraft, this thing fell off, but up until then I had to be at full power not gaining any height at all. And it's interesting because, at the end of the day, the great man enjoyed the whole thing and didn't appear to be aware of the problem* (the Captain laughs as he says this) *... anyway a satisfied customer left and that was that.*[7]

The Hurricane fighter was the aircraft of choice for use aboard the CAM ships.

Its need for catapult assistance to take off earned the plane the nickname of 'Hurricat'. Their most important mission was to shoot down or chase off the long-ranged German reconnaissance planes that shadowed convoys to send information about them to U-boat wolf packs. The spotter planes, called Kondors by the Germans, were converted passenger carriers that could easily loiter out of the range of shipborne guns.

Photographs of CAM ships show that the short catapults were often mounted forward. When needed, the ship would turn into the wind and make maximum speed to provide the greatest possible lift to the airplane as it was launched. There were no means for recovery of CAM launched planes at sea. Once his mission was completed, a pilot would either have to seek land or, as in practically all cases, circle back to the convoy to bail out or ditch close to a ship that would pick him up. In the two years that CAM ships were used a total of six enemy planes were shot down against the loss of one British pilot and twelve CAM ships sunk.[8]

### 'It Was the Smallest Aircraft Carrier in the World'
### Britain's First Escort Carrier – Made in Germany

In 1940 the German refrigerated stores *Hannover* that the British had captured earlier in the war, was transported to Blyth Shipyard in Northumberland. She was fitted with a flight deck that measured 480 feet long and renamed HMS *Audacity*. Lacking elevators, *Audacity* had to keep her entire airwing of six American-built carrier aircraft lashed down on the flight deck. Landings were assisted by three arresting wires stretched across the after portion of the flight deck. The plan was to use *Audacity* to counter German Kondor spy planes and to defend convoys against aerial and submarine attacks. The new carrier entered Royal Navy service in June 1941. She would see duty on convoys that ran between England and Gibraltar.

In September 1941 *Audacity*'s first convoy was attacked by both submarines and aircraft. Three of the convoy's twenty-two merchant ships were sunk by submarines and three others were lost to air attacks. One of *Audacity*'s planes was credited with shooting down a German attacker as it attempted to make a bomb attack on one of the convoy's ships. At the end of the month *Audacity*

HMS *Audacity*, escort
carrier, Model 1:1200

arrived unscathed at Gibraltar with the remainder of her convoy.

Captain Brown, the former CAM pilot, now the commander of *Audacity*'s air
group, 802 Squadron, spoke about the ship:

> *When I first saw* (Audacity) *it was the smallest aircraft carrier in the world,
> actually ... but to me it wasn't unusual ... we had some pilots in our
> squadron who had flown onto large aircraft carriers like the Ark Royal and
> this small matchbox terrified them. But it didn't mean much to me ... it
> was just another place to land.... And maybe that was to my advantage, I
> think, because this is what got me into test flying because the commanding
> officer of that aircraft carrier wrote to the Admiralty – unknown to me,
> of course, and said that I had a special facility for deck landing and he
> thought they ought to make use of it ... that's how I got into test flying.*[9]

Over two further convoys *Audacity's* airmen earned credit for four German
planes shot down at the cost of one of their own.

### 'Roaring Curses at the Enemy'
### The Fury of Battle

*Audacity's* final convoy departed from Gibraltar on 14 December 1941. She
accompanied a group of escorts headed by Captain 'Johnnie' Walker who was
destined for fame by, among other important deeds, directing the sinking of

between fourteen and twenty U-boats during the war. The convoy's escort group included seven Flower class corvettes and two sloops. Along with *Audacity*, the convoy included three additional destroyers and 32 merchant ships. *Audacity*'s pilots would be credited with two enemy planes shot down by the convoy's third day of steaming.[10]

Early on the morning of 17 December, Captain Walker ordered *Audacity*'s commanding officer to launch an aircraft to look for possible surfaced submarines. Before too long, one of them sighted *U-131* on the surface and vectored escorts to its position. When the submarine dived, it was attacked with depth charges. Although the contact was lost, Walker insisted that *Audacity* launch further aircraft and aggressively patrol against its reappearance. Conventional anti-submarine tactics would have called for a tightening of the defensive ring around the convoy to await an attack at which time the convoy's escorts would spring into action. Firmly believing that a good defense rested completely with a good offense, Walker sought to actively draw his enemies into combat. *U-131* had remained close at hand and, when her captain thought it prudent, the submarine surfaced in preparation for an attack. *Audacity*'s pilots, encouraged by Walker to seek trouble, caught the submarine by surprise and initiated an attack that sent the Germans into a crash dive.

The German boat remained hidden by the depth of the water and her own silent battery-powered operation. As time passed, however, the submarine's air decreased in oxygen content while carbon dioxide levels steadily accumulated. The U-boat's lack of breathable air finally forced it to surface. It was immediately spotted by several of the convoy's escorts. Walker ordered a plane from *Audacity* to attack. The pilot complied with a strafing run. The submarine returned fire and managed to shoot down the plane and kill its pilot, but a barrage of gunfire from the convoy escorts soon sank the U-boat.

The ferocity of the running battle, pitting U-boat against convoy and escorts against U-boat, gained headway. On the following morning, several of the escorts found *U-434* on the surface. The submarine had been carefully keeping track of the convoy's disposition and was prepared to share the information with other U-boats in preparation for a coordinated wolf pack strike. The U-boat dived and the escorts made several passes over the spot to drop depth charges. Soon, damaged by the shock of multiple close detonations, *U-434* was forced to the surface. As her crew piled out and jumped overboard, the submarine turned over and sank.

Later that day several German spotter planes appeared overhead. Walker radioed *Audacity* to launch aircraft to pursue. The fighters found their quarry, but gun failures allowed the Germans to escape. Walker, certain that the convoy had been reported, requested round-the-clock air patrols from *Audacity* as two of his destroyers were forced to turn for port due to low fuel. A U-boat contact was made at dusk and two escorts dashed off to investigate. They spotted the submarine and fired upon it but missed. Darkness fell and the convoy maintained a zig-zagging course towards England.

Before dawn of the following day, the destroyer HMS *Stanley* spotted *U-574* on the surface. The submarine had been working into position for an attack by moonlight. The destroyer radioed her position and turned to attack. The U-boat was not shy in turning to take on the oncoming destroyer. Walker was several miles distant, looking in its direction through binoculars, when the destroyer signaled that she had detected torpedoes passing astern. According to Walker's diary,

> At the moment when everything seemed to be sorting itself out at once and I had my glasses on her, she went up, literally, in a sheet of flame hundreds of feet high. She thought the torpedoes were passing her.[11]

Walker, who was conducting the battle from aboard the sloop HMS *Stork*, went to the spot where the destroyer had gone down. *Stork* began to drop depth charges on the intuition that the U-boat might attempt to hide itself in the noise field created by the still settling destroyer. The commander remained mindful of the danger of heavy explosions to any survivors still in the water, but acted unemotionally and decisively. Suddenly the U-boat broke surface a short distance away. Walker described the confrontation,

> As I went in to ram, he ran away from me and turned to port. I followed and I was surprised to find later that I had made three complete circles, the U-boat turning continuously to port inside Stork's turning-circle at only two or three knots slower than me. I kept her illuminated … and fired at him with the four-inch guns until they could not be sufficiently depressed.

*After this the guns' crews were reduced to fist shaking and roaring curses at the enemy who several times seemed to be a matter of feet away rather than yards.*[12]

Despite the note of humor in Walker's words, the action was both furious and vicious. *Stork* machine gunned the U-boat's bridge structure and was finally able to ram the bobbing enemy. As the submarine scraped against the sloop's hull and slipped beneath the surface, Walker ordered a group of depth charges set for shallow detonation dropped. The submarine and a number of her crew were destroyed. *Stork* was now forced to operate at reduced speed due to the damage to her bow from ramming the U-boat. The escort's damage also left her asdic inoperable. Even as *Stork* and other escorts were searching for and picking up survivors from both *Stanley* and the U-boat, one of the convoy's ships was torpedoed and sunk. The Admiralty radioed Walker that there appeared to be half a dozen U-boats in the vicinity. Thus far, the convoy's defenders had sunk three U-boats against the loss of a destroyer, one merchant vessel, and an airplane from *Audacity*. The convoy was doing very well by the standards of 1941.

*Audacity* continued to prove her value on the next day when a pair of her aircraft shot down yet another German spotter plane. Her aircraft also caught another surfaced U-boat, but the subsequent attack did not yield a sinking. Over the course of the day *Audacity*'s aircraft made attacks on several more U-boats. There were still no sinkings, but the carrier and her planes at least managed to keep U-boats at bay. The convoy now made a straight course at its best speed for home. There was no sense wasting time or fuel by zig-zagging since the Germans very clearly had them in their sights already. Walker wrote,

*The net of U-boats seems to be growing tighter around us despite* Audacity's *heroic efforts to keep them at arm's length.*[13]

### 'The Stern Just Rose High in the Air'
### HMS *Audacity* Torpedoed

On 21 December *Audacity* was hit by a torpedo from *U-571* that damaged her steering but did not cause her to lose way. She settled by the stern but, because

HMS *Audacity*

the convoy's escorts had been pursuing other U-boats intent on attacking the convoy, there could be no counterattack with which to protect the carrier. Captain Brown had just landed aboard the ship and gone below to the wardroom for a cup of coffee when the ship was hit. With its rudder damaged, the ship circled for a while before coming to a stop. The U-boat, secure in the knowledge that *Audacity* was alone, surfaced. Standing on the flight deck, Brown stated that the carrier and the U-boat were so close together that he was able to see the gold braid on what he assumed was the submarine captain's cap. The officer stood looking at *Audacity* and, according to Brown,

> *... the captain* (of Audacity) *called everyone onto the flight deck because he thought that if we had to be sunk they're going to have the best chance on the flight deck. ... One of our sailors, his nerve broke, and he rushed over to one of the 20mm cannon and opened fire with no hope really of hitting the U-boat but he did open fire and that caused the German to release his torpedoes. I think there were four fired at us and I think all four hit. But certainly the bows literally fell off the carrier and it immediately tipped up. The stern just rose high in the air. As it did so ... the aircraft were all lashed down ... with steel hawsers and as it tilted up I could hear these hawsers beginning to stretch and the twang as they broke and the six aircraft just rushed down the flight deck into four hundred odd people standing there*

*and killed a large number … injured a large number … and a lot of people just rushed for the deck and leapt over the side.*

*If you were at the stern it was a leap of about 50 or 60 feet. … You didn't know if you were going to land on somebody in the water but it was that sort of evacuation; a panic evacuation because of what happened to the aircraft.*[14]

Walker noted in his Battle Report that he felt responsible for the loss of the carrier. He wrote that he had denied her the company of an escort ship because he was hard-pressed to give one up from submarine hunting. He also felt that he should have ordered the carrier to a better and more protected position within the convoy but had neglected to do so.[15]

### 'I Was in a Favourable Position'
### A German Version of the Attack on *Audacity*

A German version of the sinking, broadcast as a radio interview on 30 December 1941 by a Frankfurt radio station, has been preserved in translated and transcribed form. A reporter spoke to Kapitanleutnant Gerhard Bigalk, the commander of *U-751*, who was credited with the sinking of *Audacity*. Although some of the ship types, dispositions, actions, and the general number of them may appear questionable, the U-boat captain was acting under less than ideal conditions for observation. He described the action.

*I was only at sea for a few days when I had to crash dive because of an English plane. In the listening instrument I heard screw noises in the water and took them to be coming from a convoy. I told myself that I should get to the surface as quickly as possible to see what was actually the matter, so I came to the surface very soon and only a few minutes later I saw clouds of smoke and a few minutes after I saw the outlines of some destroyers. Aha, there is a convoy! We were very glad to have met a convoy after only a few days after our departure. First of all I approached the convoy to see how things were. I discovered a number of destroyers zig-zagging wildly and, furthest to the left, next to the destroyers, I saw a large, long shadow surrounded by several destroyers zig-zagging crazily. Suddenly a wild firing of tracer bullets started up in the East. At this moment my other U-boat comrades who were also going for this convoy, had probably opened attack. The destroyers took course for the tracer bullets; the long shadow which I first took for a tanker, zig-zagged first Eastward, then Northward, presumably to get away from the convoy. I made for the large shadow immediately to attack it. Suddenly the large shadow turned away sharply and at the same moment there was a great firing of rockets from the convoy. The whole area was as light as day. Other U-boats must have been attacking. Ten or fifteen rockets hung over the U-boats as if spellbound. The destroyers nearby also started firing tracer bullets and suddenly I saw in the light of the tracer bullets and rockets a large aircraft carrier lying in front of us. Good God! What a chance! An opportunity such as a U-boat commander does not find every day. The whole bridge was wildly enthusiastic.*

*Now I was in a favourable position to attack. I had to fire. I fired several torpedoes, and then came the terrible tension of waiting to see, if or not, one of them hit its mark. Then suddenly a fiery detonation aft. A hit aft! The ship described a semi-circle portside, and then stopped, unable to maneuver. Apparently my torpedo had smashed her screws. I turned a short distance off to load new torpedoes. Down below in the forrard (forward) compartment there was terrific crowding since we had left just a few days before and the forrard compartment was full of provisions and all sorts of impossible things necessary for an operational cruise. My torpedo mate and torpedo crew worked like mad. We in the meantime were standing on the bridge watching the aircraft carrier and were terribly excited lest the destroyers return and mess up this unique chance. But apparently the destroyers were furiously busy, for way back on the horizon there were bangs and detonations, and tracer bullets were being fired. Our comrades were doing their work. The torpedo tubes were reported clear for action, thank God. I made another attack approaching the ship at a crawling pace so that she should under no account hear me. The water was phosphorescing like mad and could only proceed very slowly so as not to be discovered by the aircraft carrier, which had stopped. I came nearer and nearer. I didn't care anymore. I had to get so near that on no account could my torpedoes miss. A gigantic shadow growing larger and larger all the time! I had approached so closely that no torpedo could possibly miss and then I gave permission to fire. The torpedoes* (cleared) *their tubes. Seconds of great tension. There, hit forrard, twenty meters behind the stem. A great detonation with a gigantic sheet of flame. A short time afterwards, another detonation in the middle; again a great column of fire. Hardly had the column of water subsided when a strong detonation was observed forrard. Probably ammunition or fuel tanks had been hit. I presumed that petrol tanks or something of that kind had been blown up. I turned off and in doing so cast another glance at the aircraft carrier. The fore was already flooded and the deck was turning upwards. At that moment destroyers were reported starboard. They were dashing full speed towards the aircraft carrier, which was wildly firing distress signals – great stars bursting in the air. I was able to get away from the pursuit. I got a rain of depth charges but that was to no avail for the English – I escaped.*[16]

## 'The Bay of Biscay in December is Not the Healthiest Place to Be'
## Surviving in the Sea

With *Audacity* sunk and *U-751* on her way out of the area, it remained only for the small carrier's crew to be rescued. The *Audacity*'s captain died in the water as did numerous others. Captain Eric Brown related,

*… the carrier was sunk on the 21st of December, 1941 … we all found ourselves in the Bay of Biscay in December which is not the healthiest place to be. A destroyer* (or) *a frigate came to rescue us along with some corvettes from the convoy escort group but after they had rescued quite a number of people, I was not among them at that stage, and when they took off they left about 26 of us together … we tied ourselves together … there were only two pilots, myself and my flight leader and the rest were seamen from the ship. We* (two pilots) *had Mae Wests which kept us afloat nicely … they*

(the ship's company) *had only – virtually – inner tubes of tires around them and cords over their shoulder and after the rescuing (ships) had left they fell asleep; it was exhaustion, I think, and of course they drowned. Our Mae Wests would keep our heads out of the water but these inner tube affairs were hopeless for that so ... the other guys were lost. (By) morning there was only my flight leader and myself. ... the destroyer came back for us, well, just looking for anybody and when we got onboard eventually they explained that they had had a nasty 'ping' (asdic contact) that the submarine was still around and they couldn't afford to come to a stop to pick people up otherwise they were a sitting target so understandably they had to go and leave us ... so we had a fair number of casualties total overall ... from the actual torpedo strike(s) and the subsequent waiting for rescue. It was a ruthless war and it wasn't just the enemy; you had another enemy in the sea.*[17]

The Navy's escort carrier force steadily grew through the addition of seventeen more British conversions like *Audacity* and thirty-nine ships acquired through Lend-Lease from the Americans. Through Lend-Lease cooperation the United States provided Great Britain with warships – mostly destroyers and escort carriers – in exchange for basing rights in far-flung and strategically significant British territories. The act remained in effect until the end of the war.

## 'Snotties'
## An RNVR Midshipman and Times That Were Not Always Cruel

The writer and naval officer Nicholas Monsarrat, like many others, received his commission as a member of the Royal Navy Volunteer Reserve, the RNVR. The acute manpower shortage had caused the Royal Navy to originally try to fill its officer ranks with men from the Royal Navy Reserve, the RNR. A majority of RNR officers had either naval or other maritime experience prior to being activated for World War II. When the need for men could still not be satisfied, the Navy resorted to the RNVR which included men who, although lacking professional maritime qualifications, nonetheless had some knowledge or interest in the sea. Among these were yachtsmen such as Monsarrat. Still others were enlisted into the RNVR with no nautical experience at all. The RNVR was called the 'wavy navy' after the wavy uniform coat sleeve rings that served to identify the wearer's rank. Regular or RNR officers wore straight rings on their coat sleeves.

Colin Bourne recalled his entry into the Navy, selection and training for his RNVR commission, and his service aboard several Flower class corvettes. His naval career was far less harrowing than that of Monsarrat.

> *After I left school I went to work in … a publishing business called World Books, one of the earliest book clubs. This was an interlude between leaving school, my eighteenth birthday, and being called up … In the spring of 1943, I was called up to start a naval career.*

> *We went first to receiving camp … where we were kitted out; the first steps to getting into one of the services during the war. That was a very rude awakening because on the very first day there were about 12 of us at the dinner table in the mess. The food was brought to the table – meat, potatoes, and peas and (the) action started immediately. Most of the people round the table didn't wait, they just got hold of the meat with their hands and helped themselves. It left me completely bewildered. I had never seen his happen before … my first night as a naval rating … the next night I made sure I was nearer the meat dish than anyone else![18]*

Bourne spent the next several weeks as a typical recruit. He and his fellow trainees marched, drilled, ran, and partook in assault courses. The training also included time aboard ship designed to provide the novice sailors with practical experience at sea. During this time, Bourne was deemed as likely officer material. He did not know why he was selected, but he went along.

> *Starting on my officer-training career, we were sent to HMS* King Alfred *in Howe. We attended lots of courses and lectures and every now and then we had to give a talk ourselves. We did a lot of practical work, man management, etc. I was very fortunate as my digs were based about a mile from my sister and her husband who were living in Brighton at that time. We also attended Lancing College, which had a magnificent school chapel.*

*When we had passed various examinations at King Alfred, we attended a two or three week finishing course at Greenwich College ... I came out as a newly pledged midshipman. Snotties, as they were called. On my lapel jacket was a little maroon strip of cloth with a little gold piece on maroon. So, here I was, a newly pledged officer in the RNVR, Royal Navy Volunteer Reserves, the wavy navy!*

*(After leave), it wasn't very long before I received my sailing orders to report to HMCS* Lunenburg[19] *in Londonderry ... a Canadian corvette. I went aboard and followed instructions issued to all young officers that go aboard a new ship for the first time, to salute and say, 'Permission to come aboard, sir.' I was very pleased to be on one of these ships (a corvette) ... We were an escort vessel, carrying out convoy duty. The Flower class corvettes were ... uncomfortable in (the) extreme! It was also known that if you could stand a* Flower *class corvette, you could probably stand anything! That was right, because when we did get started, and I went out on the first sortie I think I was seasick for about a day and a half ... So I joined this ship* (Lunenburg). *I never knew why I had been posted to this particular ship, they dotted the officers around. There was a radar officer ... (and)*

HMCS *Lunenburg*

*he and I were the only English officers on board. The crew were super and very enjoyable to work with. I know that there was more informality on board this ship than there would have been on one of the major RN ships ... Being a midshipman and being a very young raw junior officer, I wasn't allowed to take any watches myself; my job was ... looking after the ship's office and so forth. Of course, I did my share of watchmanship but I wasn't allowed to do one myself, quite understandably and rightly, otherwise there may have been total disaster. So, first of all I shared the midnight watch with a Canadian who was about six or seven years older than I was. His name was Tom, and we became very good friends, and we kept touch throughout our lives until he died about two years ago. I had the privilege of being asked to be godfather to his fourth and youngest son, which I did with pleasure. I mention this because it shows how ties can be held together when you meet someone in wartime service. I remember Tom with great happiness ...*[21]

Bourne remained with HMCS *Lunenburg* for the next six months as the ship escorted convoys between Canada and the United Kingdom. He was fortunate in that all of his ocean crossings were relatively routine and free of trouble from commerce raiders, U-boats, or air attacks. As the 1944 invasion of Normandy, D-Day, approached, *Lunenburg* was ordered to Weymouth Bay. Due to wartime secrecy, none aboard Bourne's ship had any idea what was happening.

*(There was) no shore leave apart from the captain and the number one* (first lieutenant, or second in command). *To stop boredom setting in, we gave games to the crew to keep them occupied and we played endless games of Monopoly ourselves on the bridge. Eventually, orders came and we escorted ships, Mulberry (artificial) Harbours, and equipment over to France. In this small way, I was involved in the D-Day landings.*[21]

Bourne was detached from *Lunenburg* and sent to a duty that he did not relish in the least: submarine school. He admitted to being a marginal trainee.

*An officer in charge came up to me and said, 'You've worked hard at this, but I don't think that submarines are your forte, do you?' I replied by saying that I entirely agreed with him ... So I went home (on leave) and, very shortly afterwards, I received sailing orders to Gibraltar ... I joined (Flower class corvette) HMS Jonquil, a very happy ship with lots of different nationalities on board. We had people from Rhodesia, South Africa, and Norway; a very happy crowd. This was followed six months later by joining HMS Bellwort, also a Flower class corvette. There, I met another officer who had been to a school that played a good class of (field) hockey (as I had in Dunstable), and we decided to form a hockey team to keep the crew entertained. We bought black and yellow shirts, got hold of some hockey sticks, gave lessons, and off we went to play a match against another ship. I put a football goalkeeper into the hockey goal ... the team did really well, but when the first ball spun towards the goal, the keeper picked it up and kicked it out into the air like a football! The referee blew his whistle and looked on in horror. I tore over from my inside left position and explained the situation. We went on to blend ourselves into a nice little team, played about 15 or 16 matches and lost only one match, and that was by default ... We were tied up in the harbor (at Gibraltar) ... at the end of the war ... I was transferred home again, and that was the end of my Flower corvette saga, which I enjoyed one way or another.*[22]

### 'Send In The Rescue Party!'
### A Dubious Casualty of War

Radar operator George Lunam served aboard the *Flower* class corvette HMS *Anenome* when the ship was a part of Escort Group B4. He remembered the day when he was declared a casualty by the Escort Group Commander.

*... Escort Group B4 was moored in the harbor of St. John's, Newfoundland ... We expected to spend perhaps two nights in St. Johns (between convoys) repairing, refueling, rearming, and reprovisioning. We also hoped to get out of the clothes we had worn all the way from Londonderry, and have a bath with a bucket of hot water. ... In the midst of all this activity, we were not overjoyed to be told that the Commander of the Group was coming to*

HMS *Anemone*

*inspect HMS* Anenome. *As soon as he arrived, we were piped to action stations. My partner and I shut ourselves in the RDF (radar) hut – a five foot square steel box perched above the bridge. We switched on the set and made sure everything was clean and tidy before we settled down to await inspection. We waited and waited for about a half an hour, and eventually decided that we had been forgotten about. We got out the fags (cigarettes) and lit up. Hardly had we had a couple of puffs when we heard steps on the access ladder. The cigarettes were hurriedly nicked and put in our pockets. I grabbed the ashtray and put it in my duffle coat pocket, and my partner attempted to waft smoke up through the hatch ... By the time the Commander had undone the dogs on the door and opened it, we were seated (and) giving a good imitation of conscientious operators hard at work. The Commander sniffed, looked hard at us, scanned every surface, then got down on his hands and knees and looked under the units to inspect the, fortunately, spotless deck. He got up, looked out of the door, and shouted down to the bridge, 'Fire in the RDF hut! Two men overcome by smoke! Send in rescue party!'*

*We were dragged out of the door, bundled down the ladder, and laid out on the deck to be given painfully enthusiastic artificial respiration. With hindsight, we can be glad that the 'Kiss of Life' (mouth-to-mouth) had not yet been invented!* [23]

## 'So Another Heroic Feat!'
## Some Minesweeping Adventures

As with antisubmarine vessels, the Royal Navy was woefully short of minesweeping ships when the war began. Of the approximately forty minesweepers available in late 1939 half were of the coal burning *Hunt* class that remained from 1917–1919. Two classes were introduced during the war years: the fifty-one ships *Bangor* class and the *Algerine* class of approximately one hundred ships. The design of the *Bangor* class ships was kept deliberately simple and austere to allow them to be built quickly by shipyards that had been rushed into wartime expansion through the hiring of many new and inexperienced workers. Construction of the largest Royal Navy minesweeper class, the *Algerines*, began in 1942.

As the war progressed, pressing needs and unique circumstances led the Navy to improvise and utilize its minesweepers in a broad range of roles that included convoy escort, anti-submarine warfare, shore bombardment, at-

An unspecified *Alegrine* class minesweeper, Model 1:1250

sea rescue, ocean survey, emergency troop evacuation, and even electronic countermeasures operations. During the war the Royal Navy would lose a total of twenty-eight minesweepers.

Scrambling to fill its mine warfare needs in the early days of the war, the government sponsored radio broadcasts calling for volunteers from among fishermen to serve aboard minesweepers. The call was for men eighteen to forty-five years old who had a minimum of one year experience in deep sea fishing. Skill with nets and other gear for catching fish was deemed to be similar to that needed for the operation of mine clearing equipment. Thomas King of the minesweeper HMS *Sharpshooter* offered his thoughts on the emergency wartime or, hostilities only, sailors summoned to serve alongside the regular Navy's professional sailors.

> *... a small ship in the Navy was always preferable to serve in to the big ship. There was more comradeship in a small ship, but on these minesweepers everybody done their job and, of course, there was a certain intake of the chappies that were called up for the war, hostilities only. And they were*

HMS *Sharpshooter*

*good … They fitted in very, very well. I was an active service rating … but in all the time I served during the war I always found that the hostilities ratings worked into the Navy very well.*[24]

In addition to the purpose built ships, the Royal Navy converted or requisitioned a wide variety of small vessels that included fishing trawlers for minesweeping duties. The concept of using trawlers and fishermen as emergency wartime minesweepers went back at least to 1907. Part of the logic was that in wartime the fishing fleet would be inactive and laid up anyway, so it would be wasteful and imprudent not to put it to a use for which it was naturally suited. The adventures of a fisherman turned minesweeper crewman during the war were narrated by Sandy Ritchie who was called up as a naval reservist specifically for service aboard converted trawlers.

*When you got called up you just got a telegram to report … out of the blue … and away you went. That was the start of your Royal Naval Reserve career in the minesweeping service. You got training there in Lowestoft (in Suffolk on the North Sea coast). You were boarded out in local houses, B&B more or less, and you were trained there in the ways of the Navy. After they were satisfied with you, you were allocated to a ship. So I was posted to Dover aboard a minesweeper called the Regardo – a Grimsby trawler, I think she was.*[25]

*The sweeping we did in Dover was for magnetic mines which the Germans laid. Of course the channel is shallow water, only about 20-odd fathoms, and it is ideal for the magnetism of a ship or anything sailing over to be attracted and blown up.*

*The mines were blown up by us putting an electric pulse in the water. Now we had three ships going abreast to do that. To keep us all safe we had to be steaming at the same speed, dead abreast exactly. And for that purpose we had pulsing lights fore and aft on the ship. And these pulsing lights all had to come on three fore at the same time, three aft, so the boats could see that they were dead on. Otherwise if one lagged behind and a mine came up he would be liable to get blown out of the water. We did lose a boat. Three of us were tied together and this mine hit the sea bed behind the boat and sank it, and eight were killed. They were lads we knew, just like your pals, you know. So we had to bury them with all the palaver of the gun carriage and naval funeral.*

*We were sweeping one day and we were blowing the mines and we rather went off station. I was actually on the bridge as quartermaster steering the boat, and my head hit the roof in the wheelhouse because of the blast from this mine. It knocked the engine off its mountings. We had to be towed in.*

*We never went to bed for months and months because the Germans were using these incendiary bombs. They were in baskets. You could hear them coming down and rattling, and they landed in the docks. We had to shovel them over the side because they were phosphorus and would burn through metal, wood, anything. So you had to get rid of them.*

*This Norwegian fellow that ran the base in Stornoway* (in the western islands of Scotland) *married into well-to-do people in the area … wanted to transport about fifty sheep to Dunvegan on the isle of Skye, across the Minches* (straits between Scottish coast and some of the outlying western islands), *and we got the job. And that's what we did during wartime, transferring about fifty sheep into Loch Bay* (near Dunvegan), *chasing them out of the small boats, chasing them over the beach and on the shore. So another heroic feat!*

*We were always uptight when we got a mine disposal expert on board. We would get a signal that he was coming and all the time there were mines moored throughout the Minches. These would break loose, and we had to deal with that, and often they were on the rocks somewhere. One time we were called to Castle Bay on Barra … it is a lovely bay … and so we undid the lid* (of a beached mine) *and put a match to it. While it was blazing away, we were off back aboard again. Then this fellow, he said, 'Do you like to fish?' We replied, 'Yes.' He had a wee suitcase with detonators and*

*he'd chuck one of those overboard. And any fish that was down there
would just pop up to the surface – dead. A convenient way of fishing. It
was a funny life!*[26]

## 'People Talk About Miracles'
## HMS *Sharpshooter* at Dunkirk

The Royal Navy's ability to be versatile and adaptable was well demonstrated
in late May and early June of 1940. The British Expeditionary Force which
had been sent to the Continent in order to counter Germany's advances
across northern Europe had been pushed into a small and desperate defensive
perimeter near the town of Dunkirk, France. Almost 400,000 troops were present
and, as it appeared that they would soon be overrun by the Germans, a plan
for a conditional surrender was being considered. By good fortune, however,
the German army took a three-day halt in order to reorganise and consolidate
against any possible counterattack or breakout. The three day respite gave the
British just enough time to organise and execute a massive evacuation back
across the English Channel.

The minesweeper HMS *Sharpshooter* was one of the thousands of vessels
pressed into service for the rescue. The ship was ordered, with little explanation
to the crew and on short notice, to sail from Scapa Flow to Dover where she
arrived on 28 May. She was immediately ordered to proceed across the Channel
to La Panne, Belgium just a short distance to the east of Dunkirk. It was not until
*Sharpshooter* was underway to La Panne that the crew was made aware that they
were to assist with a troop evacuation for which they, of course, had not made any
particular preparations. All they knew was that they were, according to crewman
Thomas King, '… going to take an isolated bunch of soldiers from the beach
alongside Dunkirk'. The crew's first inkling of the true nature of the task that lay
before them came when, going towards the beach for the first time, *Sharpshooter*'s
captain hailed an outbound vessel to ask how many troops were ashore. The
reply was, '… there's bloody thousands!' *Sharpshooter* anchored several hundred
yards offshore and launched her motor whalers to run ashore to begin picking up
troops. King, assigned as coxswain of one of the whalers, recalled,

*… I had a crew of five in the whaler and I did not know what to expect … when we got closer … it was human beings waiting to come off. And there was no order … at all. It was more or less what you would say, a free-for-all. Soldiers don't know the life-saving capacity of boats. We could only take ten to twelve in a 22-foot whaler. And so we kept our distance from the water's edge because it was no good us going right up on the beach because we'd got to get seaborne again. Anyhow we got the first load of soldiers on, I think it must have been ten to twelve and put them back to our ship. But in the meantime there was other boats … were taking soldiers from the beach to our ship. And I think we made four trips all told and then the captain decided that there was enough … and we steamed back to Dover.*

King recalled that no special provisions had been made for the evacuation. Once the troops were loaded on board, they were made as comfortable as possible. The evacuees were given as much as was available from the scarce and plain stores aboard that included bread, butter, cheese, and hot cocoa for the trip back to Dover. There were numerous German planes and E-boats (torpedo craft armed with small caliber automatic guns) around that attacked, damaged, and sank ships of the evacuation force. None targeted *Sharpshooter*, however. Of the men picked up by the minesweeper King said,

*All they had was their uniforms and they seemed tired and hungry, but their spirits were still there, I suppose – I don't know whether it's the Englishman's spirit or not but they weren't really sort of beaten – to get back and then to get back at the Germans.*

*Sharpshooter* took 100 men back to Dover and returned for a second trip when they picked up an additional 273. Heading back to Dover they heard a voice call out in the dark. It was a completely naked soldier who was floating some two to three miles from shore in a large laundry basket. He was quickly picked up. With the second load delivered, *Sharpshooter* was on her way back to Dunkirk when she was rammed in the dark of night by a French mail boat loaded with 200 evacuees. The French vessel continued on its way. *Sharpshooter*, her bow damaged, sent the following message: 'From *Sharpshooter* – Have been in collision necessitating dockyard repairs duration of which not known. No casualties.' The sea remained smooth and calm as *Sharpshooter* was towed back to Dover without incident. By the end of the effort almost 340,000 of the original 400,000 man force were taken back to England. King said of the Dunkirk evacuation,

> *… people talk about miracles. But after being at Dunkirk and seeing the evacuation … miracles do happen. It was an act of God that all those soldiers got away from those beaches.*[27]

### A Minesweeper, a Secret Weapon, and a Lot of Wine

Wartime, for all its dangers and unforgiving cruelty, can still have occasional odd moments where potential disaster turns humorous. One such event involving a German magnetic mine was told by an unnamed Royal Navy veteran.

According to the sailor, the Germans had developed a moored mine that, when deployed, would itself deploy a second dummy mine of its own. Minesweepers passing overhead would cut the cable to the dummy mine and assume that the area was clear. There was also a variant of that mine that had mechanical devices placed along the mooring cable that would allow a cutting cable to pass through it without actually severing the mine's cable. Over time, the British became suspicious about how cleared areas were able to remain dangerous. A minesweeper was ordered into a potential minefield for the purpose of collecting samples of any 'secret weapons'.

The chosen minesweeper, HMS *Sutton*, steamed to the area in question and spent an entire day sweeping for mines with no luck. As darkness approached the captain decided to anchor for the night and resume the search in the morning. The anchor had been dropped to the bottom when a mine was spotted astern and drifting towards the ship. Unknown to any on board, it was snagged on the ship's sweeping cable. Overlooking the anchor in their haste, all ahead full was rung up, and the ship surged forward. The anchor, deeply embedded underwater, caused the anchor chain to unwind amidst a shower of sparks as its links banged against the ship's own metal hull. Since the final link was likely to break violently away from the ship and whip up into the air, all of the crewmen who were stationed on the foc'sl dashed hastily aft. The mine, still being pulled along by the ship, continued to follow close astern when the anchor chain fully played out and, instead of breaking, pulled the ship down hard by the head. The stern lifted high into the air just as the mine drifted underneath to explode. The ship remained sharply head down when the engine room crew, unsure of what had happened, clambered onto the deck from below with cries of, 'abandon ship!' The captain, who had quickly surveyed the damage and determined that the ship was in no danger of actually sinking, shouted 'I'll shoot the first bastard who does!'

The crew was able to shore up the damage and get under way. The ship slowly and carefully began to head towards home through a severe lightning storm. Because the Germans tended to mine it as often as the British would clear it, the channel of the harbor they entered was lined with swept but as yet disarmed mines. Passing along, the ship was greeted with one jolting underwater explosion after another as the ship's hull, its magnetic signature unknowingly altered by the lightning it had so recently sailed through, triggered the magnetic mines remaining in the channel one after another. The ship nonetheless arrived safely and without casualties. Although British naval authorities were quick to criticize the ship for its failure to retrieve one of the mysterious new German mines, all had not been in vain for the crew. The ship's well provisioned wine locker was located in the part of the ship that had suffered the heaviest damage. On inspection, however, not the least bit of harm had come to any of the wine itself. The supply included a fair quantity of Napoleon Brandy secured on the ship's previous stop at Malta. All aboard *Sutton* conspired to declare that the ship's entire alcohol supply had fallen victim to the war. As the visible damage to the ship provided reasonable evidence for it, naval authorities unquestioningly accepted the minesweeper's statement as true. *Sutton's* men were later able to secretly advertise and sell what they did not drink of their 'lost' wine to their flotilla mates.[28]

## 'I'm Proud That I Took Part in D-Day'
### Action off Normandy

Even before the battleships, cruisers, and destroyers could dare to get close enough to provide covering fire for D-Day at Normandy, and before the first transports could move into position to deploy the first troop laden landing craft, the minesweepers had already been hard at work. They plied the English Channel to clear the way for the thousands of invasion craft soon to come. They were required to remain on duty even well after the landings of 06 June since additional mines were dropped every night by German aircraft. Sweeps continued by night and day under heavy fire from German shore batteries. The enemy was as clever as he was dangerous. The shallow waters where landing craft had to go, for example, were replete with what were called 'oyster mines'. These were a pressure sensitive device that operated by means of a bellows. A passing craft would create a downward pressure field that compressed the bellows to trigger the mine. Oyster mines had been created with the knowledge that, even though it was a shallow drafted ship, a minesweeper would still be too big to get into an area sown with them. The British minesweeping forces were no less creative than the Germans. They devised a solution, as simple as it was ingenious. They employed long tubes or pipes through which they rolled hand grenades. The concussion of the exploding grenades set off the mines.[29]

The clearing of mines was not the only dangerous task to which minesweepers were assigned at Normandy. A former crewman aboard HMS *Pickle,* recalled that his ship was ordered to move close to shore to deliberately draw the enemy into shooting so that his gun positions might be better targeted for counter fire by the guns of the bombardment force. One of the British sailor's many feelings was that of, 'we were ready to be sacrificed'.

*I was just eighteen on D-day … It was all top secret and we weren't to mention anything (about it) in letters home … On the fifth of June the lower deck was cleared and the Flotilla leader told us we were able to go. We were to spearhead the whole invasion fleet sweeping to France with a couple of battleships or heavy cruisers backing up each one. We were to bomb the coastal defenses until the point of arrival and then to drop anchor half a mile or so off the beach to act as decoys in case any of the shore batteries were still alive. That meant, if necessary, we would be sacrificed!*

*We sailed on the 5 June just after noon with all sorts of craft trailing in our wake. We started sweeping five or six hours later. By midnight we were at action stations sweeping about five miles off the French coast … I wasn't thinking about being frightened. The overriding feeling we had was one of excitement. But as we approached France, I started to wonder how I would react to the fighting. Would I be a coward? It's not that I doubted myself, but … I had heard of some who were petrified with fear, for example during World War I, but I didn't react in this way nor did I see anyone who did.*

*We anchored quietly a mile or so off the coast of Courseuilles – at Juno Beach. We could see the dim outline of the land and soon after, the houses opposite; later whilst we lay hardly daring to breathe, the battleships some miles behind began shelling. It was an odd sensation to hear these huge shells hurtling over us and exploding inshore. Later, destroyers came closer and began shelling and we had grandstand view of the landing craft going beyond us and up the beaches – and all hell was let loose! The main danger seemed to be avoiding a collision with landing craft weaving in and out. We were lucky – we did have a collision but suffered only slight damage to the hull. Later as the invasion moved inland we swept around the anchorages and then we sailed back to Pompey (Portsmouth). It was an incredible sight to see the ocean covered with thousands and thousands of ships and craft of every description. After a day and half we went back to and Normandy. We would do ten days there and two or three in Pompey – this routine went on for a while …*

*As I reminisce I can recall lots of experiences, too many to mention and lots that I had long forgotten; sad ones such as seeing the corpses of American sailors – and, probably from the same sunken American ship, picking up a crate containing thousands of American cigarettes! … I'm proud that I took part in D-Day … (and as for the Germans) they're different people now, and if we can't be friends with them there's no hope. We're all part of Europe now.*[30]

Another look at a minesweeper's lot at Normandy was provided by George Lamming in a journal format. Lamming was an asdic operator aboard HMS

*Orestes* of the 18th Minesweeping Flotilla. His report gives a day-by-day and hour-by-hour account of events in the English Channel and off the Normandy coast from 5 June until 10 June.

*Monday, 5th June, 1944: This seems to be the day, ship's company has been issued with action rations, field dressings, and a piece of rope to tie round our waist to enable (us) to pick up any survivors (of ships or landing craft expected to be sunk). Also a check-up has been made of all life belts and life-saving lights … We are under way now. Just received a signal from HMS Tyne (a depot ship), 'Good Luck. Drive Ahead.' … Hundreds of small landing craft are underway along with us and getting into formation as we leave the solent. This is definitely 'the day' we have long awaited. I don't think anyone is sorry. We will be able to see the end of this war in sight once we get this over … 18.00 hours: We have been steaming slowly all day long. Nothing but invasion craft as far as the eye can see … 20.00 hours: … everyone is a bit more serious. Being the first ship in (to clear mines) does not make us too happy. No one thought our job would be dangerous, however everyone hides their feelings the best way they can. Some make a few wise-cracks and cause a laugh. I think we would laugh at anything for the sake of laughing … 22.00 hours: 'Sweeps Out.' Everyone is on their toes, life-belts are inflated and tied to them are small waterproof bundles with any photographs etc. of any sentimental value. In line ahead is the 18th Flotilla – Leader, HMS* Ready *– Orestes – Hound – Hydra – Onyx – and* Cockertrice *… 23.00: There goes the first mine, swept by HMS* Ready. *After this, they come up regularly, some exploding near, unexploded mines are floating uncomfortably near. Ready has now lost both her sweeps by exploding mines and has fallen astern to repair them. We are now in the lead, but not for long, our sweeps soon go the same way as the* Ready's, *however we quickly have them repaired and take up position again.*

*Tuesday, 6th June, 1944, 02.30 hours: We are now through the minefield and within a few miles of the enemy coast.[3] All that has to be done now is to clear an anchorage for the invasion fleet behind us … 04.00 hours: The bombardment of the coast has begun by the big guns of the Royal Navy.*

*Some of those seen include HMS Enterprise – Emerald – Belfast – Glasgow – Hawkins – Roberts – Frobisher – Orion and heaps of destroyers and battleships, including* Ramillies – Richelieu *(French)* – Nelson – Rodney – Warspite – *and* Texas *(USA). The bombardment from these ships is terrific. Landing craft are now seen to be making their way inshore. I wonder what sort of reception they will get (Good Luck to them all). No one can feel more proud than we do, we have done a good job, no ships have been sunk by mines so far, and this speaks to the success of our sweep. Enemy gun emplacements are being shelled by the fleet and bombed by the RAF. Aircraft fill the skies and so far there are no signs of the Luftwaffe.* Lightnings *and* Spitfires *are everywhere and large formations of troop carrying planes and gliders are going across. We have complete mastery of the skies and the seas up to now.*[31]

*Tuesday, 6th June, 1944, 12.00 hours: Heavy explosions are coming from the shore and the troops are apparently meeting strong opposition on the beach head, while all the time landing craft are heading to shore. A few of the craft are drifting about helpless. One can be seen with a heavy list. She has been taken in tow by a sister ship … 14.00 hours: Bombardment still heavy and landing craft are still heading for the shore. The ship shakes with heavy explosions and I think the ship's company would welcome a wash and a shave. Five amphibious 'ducks' are floating by helpless. No one seems to be aboard them, except one with two US soldiers on it which has been taken in tow by one of our motor launches attached to our flotilla … 21.00 hours: Troops still landing - aircraft still shuttling back and forth – all aircraft have been painted with black and white stripes for identification purposes … 23.00 hours: At last, the long awaited (aerial) attack by the enemy is taking place, what a reception he gets. The sky is lit with the flak from the fleet. A plane has just swooped down over the ship, and crashed down into the sea with a terrific explosion near to one of our landing craft. At first it seemed to have struck it …*

*Wednesday, 7th June: All night long we have been at action stations and we could do with a good night's sleep, necks and backs are sore through constantly wearing life belts and all essential gear, still no one moves to take them off … 10.00 hours: (after resuming sweeping at 08.30): In the last half hour we have swept up 12 mines, two by* Ready *who has again lost her sweeps. She falls astern again to repair them. We have bagged four of the 12 bringing our total to about 15 and the whole flotilla has swept up 51. As we sweep, landing craft full of troops are still passing by … 17.00 hours: Quiet afternoon, those off watch are taking the chance of two hours sleep. Ships of all descriptions are passing by all day long … 18.45 hours: Body of airman drifts by ship and we learn that 26 enemy aircraft were shot down last night … 20.00 hours: Just cleared two mines. Four mines floating by unexploded. We have been detailed to finish them off. Mines sunk by rifle fire. We also have the anti-tank gun out (presumably to make easier work of shooting at mines) … 23.45 hours: Smoke screen put up by all ships. Reason not known. We are now at anchor, all minesweepers are forming a gigantic defence around the beach head coast. Air-raid in progress – terrific barrage going up ashore. Wreckage and bodies float past ship … 08.00 hours: Out again sweeping Channel for convoys to come through … 10.30 hours: Action stations – submarine for a change. Two U-boats reported on surface. We search but have no luck … 11.00 hours: Secure* (from action stations), *tot time. Everyone is fed up with carrying this gear around and only taking it off for a hurried wash. Most of the boys are thinking of home and wishing they could get word home to say they are OK …*[32]

*Thursday, 8th June, 12.00 hours: Sweeping the Channel again … 18.30 hours: (done with day's sweeping). Air raid – at anchor a few miles from beach head – explosions can be heard, big ships are nearer the shore putting up a big bombardment. Columns of smoke are rising all along the coast. I suppose the Luftwaffe will be over again tonight. Just heard E boats* (fast attack patrol craft) *attempted to attack convoy in Channel unsuccessfully. Also, over 70* (enemy) *aircraft shot down over beach head on Wednesday night … 20.30 hours: Explosions coming from coast, otherwise everything is quiet, for how long I wonder. Plenty of gear floating past; soldiers' haversacks, petrol tanks, etc. Convoys, landing craft, and hospital ships still going in … Friday 9th June: Just settled down when alarm bells go. What a life. This time another aircraft shot down … 00.30 hours: We can see a ship on fire out at sea, lighting up for miles around it. We later found out that it was a petrol carrying ship … 03.00 hours: E-boat battle out at sea. Tracers seen and gunfire heard. Bombardment by the fleet has not yet ceased … 09.00 hours: We have just learned we are stand-by M/S flotilla for today giving us a chance to have a good scrub-out throughout the ship. No action stations this forenoon but no sleep owing to the scrub-out. Trust the Navy, they would scrub-out if the ship was sinking … 12.00 hours: Weigh anchor and proceed further inshore. A corvette can be seen sunk, her stern is sticking out of the water (K-514).[6] Wonder what are losses in ships are to date … 18.30 hours: Action stations. They won't even let us get our supper … 18.45 hours: Secure but supper is cold … 19:00 hours: Very heavy explosions coming from shore. Plenty of wreckage passing the ship including a barrage balloon which we hauled aboard. All the boys are cutting pieces of the water tight material; what for I don't know. One chap says it will be a good cot sheet … 23.35 hours: Air raid. Bombs dropped on beach head. Enemy aircraft are now using the allied markings of black and white stripes. Terrific sheet of ack-ack meet them. Aircraft passing overhead going towards beach. Plane comes down in flames. Some of the ship's company sleep out on deck while the barrage continues … Saturday, 10th June, 08.00 hours: Weigh anchor. Out sweeps again. Buzz around the ship, we are going back to Portsmouth tomorrow for oil and stores. Wonder if we shall get any shore leave if we go back … 17.00 hours: This is the quietest day we have had so far … 19.00 hours: Heading towards the beach head. Plenty of wreckage and oil float past; life belts, stores, etc. Body of a sailor on a raft drifts past the ship. Nobody stops to see who he is. Seas still choppy … 20.00 hours: We have been sweeping all day long but have not cleared any mines. I think that this is more of a precaution sweep than anything else.[33]*

## 'It Was Dangerous Work at Times'
## Clearing Mines After the War

Even after the war was over thousands of mines sown throughout the world's oceans and littorals remained to be cleared. The 16 December 1945 edition of the *Sunday Malta Times* newspaper estimated that in the Mediterranean alone about 40,000 of some 100,000 mines dropped during the war remained dangerously in place. Mediterranean ports and the access lanes to them that needed sweeping included Malta, North Africa, Sicily, Salerno, the entire Italian west coast, and the Dardanelles. According to the 2 December 1945 edition of the newspaper,

> *Where there's a mine, there's a minesweeper … the vast task of mine clearance is still urgent … now that peace has come the men for whom the war is not yet over, must spearhead the vast fleets of merchant ships that have still to succor a starving and war-torn Europe … In this they are assisting in great measure in winning the Battle of the Peace, for without the minesweepers and the men that man them there can be no free flow of shipping to convey supplies to the empty larders of an exhausted continent …*[34]

Patrick Fitz who had helped bury men at sea in Italy, eventually found himself aboard the minesweeper HMS *Albacore*. Long after the war, he spoke about his time on post-war mine clearing duty,

> *… we were sweeping in the North Sea … it was dangerous work, at times; it was hard work; it was long, long days … but I enjoyed it … (Albacore) was what I considered to be a happy ship (and) I enjoyed it on there (with) a good crew. I think the work was interesting (and) they kept you busy … we would be at sea for 10 days then we would come back in for five. We were based at … a bit of a dump (so we mostly just stayed aboard the ship) … (as) minesweeping operations were coming to an end we went down to Portsmouth and now we started having leave … (it was during) the cold winter of '46 and '47 and it was a jolly hard life, then because you had practically no heating on the ship and we were in dry-dock and if you wanted to clean up we used to go ashore and have a bath at Aggie Weston's place…*[35] *(which) was very good; they were first class. There was canteen messing (where) we used to feed for ourselves … several mates (and I); we used to go ashore, have a bath at Aggie Weston's … where you could (also) have a meal or a bed, if you wanted but we used to always*

*come back on board , then we'd go 'round to Charlotte Street to the market where we'd do a bit of shopping (and) bring (food) back on board for the rest of the week … we were (just) looking after ourselves.*

*In the end I'm glad I was in the Navy rather than the Army or the Air Force … I was quite happy there … met some jolly good mates … still have got them.*[36]

The officers and men of Royal Navy's minesweeper force were thanked and congratulated by the following message from Prime Minister Churchill,

*Now that Nazi Germany has been defeated I wish to send you all on behalf of His Majesty's Government a message of thanks and gratitude … The work you do is hard and dangerous. You rarely get and never seek publicity; your only concern is to do your job, and you have done it nobly. You have sailed in many seas and all weathers … This work could not be done without loss, and we mourn all who have died and over 250 ships lost on duty … No work has been more vital than yours; no work has been better done. The ports were kept open and Britain breathed. The Nation is once again proud of you … W.S. Churchill.*[37]

ENDNOTES

1.  Keegan, John. *The Price of Admiralty*. Penguin Books. 1988. p. 263.

2.  Morison, Samuel Eliot. *History of United States Naval Operations in World War II, Vol. I*. Little, Brown & Co. 1947. p. 17.

3.  Turner, Dick. Autobiography updated in 2008 for the HMS *Hood* Association. hmshood.com. Accessed July 2013. Additional anecdotes and quotes by Turner can be found in Edwards, Bernard, *The Cruel Sea Revisited*, Naval Institute Press, 2008.

4.  Turner.

5.  The novel features two ships aboard which the author's protagonist, a young naval reserve officer, served. The first, HMS *Compass Rose*, was based on one of Monsarrat's real ships, HMS *Campanula* of which he was the 1st Lieutenant. The novel's second ship, HMS *Saltash* was a River class ocean-going frigate that was based on either HMS *Ettrick* or HMS *Perim* which were the author's last two actual ships. *Ettrick* was a River class frigate and *Perim* was a Colony class frigate which was the American-built version of the River class ships.

6.  Monsarrat, Nicholas. *The Cruel Sea*. Buford Books. 1961. pp. 230–232.

7.  _____ 'Extracts From an Interview With Captain Eric Melrose 'Winkle' Brown.' deltaveemedia. co.uk. Web. Accessed January 2014.

8.  _____ 'Merchant Ships Used as Fighter Carriers in World War II.' nauticapedia.ca. Web. Ac January 2014.

9.  _____ 'Extracts From an Interview With Captain Eric Melrose 'Winkle' Brown.'

10. _____ 'HMS *Audacity*.' royalnavy research archive.org.uk. Web. Accessed January 2014.

11. ateamatwar (contributor). 'Captain Frederick John Walker.' BBC WW2 People's War. Article ID A 5024224. 2005.

12. ateamwar (contributor).

13. ateamwar (contributor).

14. Royal Aeronautical Society. 'Interview With Captain Eric 'Winkle' Brown.' youtube.com. Web. Accessed January 2014.

15. ateamwar (contributor). 'Captain Frederick John Walker, U-boat Killer, Part 2.' BBC WW2 *People's War*. Article ID A 5102876. 2005.

16. Clare, Peter (editor). 'German Account of Sinking of HMS *Audacity*.' WW2-talk.com. Web. Accessed January 2014.

17. _____ 'Extracts From an Interview With Captain Eric Melrose 'Winkle' Brown.'

18. Dunstable Town Centre (contributor). 'Memories of Flower Class Corvettes.' BBC WW2 *People's War*. Article ID A 5203775. 2005.

19. Royal Canadian Navy (RCN) Flower class corvettes were not named after flowers. Many, like HMCS *Lunenburg*, were named after Canadian towns.

20. Dunstable Town Centre.

21. Dunstable Town Centre.

22. Dunstable Town Centre.

23. Lunam, George (contributor). 'Life on a Flower Class Corvette.' BBC WW2 *People's War*. Article ID A 2060588. 2003.

24. Imperial War Museum. Sound recording archive. 006973. King, Thomas. 1983.

25. Regardo was built in 1915 and was almost immediately requisitioned by the Navy for emergency minesweeping service. She was returned to owners after the war, but was requisitioned once again for World War II.

26. _____ 'Minesweeper.' Remembering Scotland at War, oral history. rememberingscotlandatwar. co.uk. Transcript accessed April 2014.

27. _____ Interview With Thomas Phillip Edward King of HMS Sharpshooter,' Transcript from the Imperial War Museum's sound recording archive 006973. Halcyon-class.co.uk. Accessed March 2014.

28. Imperial War Museum. Sound recording archive. 19584. Interviewee not named. 1979.

29. Beckisle (contributor). 'Minesweeping in the Royal Navy.' BBC WW2 *People's War*. Article ID A 3531232. 2005

30. Chippendale, Bill. 'We Were Ready to be Sacrificed.' news/bbc.co.uk. Web. Accessed April 2014.

31. CSV Action Desk/BBC Radio Lincolnshire (contributor). 'Account of D-Day, Part 1.' BBC WW2 *People's War*. Article A 5264101. 2005.

32. CSV Action Desk/BBC Radio Lincolnshire. 'Account of D-Day, Part 2.' BBC WW2 *People's War*. Article ID A 5306005. 2005.

33. CSV Action Desk/BBC Radio Lincolnshire. 'Account of D-Day, Part 3.' BBC WW2 *People's War*. Article ID A 5327787. 2005.

34. _____ 'War and Post-war Minesweeping in the Mediterranean.' Article 194520205. minesweepers. org.uk. Web. Accessed April 2014.

35. There were several establishments at Royal Navy ports in England as well as overseas called 'Agnes Weston's Royal Sailors Rest.' The original was established in the 1870s by its namesake founder who felt that many men needed a safe, clean, and alcohol-free environment where they could find meals, lodging, and recreation. The Portsmouth Aggie Weston's was bombed during the war, but was later rebuilt. A branch of Aggie Weston's remains at Helensburgh near Clyde Naval Base and, according to its current website, '… offers quality 3 bed and breakfast accommodation (16 ensuite bedrooms). There is a bustling coffee shop which serves light lunches (and there are also) a gym, and a sauna.'

36. Imperial War Museum. Sound recording archive. 21284. Fitz, Patrick Walter. 2001.

37. _____ 'Halcyon Class Minesweepers and Survey Ships of World War II.: halcyon-class.co.uk. Web. Accessed April 2004.

# EIGHT
# THE NAVY'S PILOTS, PLANES AND CARRIERS

British aircraft carrier, *Ark Royal*, with a flight of Swordfish bombers overhead, *c.* 1939

At the beginning of World War II the British fleet had but one modern aircraft carrier, HMS *Ark Royal,* which had commissioned in December 1938. All six of her predecessors were still in service, but only one of them had been designed and built from the keel up as a carrier. That ship was commissioned in 1924 and had served more as an experimental vessel than a true naval combatant. Of the Royal Navy's other early carriers, four were re-built capital ships and one was a converted ocean liner. None could carry more than fifty aircraft. Although the

Royal Navy had been an original innovator in the field of naval aviation, Japan and the United States had each forged ahead during the 1930s. Two critical areas in which the Japanese and Americans had advantages were in shipboard aircraft capacity and maritime aircraft. It took three British aircraft carriers to operate the same number of planes as just two American or Japanese ships and the aircraft of the latter two navies were newer, faster, and generally superior to their British counterparts. One very notable British advantage was that Royal Navy carriers bore armoured decks. They would prove their value late in the war when wooden-decked American carriers, their larger complement of aircraft notwithstanding, would consistently suffer far heavier damage and casualties from Kamikaze hits than their British counterparts.

Due to its subservience to the Royal Air Force, the pre-World War II Fleet Air Arm was burdened with aircraft that were usually old and even obsolescent. Among the planes that flew off of British carriers in the years leading up to the war was the biplane Fairey Swordfish torpedo bomber which would prove durable and effective despite its antiquated appearance. Less worthy aircraft included the monoplane Blackburn Skua dive-bomber, and the Roc, a fighter plane variant of the Skua. The fighter proved too slow and vulnerable so, by 1941, it was no longer a front-line aircraft. The Swordfish's maximum speed was 140 miles-per-hour and it had a range of about 550 miles when carrying either a torpedo or a 1,500 pound total bomb load. The Swordfish were only replaced when American war production hit its stride midway through the war. By then the Navy's preferred torpedo plane was the faster and significantly more powerful US Navy Grumman Avenger. Still, for all the Avenger's virtues and all the Swordfish's deficiencies, the venerable bi-plane was never fully replaced. Swordfish served until the very end of the war.

### 'One of the Crew Fell Out Over the Side'
### Remembering the Swordfish Torpedo Bomber

Swordfish pilot Bruce Vibert joined the Royal Navy at age seventeen after seeing a newspaper article about the sinking of the carrier HMS *Courageous* in 1939. His precise ambition was to fly the Swordfish which he recalled as a much better plane than history has given it credit for being.

HMS *Courageous*

*The Swordfish was the most capable aircraft anywhere in its given role ...*
*I'd flown the Blackburn Shark* (a torpedo bomber of 1933 vintage that the
Swordfish replaced) *which handled like a grand piano with wings. The*
*Swordfish was entirely different. Some history books have recorded the*
*Swordfish as ponderous but that simply was not the case. The Swordfish*
*could turn on a pinhead. It was anything but cumbersome ... no aircraft is*
*easier to land on a pitching and rolling (carrier) deck. There the Swordfish*
*was easier to land than any other aircraft. Its qualities made it uniquely*
*suitable in those conditions which, at their worst, kept more modern aircraft*
*in the hangar. Performance was agile – it had not one single vice. In my*
*mind only the Japanese Zero was capable of out-turning the Swordfish.*[1]

During the war Vibert was assigned to a Swordfish squadron that embarked
aboard an escort carrier for convoy and anti-submarine duty of which he said,

*One did a boring job ... unexciting, unglamorous, but useful. Throughout*
*each run* (shipboard deployment) *each lasting several weeks, one never*

*saw land. But we were saving the lives of merchantmen, and whilst our aircraft is best known for (other, more memorable, actions) I suggest that it was against (U-) boats threatening our convoys that it made its greatest contribution to our war effort.*

*Starting before dawn, until after dark, patrols of two to three aircraft were flown. Carrying either depth charges or rocket projectiles, these were made ahead of the convoy at no more than 3,000 feet* (altitude) *and lasted up to three hours. Equipment was the 'Mark 1 eyeball', an air to surface 'radar' of very limited range. W/T* (radio) *silence was kept and communication with the ship or another aircraft was by Aldis* (signal) *Lamp or hand waving. One watched the wave tops for that which did not break and for white water in the distance which could be a U-boat on the surface. The dusk patrol was* (made from) *far astern, to put down any (U)-boat aiming to catch up overnight on the surface. The convoy showed no lights and kept* (radio) *silence.*[2]

Vibert described the conditions aboard a Swordfish aloft and the duties of its crew,

*Apart from local wind and weather* (typically provided by the ship's meteorologist) *at the time of departure the observer had little more than a blank sheet of paper, dividers, and rule. Hopefully, also a pilot could fly an accurate compass course. The telegraphist/air gunner kept a listening brief on his W/T* (radio) *set and watched the waves. In their bath-sized cockpit, he and the observer were more exposed to the elements than the pilot. There was no heater in the aircraft. However, this open cockpit was a contributory factor in us having markedly the best chances of survival in a Swordfish, whether in action or accident. The open cockpit was far easier to vacate in a hurry.*[3]

An incident involving a Swordfish in flight recalled by Ken Hutchinson provides a perspective on the plane's open cockpit that Vibert may have overlooked,

*During a training air gunnery flight in a Fairey Swordfish, which was an*

*open cockpit aircraft, as the two crew members were changing places for the firing exercise, the pilot banked the plane. One of the crew fell out over the side – which would not have happened had he not released his safety hook too early. I leant out of the cockpit and held on, initially, to the airman's boots, but as these are looser fitting than shoes, he began to slip out of them. I had to stretch further out and managed to grab his belt, and eventually pull him back in. In those days there was no 'mike' contact in a Swordfish, simply a rubber voice pipe, which had to be held to communicate. So the pilot knew nothing until the rescue had been carried out.*[4]

### 'They Put Up a Lot of Flak at Us'
### The Raid on Taranto

High on Benito Mussolini's political agenda were ambitions to reclaim the glory of Imperial Rome for Italy. The rapid success of Germany's military aggression in Europe led the Italian fascist head of state to believe that the war on the continent would not last long. Eager to capitalize on the opportunity to gain territory from England and France and to strengthen his own colonial holdings in North Africa, Mussolini brought Italy into the war on Germany's side on 10 June 1940.

The Italian fleet of 1940 included seven battleships, eight heavy cruisers, eight light cruisers, about sixty destroyers, and over one hundred submarines. Of the battleships three were modern ones designed in the mid-1930s and four were renovated World War I ships. The cruiser fleet, constructed with control of the Mediterranean in mind, consisted of ships that were mostly designed from the late 1920s through the mid-1930s. A large portion of the submarine fleet was less than fifteen years old. Although it had one such ship under construction in 1940, the Italian navy did not have any aircraft carriers.[5]

In order to counterbalance Italy's navy, the Royal Navy counted on a Mediterranean presence of four battleships, the aircraft carrier HMS *Eagle*, nine cruisers, twenty-five destroyers, and a handful of submarines. The key British Mediterranean positions were Gibraltar at the sea's western extreme, Malta occupying a central position, and Alexandria which guarded access to the Suez Canal and the oil fields further to the east. Despite being few in number, aircraft and submarines based at Malta were proving to be a major disruption against Axis shipping bound for North Africa. Until late in 1942 a great deal of Italian and German military energy and resources were to be directed against the island in desperate hopes of neutralizing it.

In November 1940 HMS *Illustrious*, which had only commissioned six months earlier, was ordered to execute a surprise air attack against the core of Italy's naval power at the Taranto naval base. *Illustrious* was supposed to have been supported by a second carrier, HMS *Eagle*, but prior combat damage kept the latter ship out of the action. *Eagle's* contribution would be limited to the loan of some of her airwing to *Illustrious*. Six battleships and six cruisers were anchored at the Italian base which the British had thoroughly scouted, studied, and photographed. The chosen time for the attack was mid-month when a full moon would provide illumination for the attacking aircraft. The reliance on darkness was at least in part based on the fact that the attack was to be carried out exclusively by Swordfish torpedo bombers. The plane's slow speed made it vulnerable to Italian air defenses and darkness had to be counted upon as its best protector.

HMS *Illustrious*

David Goodwin was an air crewman with one of the incapacitated *Eagle*'s aircraft on loan to *Illustrious*. Prior to the carrier's departure from Alexandria none of the fliers had any idea what their mission was to be. Once the ship was at sea, however, they were briefed by RAF intelligence personnel. The pilots were shown maps drawn from aerial reconnaissance photos which included the exact location of each Italian ship.

According to Goodwin, two waves of Swordfish, each with ten planes, were launched against Taranto. Eight planes in each wave were to attack with torpedoes. Two from each wave were to act as dive bombers. An additional two Swordfish, laden with flares, accompanied the strike groups. The flares would be dropped to help light up and silhouette the Italian ships for the attack. Goodwin's plane was one of the dive bombers in the first wave.

> … (W)e took off and it was a very dark night. We formed up formation over (an illumination) flare and then climbed and set off for Taranto. There was quite a lot of cloud about and, as a matter of fact, our aircraft and a number of others got separated from the rest. So, from our point of view, we seemed to be flying on alone. Although (eventually) all of the aircraft did arrive over Taranto. The Italians had detected us on their sound locators before the aircraft got there, and, by the time we started to fly over the harbor, the amount of AA flak with tracers was really quite terrific. I had been in quite a number of night bombing raids over other Italian harbors in the Mediterranean and there's always a lot of flak there, but never so much as I'd seen over Taranto.
>
> My aircraft, with my pilot, was one of those dive bombing the cruisers in the inner harbor whereas the majority of the attack was with torpedoes on the bigger ships (the battleships) in the outer harbor. We, of course, didn't see any of our other aircraft. One felt rather quite alone … Anyway, we dive bombed the cruisers and we thought we got some hits on them and then my pilot jinked out and we got away. As we went out, we flew over the seaplane base and they put up a lot of flak at us, too. Finally, we set course, all of us individual aircraft, back to the Illustrious some 180 miles to the eastward. In those days, before radar was outfitted … it was purely

*a matter of (human) navigation to find the ship … Anyway, we did find her without any trouble and my pilot made a perfect landing on Illustrious. And I think all of us, as we counted the aircraft coming in to land, were amazed to find that in our wave there was only one missing. And in the second, later, wave another aircraft had been shot down.*[6]

Goodwin added that his emotions were largely of apprehension as his plane was launched from the carrier. Among his worries were those of being able to find the target. After the shipboard briefings the fliers had been given, Goodwin understood the magnitude of the mission. He was more than a little concerned that his efforts at navigating might somehow cause his aircraft to miss Taranto altogether. During the attack, he admitted to a blend of emotions that included fear and exhilaration. The glare from exploding antiaircraft munitions and enemy searchlights seeking targets dazzled the fliers' vision. Along with his pilot, Goodwin feared that they would not be able to see their targets well enough to hit them. Goodwin worried on the long and steep dive downward that his pilot might somehow not be able to pull out of it. When the Swordfish did, indeed, come out of its dive, however, Goodwin was more than elated. The return flight brought on more anxiety as, lacking radar or even radio signals, it was once again his and the pilot's responsibilities to find the proper way. While a concerned pilot might request a radio beacon with which to steer his plane, no ship in the fleet would ever provide one. The risk of detection was too great and strategic logic dictated that it would always be better to lose a few aircraft than an entire ship.

Photo analysis from the morning after the raid showed that three Italian battleships had been sunk. Goodwin attributed the raid's large number of damaging torpedo hits to what was then a relatively new type of detonating device. Traditionally, a torpedo carried a detonator that would cause it to explode on contact with its target. Such a hit often took place against a hull that was protected by armour or blisters. A fair amount of the impact would be absorbed to limit any damage. The new detonator, however, was triggered by the magnetic field created by a target ship's hull. The torpedo, therefore, could be set to travel at a depth that would bring it beneath the ship. The resulting explosion would produce heavy upward moving shockwaves that could break a ship's back.[7]

Of the three battleships that sank in the shallow water of Taranto harbour, two, one each new and old, were repaired after about six months and returned to service. The third, one of the older vessels, remained inactive for the duration of the war. The bombing of the cruisers resulted in only two hits by bombs that failed to detonate.[8]

Despite the tactical brilliance of the Taranto raid, the balance of naval power in the Mediterranean remained unchanged. The final analysis has shown that the British objective of eliminating Italian naval power from the Mediterranean in that one blow was not met. Too few aircraft carrying too few bombs and torpedoes did too little damage to the Italian ships. By comparison, the Japanese who studied the raid in detail were to employ all six of its front line carriers and over 400 aircraft at Pearl Harbor. Had the lone Royal Navy carrier at Taranto and its attack wave of a mere two dozen planes been supported by a second, and even a third carrier, the end results of the strike might have been different. That cannot be known, of course, and critics, granted the wisdom of hindsight, have argued that, with a stronger attack force, the damage inflicted against the enemy could have been critical rather than a mere inconvenience. The struggle for control of the Mediterranean continued unabated.[9]

### 'Dice With Death'
### Carrier Takeoffs

Tony Inman a radioman/bombardier described the process by which aircraft were prepared and sent into the air from a moving aircraft carrier.

> *'Hands to flying stations,'... was the signal for the flight deck party to muster, put the aircraft that were about to fly in their correct places* (also called 'spotting' aircraft), *test engines, and see that everything was ready. In the meantime the crews and pilots who were about to 'dice' were briefed* (dice was the abbreviation for 'dice with death,' the casual throwaway phrase used for flying originally from the RAF). *We would then wander out onto the deck and get into our aircraft and make ready. (I don't remember that we had the American phrase, 'Pilots, man your planes!'). When we were ready, strapped in, equipment out of the way ... we would tell (the*

*pilot) who would indicate our readiness to the Flight Deck Officer. He was the man in charge of the flight deck, and I mean in charge. When all planes were ready he would signal to the bridge where Commander Flying would have the affirmative flag put out. Flying could now begin.*[10]

The 'affirmative flag' would have been a green one. Displaying it during flight operations indicated that everything was safe and ready for takeoffs or landings. A red flag was used to indicate a problem. Flight operations would be suspended until the difficulty could be remedied.

*The ship now turned into the wind* (to provide additional lift to the planes) *and engines were started. When … the ship was going full speed* (about 17 knots) *the Flight Deck Officer brought down his flag* (or pointed emphatically forward with his hand) *and the first aircraft took off. This was the Avenger, which having a shorter takeoff was always in front of the fighters. Open the throttle wide, stand on the brakes, and, just when you thought everything would shake to bits, release the brakes. The tail was up by the time we passed the bridge and if the wind was strong enough we were just about airborne when we were at the end of the deck, so bank away to starboard to get our slipstream clear of the deck where the next plane was already on its way.*

*If the wind was less strong we would not be airborne by the end of the deck and would sink down towards the sea. The drill was then to raise the undercarriage and put on less flap which all had the effect of increasing air speed to a safe amount before climbing away.*[11]

By mid-war aircraft carriers, large and small, had been equipped with hydraulic catapults at which time radioman/bombardier Inman was assigned to the three-man Grumman Avenger torpedo bomber. The other Avenger crewmen were the pilot and turret gunner. Inman described being launched from a carrier by catapult.

*(The Avenger was) … 'On the 'Squirter' (as) … there (was) not enough wind. There she was on the catapult looking unhealthily close to the (front)*

*edge of the deck. The catapult was a slot at the edge of the flight deck probably about 50 feet long, with a hooked traveler in it. The aircraft was placed astride the slot and the tail wheel was attached at the back end. My recollection is that a rod of mild steel passed through the tail wheel and was secured to the deck. On the strut of each wheel* (near the base and leading edge of the wings) *was a downward facing hook and a steel hawser – looped at each end – was looped over these hooks and round the traveler on the catapult slot. One of the engineering officers was in charge of this contraption and he moved the traveler far enough to take up any slack on the hawser. The crew boarded, strapped themselves in, anchored anything loose, and signaled the pilot. He gave thumbs up to the flight deck officer who, after receiving permission from the bridge, waved his flag round and round his head. This was the signal to the pilot to open the throttle to its full extent, tighten the wing nut so that it would not slip with acceleration, and for the crew to brace themselves … Down came (the flight deck officer's) flag, the engineering officer pressed his button, and we were off. The catapult went off with a thump that could be heard and felt all over the ship. Great pressure was applied to the traveler until it passed the breaking strain of the mild steel rod. When this broke the plane was free, the traveler shot to the end of the slot, pulling the plane via the hawser and flicked us off the end. As we passed, the end of the loops on the end of the hawser slid off the hooks, and could be recovered for future use as it was tied to the ship by a piece of rope. As the plane went from rest to 65 knots in 60 feet the acceleration was fierce …*[12]

### 'Sometimes They Crashed'
### Carrier Landings

The general nature of returning and landing aboard a carrier was described by a former enlisted air crewman Raymond Wills.

(Being trained as an aircraft mechanic) … *my job (aboard the carrier) was to inspect the planes. I would check the panels and oils* (possibly including hydraulic fluids and engine coolants) *before takeoff … The pilots used the runway* (flight deck) *to practice landings, the batman would bring them in but sometimes they crashed. If the plane was badly damaged it would be taken ashore, we only did small repairs on ship, such as small dents … Some planes crashed into the captain's tower, the bridge, this caused too big a repair to do on the ship. They seldom burst into flames. Some planes went into the water; we had to be quick to retrieve the pilot because he had heavy gear on. When this did happen we quickly lowered the boat to rescue the pilot. On many occasions the planes got caught … and hung over the sides of the ships. I would have liked to have flown a plane but I was colour blind.*[13]

A 'batsman' was a landing officer. He was usually an experienced naval aviator who would stand on a platform near the after end of the flight deck to provide guidance via hand signals for incoming pilots. He held paddles that he used to inform each plane's pilot as to his position, angle, and altitude relative to the flight deck for a safe landing. If all was in order and the plane had its wheels down, flaps down and hook down, he would signal the pilot to cut his engine to complete the landing. If anything were amiss, he would give a wave off signal to tell the pilot to avoid landing. In such a case the pilot would have to instantly apply full power to his engine and circle around for another attempt. It was often the practice to have a destroyer trail behind an aircraft carrier during flight operations. Any pilot who wound up in the water would be rescued by this ship that was called a plane guard.

Air crewman Inman offered his description of landing on a carrier.

(The carrier had) … *a wooden deck. Along each side of the deck was a catwalk set a bit lower so that when walking along it the deck was about level with your chest. Several large radio masts were arranged down the sides and these were normally in a vertical position but when flying was taking place they were lowered outboard to a horizontal position … there were six, I think, arrestor wires which, for landing on purposes were raised from each end to about nine inches to catch the plane's arrestor hook, and pilots were expected to catch the third or fourth wire when landing. If, by some mischance (or poor airmanship) all wires were missed there was a safety device, which, I'm glad to say, I never had to try. This was a barrier further up the deck which consisted of two steel cables stretched across (the width of the flight deck) between two steel stanchions which could be lowered to deck level out of the way. The height of the wires could be varied according to the type of aircraft and were at such a height that the bolting (having missed all arresting wires) aircraft would meet the wires which were joined vertically to stop the wires separating to slide over the engine. (The batsman) … was the man who controlled all the landings. His instructions (given by hand signals) were mandatory! They had to be obeyed. If he raised his arms (it meant) go up; if he lowered them (it meant) come down. And if he waved one arm over his head (it meant) open the throttle and go round again for you were making a right mess of everything.*

*For the batsman's benefit there was a safety net out from his platform into which he could fling himself when some pilot drifted (too close to him) when landing and was likely to clip him. The safety net was angled so he would slide down under his steel platform for added protection. This was tested when one pilot drifted over to port when landing and although he caught a wire he ran over the edge of the deck before the hook broke and the aircraft fell into the sea smashing the Captain's barge on the way. I expect the pilot is still paying for it. The batsman, meanwhile, was probably having a stiff gin to recover his nerve.*[14]

The narrow catwalk along the flight deck's edge was where numerous personnel essential for flight operations were stationed. As soon as a plane caught a wire, the men, each with a specific job that needed to be quickly and efficiently done, would rush onto the flight deck. Among these personnel was the man who manually disengaged the tail hook from the wire. Others unbolted the plane's wings to push them back to a space-saving folded position (although they were hydraulically operated by the pilot on the Avenger). Still others got behind the plane to push it along the deck and out of the way of the next plane to land. There was also a plane director who gave hand signals directing the pilot and flight deck crew where to park the landed plane. Crashed or damaged planes were lowered, as expeditiously as possible, by elevator to the hangar deck. If severely damaged or hung in a difficult position along the deck edge, a plane would be manhandled over the side. Aboard the carriers, nothing could be allowed to slow the launch and recovery cycle.

### 'I Enjoyed Life on the Ship More Than on Shore'

HMS *Premier*

Life aboard a carrier – or any ship at sea – was not always as frantic as during flight operations. Air Crewman Wills, of the escort carrier HMS *Premier*, remembered some easier times aboard his ship.

> *Smoking was absolutely prohibited when refuelling the ship. It was too dangerous. The tanker would run alongside the ship to fill the tanks ... If you were caught smoking you were slapped in jail. My friend was put in jail for smoking; he was in the toilet and did not hear the tannoy. He had to go before the Captain, who proceeded to sentence him to several days in the cells. It was a shame because it went on his permanent record ...*

*… The atmosphere on the ship was pretty good; I enjoyed life on the ship more than on shore. I always felt safe on the carrier. We got American cigarettes, American chocolate, and tinned fruit. These products were short in Britain, but we could get them from the US (when Premier went between Norfolk, Virginia, and England three times in February, April, and May of 1944). I sent the chocolate home to my family in Cranfield. We were well fed on HMS Premier; we had three meals a day … We always had good wholesome food. When the chefs would shout, 'it's eggs for breakfast' everyone would storm the galley because they were so hard to get. I remember spending Christmas on board in 1944, we sang songs and watched films on a pull down screen in the hangar. I remember singing … then someone would shout, 'ladies only' and everyone would sing in a high voice. When we were not working, we held services in the hangar and played football on the deck with a rag ball, real footballs would have bounced off the ship. We patrolled the coast and visited Belfast a few times; you could get a bed for one or two shillings a night. I really liked the Guinness. We really did drink a lot of it. I remember when the time came to board the ship again many men could not climb down to the (liberty) boat … The Captain knew of our exploits and instructed the returning crew to climb aboard … by rope ladder instead of the easier means.*[15]

Torpedo bomber crew member Inman also had good memories of the quieter and more routine days aboard his escort carrier. Many of the aspects of shipboard life that he experienced in World War II endured with him long into the post-war years.

*After a couple of days at sea there was no fresh milk, of course, beer had run out, and fresh water was severely rationed. Apart from cooking, fresh water was only on for a very short time in the morning and was not available for showers or baths which were in great demand. We were in the tropics (and) the ship did not have the luxury of air conditioning so there was condensation everywhere and copious sweating. Salt water showers, even with salt water soap, only cooled you for a short time and left you sticky. Occasionally the tannoy would pipe, 'There will be an opportunity for a fresh water shower in about five minutes' which meant that a rain squall was approaching that was likely to hit the ship. In no time at all the flight deck would be crowded with near naked bodies clutching a bar of soap and with a towel tucked out of sight where it would not get wet. You then hoped that the squall would hit the ship and that the cool drenching rain would last long enough to get yourself wet, soaped up and rinsed off.[16]*

### 'I Won't Have My Ship be Shot From Under My Ass!' *Bismarck* Meets *Hood*

*Bismarck,* 1:1200 and *Prinz Eugen,* Model 1:1200, present for the sinking of *Hood*

In May, 1941 Germany's newest and most powerful battleship made a move towards the Atlantic shipping lanes. A host of Royal Navy ships was sent after her. On the 24th *Bismarck* engaged the Royal Navy's own new battleship *Prince of Wales* along with the long-time pride of the fleet, battlecruiser *Hood*. *Hood* was sunk with all hands save three and *Prince of Wales* limped off badly damaged. *Bismarck* was now dangerously close to the open seas.

Bruno Rzonca was assigned to *Bismarck* in May 1940 while the ship was still under construction. After training, operational readiness preparations, and a surprise inspection visit by Hitler, the new battleship steamed from Gotenhafen (near Danzig on the Baltic Sea) towards the Atlantic for her one and only combat mission. According to Rzonca:

*I was at my duty station* (below decks) *and once they sounded the alarm nobody could go topside. (The British were), I think, 15 miles (away). They started shooting and the shells came closer and closer, and we were wondering in the ship, why we don't shoot back … This crazy Admiral Lutjens* (overall commander of the German force), *he wouldn't give the order to shoot back until we had already received three hits. Then the skipper* (Captain Lindemann) *got mad and said, 'I won't have my ship be shot from under my ass!' That's what he said in words, and we were ordered to shoot back. It took us five minutes to sink the* Hood. *Distance of 15 miles. We could reload the big guns in 20 seconds.*[17]

One of *Hood*'s survivors was Robert Tilburn, born in Leeds, the son of a policeman, and a sailor with the Royal Navy since he was sixteen. He joined *Hood*, his first ship, as an ordinary seaman at Gibraltar. The young sailor thought that she was 'a marvellous looking ship'. He felt special for having been assigned to her. When the war began, Tilburn was apprehensive, but felt confident that *Hood* would fare well against any enemy and thought her to be practically unsinkable.[18]

On 24 May 1941 Tilburn was at his action station on one of the 4-inch anti-aircraft guns as *Hood* headed for her encounter with *Bismarck*. He was anxious but confident that, no matter what, 'we would win in the end'.

*… at six o'clock or slightly before … in the morning, it was clear with a heavy swell and we sighted the two ships … we'd been at action stations since … the previous evening … we immediately started to close the range and then at approximately six o'clock we opened fire with A and B turrets. The* Prince of Wales *followed and then we had return fire from the* Bismarck *and* Prinz Eugen. *The first shells were over but in our wake. I think they fired two or three. The third shell hit us on the upper deck and started a fire (around) the open ammunition. Most of the upper deck's guns crews – thinking back to what had happened at Oran (Mers-el-Kebir against the French fleet) – had been ordered to go forward into a space below the bridge … as soon as the ready ammunition started to explode (a) gunner's mate (named) Bishop came to three of us who had not gone forward (and*

*told us) to put the fire out and we said, 'wait until the ammunition stops exploding' … the next shell came and blew the (gun) director away (and) the three of us were laying down next to a u.p … a funny thing that fired rockets and had a blast shield around it. An then, we were hit … a terrific explosion … and suddenly the whole ship – dead silent – maybe I'd been deafened … the (sailor) lying (nearby) had his side cut open as if a butcher had got him … his innards were coming out, and I thought, 'ooh, I'm going to be sick,' and I got up and went to the ship's side and noticed that the water was much closer than it was and the bows were coming out of the water. I went to the forrard end of the boat deck, dropped onto to the foc'sl … I realised the ship was sinking … she was rolling over and the bows were coming up … I stripped off my tin hat, anti-flash gear, overcoat, by then the sea reached me and I was in the water.[19]*

Another of the three *Hood* survivors, Ted Briggs, remembered that,

*When the action started it was wildly exciting. But this feeling was quickly taken over by terror.* Hood *was hit three times and the third hit blew up the magazines.*

*There was no sense of anything being wrong with the ship that day. We knew two powerful ships were coming, but there was no sense that we were going to get sunk or pounded or anything like that. Gunnery on the Hood was good, but not as good as on the* Bismarck. *We fired a couple of salvoes at what we thought was* Bismarck *before* Prince of Wales *said we were firing on the wrong ship and we changed over. At that distance you could only see the superstructures. We fired about six salvoes before* Bismarck *answered – we took her by surprise. She'd no idea there were heavy units in the vicinity because of radio silence. We had hit her with one which caused a fuel leakage but it wasn't all that serious. When she did reply – her first salvo fell short – you could see the splashes. The next went over (long) and you could hear the roar (of the shells flying overhead) like a thousand express trains. The third hit the base of the mainmast causing a fire in the four-inch ready use ammunition lockers. Then there was a fourth and fifth. There was no explosion that I could hear. We were thrown off our feet and I could see a gigantic sheet of flame which shot round the compass platform. The ship started listing to starboard about 10 to 12 degrees, then it started to right itself. The quartermaster* (in charge of steering operations) *reported that the steering gear had gone and we were to go to emergency conning. But as we did, the ship started to go to port and it kept going. It got to 30–40 degrees and we realised the ship wasn't coming back. There was no panic – it was uncanny but everything seemed to be going in slow motion. We tried to get out the starboard door. The gunnery officer was just in front of me and the navigating officer stood aside to let me through.*[20]

## 'They Came in Flying Low Over the Water'
## Swordfish Versus *Bismarck*

Even with *Hood* and *Prince of Wales* no longer present, ships from the Home Fleet and Force H based at Gibraltar continued to chase after *Bismarck*. Two of the battleship's pursuers were the aircraft carriers *Victorious* and *Ark Royal*.

Newly commissioned on 15 May 1941, *Victorious* had been scheduled to perform a shakedown cruise with an aircraft delivery mission to Malta. Plans suddenly changed with *Bismarck's* move towards the shipping lanes. The carrier detached from her planned club run with crated and unassembled aircraft slated for Malta still stowed in her hangar deck. She had orders to close on the German battleship's most likely position. The Admiralty was hoping that *Victorious'* aircraft would at least be able to slow the German battleship down. The Royal Navy's big gun ships would then catch up to finish her off. *Victorious* reached the Denmark Strait on 23 May, just eight days after commissioning and with scores of civilian construction workers still on board. The workers stood side by side with crewmen to show them how the ship's machinery, equipment and systems worked. Nine of the carrier's embarked 825 Squadron Swordfish had been loaded aboard the carrier specifically for the purpose of making torpedo attacks against *Bismarck*.

The Swordfish were launched at about midnight of the day on which *Hood* had been sunk. They flew towards where the *Bismarck* was thought to be. The weather was poor with high winds, heavy seas, and rain. Although the days of May were long in the northern latitudes, visibility was much diminished as the sun began to set. The squadron had yet to practice combat techniques or tactics. Several pilots were so new that their only carrier landing to date was the one they had just made to report aboard *Victorious* four days earlier. On launch from the carrier the squadron was divided into three plane sections that would attack the battleship by turn. By the mission's completion only one of all the torpedoes dropped resulted in a hit. Bismarck's gunners did not down any of the planes, but were effective in making their job as difficult as possible. The battleship's helmsman alertly and adeptly steered the ship clear of all but the single torpedo that hit the armoured belt.

A German report on the attack stated,

> They came in flying low over the water, launched their torpedoes and zoomed away. Flak was pouring from every gun barrel, but didn't seem to hit them. The first torpedo hissed past 150 yards in front of Bismarck's bow. The second did the same, as did the third. Helmsman Hansen was operating the press buttons of the steering gear as, time and time again, the Bismarck maneuvered out of danger. She evaded a fifth, then a sixth, when yet another torpedo darted straight towards the ship. A few seconds later a tremendous shudder ran through the hull and a towering column of water rose at Bismarck's side. The nickel-chrome-steel of (the ship's) side survived the attack ...[21]

Philip Gick, who would rise to admiral's rank after the war, was a Swordfish pilot in 1940. His air crew included Telegraphist Air Gunner (TAG) Leslie Daniel Sayer. The two men embarked aboard *Victorious* with 825 Squadron. With neither 825 Squadron nor *Victorious* fully worked up to operational standards, it was, according to Sayer, a mission of the blind leading the blind. Just prior to launch, the squadron received a minimal briefing that did not include bearing, range, or speed of the targeted German battleship. The Swordfish crews were merely instructed to keep a sharp lookout and to immediately attack *Bismarck* if they were to locate her.[22]

HMS *Victorious*

*Bismarck*

The Swordfish pilots aboard *Victorious* had been told that the key factor for a successful torpedo drop was to avoid excessive height and speed lest the weapon bounce off course or break apart upon striking the water. In pre-deployment practices gun cameras had originally been used to record practice drops. Photo analyses made after the exercises allowed for the calculation of the ideal attack parameters. The optimal altitude for a drop had been determined to be 20 feet. Excessive speed, according to Gick, was never a problem as the Swordfish was a painfully slow moving aircraft even at full throttle.[23]

Both Gick and Sayer looked upon the slowness of the Swordfish as a mixed blessing. On the one hand, it made the plane and its crew extremely vulnerable to antiaircraft gunfire. On the other hand, a crash landing could usually be managed at just 50 miles per hour. There was a very good chance that such a low speed crash could be escaped with minimal injury. The open cockpit made for extremely cold flying, especially since extra clothing could not be worn because of the tight spaces in which the crew had to move about to perform their jobs. The best they could do was to put on a second pair of socks and constantly wiggle fingers and toes to keep them warm and functional. The men who flew in the Swordfish often complained that, on landing, their limbs would be so stiff that they would barely be able to lift themselves out of the plane.

Following an uneventful takeoff, 825 Squadron, largely by luck, found *Bismarck*. The German ship was shrouded beneath low patchy clouds in the grey light of dusk. *Victorious'* pilots made their attacks. The low altitude used by the Swordfish in their attack approaches helped preserve them from the *Bismarck's* guns which could not be depressed far down enough to hit the planes. Also, the ship's fire control system had not been calibrated to track such unexpectedly slow moving targets. Gick recalled that when he first saw the *Bismarck* he thought that she was such an 'absolutely incredible' and 'marvelous' ship that he felt a reluctance to sink her. The pilot also felt that it was 'a bloody shame that we couldn't preserve her; capture her, instead of destroy her'. Despite such misgivings, he also realised that she was a 'terrible menace' that would have wreaked havoc among the convoys and that it was 'vital to get her'.[24]

While the other planes of the squadron made their attacks, Gick's plane could not get a satisfactory line on the battleship. He turned wide to circle around for a second run at her. TAG Sayer recalled his dismay as they had already endured and survived the Germans' intense defensive barrage once. Now they were going to go back for more. Having decided beforehand that he was not likely to survive the war, the TAG forced himself not to dwell on the present danger. Initially, *Bismarck's* gunners did not see Gick's returning Swordfish, so it was able to close unmolested. Once they were sighted, however, the Germans opened up with all available guns. While the plane was not actually hit, the splashes of water caused by the battleship's shells shredded the underside of the Swordfish's canvas fuselage. Sayer was certain that the battleship even fired her main battery's 15-inch guns at his plane. The fliers managed to drop their torpedo and the TAG, facing aft in the aircraft, could see a large column of water spout up against Bismarck's side. He was convinced that it was a hit. [25.] This could well have been the hit against the ship's side mentioned in the previously cited German report. The damage was not significant, however. It would take a follow up strike by planes from another carrier, *Ark Royal*, to cause any serious difficulties for *Bismarck*.

Because the ship and crew were so new to combat air operations, there was not much talk aboard *Victorious* about the *Bismarck* action after the torpedo planes had returned to the carrier. None of the pilots or air crewmen could really say that he had seen much of anything once his plane had dropped its torpedo. Most information came from second and third hand stories based on the random comments that were claimed to have been heard from one or another of the pilots. A number of Fulmars and Swordfish were launched over the next several days to shadow *Bismarck*. Several of these planes were lost due to the difficult flying conditions but *Victorious'* part in the action was done. *Bismarck* would be left to the likes of *Ark Royal* and the battleships *King George V,* and *Rodney*.

### 'The Torpedo Hit Astern Was the Decisive Blow'
### The Pilot Who 'Sank' *Bismarck*

During her engagement against *Bismarck, Prince of Wales'* guns had managed a couple of hits that left the German ship leaking oil; a telltale sign that would permit the British to better track her. On 25 May, *Ark Royal*, already at sea with other Force H ships, was ordered to intensify her search for *Bismarck* as it was determined that *Victorious'* earlier Swordfish strike had not been effective. It was imperative for the British fliers to slow *Bismarck* down in order to give the pursuing British heavy units a chance to catch up to her.

The following day, *Ark Royal* launched fourteen Swordfish in seas so heavy that water was washing over her flight deck. The planes located a target and were making low level torpedo runs before they realised that they were attacking the shadowing cruiser *Sheffield*. The cruiser did not shoot at the Swordfish which she recognized as friendly, but made evasive maneuvers that caused all torpedoes launched to miss. Since only three planes had not dropped a torpedo, the flight returned to the carrier to rearm. A second strike of 15 Swordfish was launched and they all vectored onto *Sheffield* so that the radar equipped cruiser could then point them in the right direction. *Bismarck* was only 12 miles from the cruiser and the planes readily found her. The Swordfish made their attack against both sides of the *Bismarck* thus forcing her have to turn into a torpedo track if she maneuvered to avoid one from the opposite side. Still, it was a daunting task for the pilots who had to fly low and straight at the very slow maximum speed of which the Swordfish was capable. The longer the time of approach, the longer the attacking planes were exposed to defensive gunfire. All the planes returned but few, if any, of the pilots believed that they had caused any damage to the battleship. In exchange for their troubles, three Swordfish crash landed upon return and several others were so badly shot up that they were no longer flight worthy. Unknown to any of the British at the time, however, was that they had managed two hits, one of which had struck and jammed one of Bismarck's rudders hard over. The hoped for result of slowing her down could not have been any better. The battleship could only steam in circles. The next morning, Royal Navy battleships *King George V* and *Rodney* would arrive to put an end to *Bismarck*.

According to the official German report written after she had weathered the *Ark Royal's* aerial strike:

> *The torpedo hit astern was the decisive blow; by destroying the steering gear it made the ship incapable of holding a course for our bases.*[26]

The pilot of the Swordfish whose torpedo made the 'decisive blow' remained unaware of his accomplishment for almost sixty years. Only when the Fleet Air

Arm contacted him in 2000 did he finally realise what he had managed to do. He spoke to the *Daily Mail* which reported the story in 2009. The veteran flier said,

> *What nobody talks about were the conditions – they were unbelievable … the ship was pitching 60 feet, water was running over the decks, and the wind was blowing at 70 or 80 miles per hour … and nobody mentions the deck hands who had to bring the planes up from the hangars – they did something special. After they brought them up they had to open the wings which took ten men for each wing. And then they had to wind a handle to get the starters working. I only stopped flying nine months ago and there are no other planes in the world that could have done what the Swordfish planes did that day. After take-off we climbed to 6,000 feet to get above the really thick cloud, and we knew when we were near because all hell broke loose with* Bismarck*'s fire. We got the order to attack and I went down and saw the enormous bloody ship. I thought the Ark Royal was big, but this one, blimey.*

> *I must have been under 2,000 yards when I was about to launch the torpedo at the bow, but as I was about to press the button I heard in my ear, 'Not now. Not now.' I turned round and saw the navigator leaning right out of the plane with his backside in the air. Then I realised what he was doing – he was looking at the sea because if I had let the torpedo go and it had hit a wave it could have gone anywhere. I had to put it in a trough. Then I heard him say, 'Let it go' and I pressed the button. Then I heard him say, 'We've got a runner' – and I got out of there.*[27]

The pilot, John Moffat, was one of the fliers whose Swordfish was not so damaged that it could not go on a second strike. By the time the planes arrived, battleships *Rodney* and *King George V* were already taking care of business. Moffat did not linger, but still saw some of *Bismarck*'s crew jump off the flaming wreck and into the cold sea. He recalled that the scene below him continued to haunt him practically daily and that he had never ceased to feel terrible that all those men caught in the water had absolutely no chance of being saved. As a sailor at war, Moffat understood that, through the quirks of war and fate, it

The 16-inch guns on the battleship HMS *Rodney* open fire on German battleship *Bismarck* in 1941

could very easily have been him in the water. He later wrote a book about his adventures, *We Sank The Bismarck* which the editors changed to *I Sank The Bismarck*. Moffat told them that the change was personally embarrassing and would be controversial. Staunchly loyal and extremely proud of the Fleet Air Arm and the men who served in it, he was frustrated that the credit directed only at him detracted from what he firmly believed was a team effort by the Fleet Air Arm and all its airmen.[28]

### 'They Laid a Charge Against Me For Damaging an Aircraft' The Pacific Theater

In 1945 the carrier *Victorious* was attached to the British Pacific Fleet headquartered in Sydney, Australia. Air operations against Japan for *Victorious* and her air wing mainly involved targeting air fields on the islands leading towards the home islands. The ship's Avenger torpedo bombers were loaded with 500-pound bombs fitted with delay fuses set for anything from '0' for immediate detonation to six hours. Delayed explosions, unpredictable by the enemy, would make repairs difficult. They would also destroy more aircraft and kill or, at least, demoralize additional enemy personnel. By June or July very little threat remained from ground-based Japanese air defenses or from enemy fighter cover. The diminishing opposition allowed British pilots to destroy practically all of their assigned targets. In the last month of the war, *Victorious'* planes were hunting down the scattered remnants of the Japanese fleet and any of the few remaining enemy aircraft.

The BPF carriers normally cruised some 25–30 miles off shore. They would launch air strikes for about two days before pulling further out to sea for replenishment. The Royal Navy fleet train included two brewery ships that supplied beer for enlisted ratings but, much to their chagrin, not to the officers. Although all aboard the ships of the BPF understood that Japan was losing the war, they believed that it would take another full year to end it. Their greatest worry was that the end would only come with a full scale invasion of Japan. From what they had seen of the Kamikazes, all knew that the Japanese would have been a formidable and difficult people to fight. The entire population would have sacrificed themselves one after the other to defend their homes.

British pilots were as dedicated and determined as their Japanese enemy in their efforts to win the war. They performed under harsh and frightening conditions in what were often very impersonal circumstances. Unlike their Japanese counterparts, however, British airmen were very strongly disinclined towards suicide. Former Telegraphist/Air Gunner Derek Foster recalled a time during *Victorious'* BPF service when his Avenger's landing system was in danger of failing due to a leak in the hydraulic fluid reservoir. Such an unwelcome failure could have spelled total disaster for Foster, his aircraft, and even the ship.

*(The reservoir) would hold hydraulic if you filled it up again. So I remembered that there was a tap on it, a screw type tap, and the instruction was always for the flight mechanics to leave this finger tight. Well, my fingers wouldn't open it so I was stuck with this thing tightly sealed. The only thing to do was to get the jungle knife that we carried, make a hole in it near the top, (and) get the fluid into there … Of course it wasn't easy to*

*get the fluid in with the aircraft swinging about so I remember(ed) there was a funnel for the urine tube* (the plane's basic bathroom system) *... so I used that for my funnel and got the fluid in and took it out but this big hole* (made by Foster) *meant that it wasn't air tight (and) wouldn't operate ... I also carried a pack of chewing gum which I hated (chewing) ... anyway I chewed off a large piece ... managed to seal this hole and the hydraulics started working again ... (the pilot) could get the flaps down and we landed OK (although) we landed with the bombs still in the bomb bay and although I'd armed them ready for being dropped and I'd gone back and turned (them) to disarm, I'd never done this before so I didn't know if this worked or not, you know! (M)y pilot had to speak up for me quite a bit when the stores officer ... got very annoyed that I'd damaged this hydraulic tank and he hadn't got a spare one so the aircraft was not able to be used until they could get one. They laid a charge against me before the commanding officer for damaging an aircraft but my pilot spoke up for me and I wasn't punished for that.*[29.]

No aircraft carrier can conduct flight operations without mishaps. Whether at war or peace, aircraft carrier crews remain on full alert for accidents that can occur at any time and in any part of the ship. A good percentage of naval aircraft lost during World War II were due to accidents of one type or another. Such losses were labelled as 'operational' as opposed to 'combat related'. In the absence of official Royal Navy statistics, US Navy data showed that, during World War II, approximately 47 per cent of its naval aircraft losses, whether carrier borne or land-based, were operational in nature.[30] Some of the accidents were tragic and others, once all had been said and done, turned out to be comical. All, however, were generally nerve wracking.

Graham Evans of *Indomitable* told about an attempted landing by a Hellcat fighter:

*Each aircraft had just one attempt to come aboard once committed ... there were just half a dozen wires to engage the hook or you would hit the barrier of steel cables raised halfway along the deck to protect the deck park (which) … was the forward deck area where those aircraft that had already succeeded to land-on would be tightly marshalled, if possible with the wings folded. The barrier was not foolproof as aircraft did, on occasion, bounce over the barrier and into the park with dire consequences. One spectacular land-on was presented by a Hellcat returning from combat seemingly unscathed, but later found to have a hook problem that led to its failure to engage. The Hellcat touched down but bounded on across the deck drifting to starboard unchecked. It slammed into the starboard after pom-pom gun emplacement on the edge of the flight deck. The impact shattered the starboard wingtip and broke the fuselage clean in two behind the cockpit rear bulkhead. The tail was flung across the deck and came to rest further aft on the portside near the ship's arrester gear. The nose, cockpit and wings were sent spinning on partially collapsed landing gear and bent propeller blades into the base of the island. As the rescue crews rushed across to the shattered remains, the pilot amazingly eased back the canopy hood and climbed onto the wing root. The pilot was even in quite a jolly mood as he assured the assembled party that he was alright despite his spectacular arrival and required no further assistance. With that he accidentally trod on a wing flap which dropped away sharply dumping the poor soul unceremoniously onto the armoured flight deck … unfortunately the pilot … broke his arm in the fall.*[31]

If a plane wrecked itself on landing during combat operations, air crews were given no more than ten minutes to salvage all that they could of value from the aircraft. The most important items, according to Evans, were gun sights, bomb sights, guns, ammunition, radio, and any useful airframe parts that could be quickly stripped off. In the case of the Hellcat described earlier by Evans, both engine and propellers had been damaged by the collision. Those parts and the rest of the plane were shoved overboard. A second story from Evans involved the landing of an Avenger with an armed bomb stuck in its bomb bay.

*After … returning from a raid, an Avenger pilot had called the ship to advise that he had a bomb stuck in the bomb bay and that the bomb bay doors would not close. Standard procedure would normally have been to ditch the aircraft to avoid blowing up the ship but somehow the Avenger had landed-on successfully. With the state of the bomb still in question, I was summoned before the captain, who ordered me to carefully find out the answer. For its mission the Avenger had been armed with a load of 500 pound MC* (Medium Capacity or general purpose) *bombs. Each had a nose fuse propeller (which) spins in the slipstream of the falling bomb to wind out the detonator thus arming the weapon for explosion on impact. With sufficient opening between the doors, any unreleased or trapped bomb may have been in such a slipstream. As I made my way out towards the abandoned aircraft 'clear the flight deck' was piped. This obvious precaution seemed like an omen to me as I made the lonely walk to the abandoned Avenger, and it did nothing for my nerves. The bomb bay doors were ajar sufficiently enough for me to insert my arms between them. The doors were being held open by a 500 pound bomb which now lay on the actual doors and not secured in the top of the bomb bay thus precluding opening the doors further. I carefully looked into and felt around inside the opening to ensure that there were no further surprises. There was only one bomb but that was enough. I felt tentatively around the bomb nose until my fingers finally touched the blades of the arming propeller. Finding it brought no relief as I could feel the screw threads meaning the propeller had unscrewed quite a bit arming the detonator … I began to coax the propeller round … with two fingers slowly completing a whole turn, then another. Intermittently I would feel the threads for any discernible change. I became bolder with the revolutions as the propeller was obviously screwing the detonator back in. Finally I got (it) in a relatively safe handling state … with some assistance the doors were slowly cranked open and the bomb was man-handled onto the deck. The aircraft, I, and the ship all remained intact. I felt this surely warranted some high award but none was received.*[32]

Many years later, Evans said that it was very difficult to get an award from the Navy during the war, but if the bomb had exploded he likely would have gotten one posthumously.

When VE Day came in May, *Victorious* and the other British carriers in the Pacific theater were still fighting off Kamikazes. When they had time to think about things, the men felt that the war was completely unfair. Back home crowds in Trafalgar Square were getting drunk, carousing, and unabashedly enjoying life. The British Pacific Fleet, however, just suffered bad food, crowded living conditions, and a murderous enemy. The men in the Pacific felt as if they had been forgotten. The war was not only over in Britain, but even their recent enemies in Germany and Italy could lay down their arms. The BPF men were 'peeved' and 'running out of steam' over the hard life and the ever present threat of death in the Pacific.

In early August, everyone aboard *Victorious* was puzzled that all ships were ordered to move away from the Japanese coast to positions at least 100 miles out to sea. They only found out by radio broadcasts that something called an atomic bomb had been dropped on Hiroshima. The news was followed a few days later by reports of a second such bomb being dropped on Nagasaki. Slowly, the magnitude of what had happened began to sink in. The men were grateful that there was no longer a need for the dreaded invasion of Japan. Some of the pilots who had been feeling that the longer they had to fly, the greater were their chances of being killed, were ecstatic. When VJ-Day was announced the men were given an extra tot of rum, but there was no real celebration or outward exhibit of jubilation. All on board knew better than to let down their guard. To a man, they very much appreciated the words of American Admiral Halsey, who encouraged them that, with the war finally over, the only thing to do differently would be, 'to shoot Japanese planes down in a friendly manner'. Celebrations were delayed until *Victorious* returned to Sydney.

ENDNOTES

1.  Barber, Mark. 'Memoirs of British Veterans: Bruce Vibert.' Originally published in *FlyPast Magazine*. April 2013. Web. Accessed February 2014.

2.  Barber.

3.  Barber.

4.  Ogonovsky, June (contributor). 'Some Fleet Air Arm Memories.' BBC WW2 *People's War*. Article ID A 4456307. 2005.

5.  _____ 'Italian Navy in World War Two.' Web. Accessed February 2014.

6.  Imperial War Museum. Sound recording archive. 11282. Goodwin, David G. 1990.

7.  Imperial War Museum. 11282.

8.  Roskill, S.W. *The British Navy at War, 1939–1945*. Naval Institute Press. 1966. pp. 110–111. Roskill's account of the raid differs slightly from that of ex-air crewman Goodwin. Roskill lists eight Swordfish in the first attack wave and twelve in the second.

9.  Caravaggio, Lt. Col. Angelo N. 'The Attack at Taranto: Tactical Success, Operational Failure.' *Naval War College Review*, Vol. 59, No.3. Summer 2006.

10. Inman,Tony. 'A View From the Back: The Recollections of a Fleet Air Arm Observer 1941–1946 (Part 11 of 14).' BBC WW2 *People's War*. Article ID A 8109209. 2005.

11. Inman.

12. Inman.

13. threecountiesaction (contributor). 'Raymond Willis Memories of HMS Premier.' BBC WW2 *People's War*. Article ID A 5879983. 2005.

14. Inman.

15. threecountiesaction.

16. Inman.

17. _____ 'An Interview With Bismarck Survivor, Bruno Rzonca.' KBismarck.com. Web. Accessed November 2013. When Rzonca was asked, 'Were you looking at the Hood at the time she blew up?' and 'Did you see Hood blow up with your own eyes?' he replied, 'No, but I did get reports from those who did see Hood go down with field glasses.'

18. Imperial War Museum. Sound recording archive. 11746. Tilburn, Robert Ernest. 1990.

19. Imperial War Museum. 11746.

20. Imperial War Museum. Sound recording archive. 10751. Briggs, Albert Edward Pryce 'Ted.' 1989.

21. Horan, Mark E. 'With Gallantry and Determination: The Story of the Torpedoing of the Bismarck.' kbismarck.com/article2. Web. Accessed February 2014.

22. Imperial War Museum. Sound recording archive. 18574. Sayer, Leslie Daniel. 1998.

23. Imperial War Museum. Sound recording archive. 12097. Gick, Philip David 'Percy.' 1991.

24. Imperial War Museum. 12097.

25. Imperial War Museum. 18574 (Sayer).

26. Polmar, Norman and Genda, Minoru. *Aircraft Carriers: A History of Carrier Aviation and its Influence on World Events, 1909–1945*, Volume I. Potomac Books, Inc. 2006.

27. *Daily Mail,* 10 June 2009. 'I Sank the Bismarck But Only Found Out 59 Years Later: British Pilot Learns of His Place in History.' Web. Accessed February 2014.

28. Graham, David. 'Lost Sailors Haunt Pilot Who Helped Sink Bismarck.' Reuters US Edition, 29 December 2010. Web. Accessed February 2014.

29. Transcript from an audio interview with Derek Foster. warexperience.org/collections/sea. Web. Accessed February 2014.

30. Air Branch, Office of Naval Intelligence (OPNAV-P-23V No. A129). Table 4: Combat Air Operations and Results, Carrier Based and Land Based, by Theater and by Year. 17 June 1946. p. 18.

31. Robin Marie (contributor). 'RNVR HMS Wanderer and HMS *Indomitable* (1941–1945), Part 4.' BBC WW2 *People's War*. Article ID A 9031493. 2006.

32. Robin Marie.

# NINE
# DECEMBER CATASTROPHE: HMS REPULSE AND FORCE Z

'A Proud Sign of Continuing British Sea Power'
*Repulse* and Her Men

HMS *Repulse* docked at Haifa, Palestine, July 1938

HMS *Repulse* was laid down at the John Brown shipyard on the exact same January day in 1915 as her sister ship HMS *Renown*. *Repulse* was still incomplete at the time of the May 1916 Battle of Jutland. The battlecruiser was completed in August 1916 but did not participate in any action during World War I. Except for certain periods of refit she remained active for the entire interwar period. Following a major refit in the early 1930s the ship was given a second, but less extensive refit from late 1938 through early 1939. She was deployed with the Home Fleet at the outbreak of World War II.

Torpedoman Richard Smith fondly referred to *Repulse* as simply being 'The Ship'. He elaborated by stating that aboard her, 'you felt like you were above other ships in the fleet'. Smith added that he considered her to be fast, efficient, happy, and lucky.[1]

While there is no single definitive definition of what constitutes a happy ship, sailors the world over would tend to characterize such a ship as one where the men are smart in the naval sense, efficient, team-oriented and extremely proud of their ship. Further signs of a happy ship include men and officers who are mutually respectful and supportive while serving with a captain who is held in high esteem by all aboard.

Seaman Robert Fraser considered *Repulse* a 'home' where all mixed in together well with the old hands being very welcoming to the new. He called her a 'beautiful ship' and defied anyone to say otherwise.[2]

Ian Hay started his life in the Royal Navy as a boy seaman at HMS *Ganges* in 1937. He served aboard the battleship HMS *Revenge* prior to transferring to *Repulse*. Hay offered his impressions of his first days aboard the battlecruiser,

> On the 3 January, 1939 an era began in my life, which I still hold close to my heart, the memories will never fade of the wonderful times I had onboard this ship … The setting where Repulse *was berthed couldn't have been more fitting, moored alongside Nelson's* Victory, *a proud sign of continuing British sea power. The only trouble was, the whole ship looked like it had just been salvaged from the depths of the ocean. I had a job to walk on the decks, in fact in certain places on the ship the deck wasn't visible because of coils of electrical cable, riveting and welding equipment.*

> … *I was sent to my mess (and shortly discovered) that* Repulse *had been chosen to take the King and Queen to Canada on a Royal Cruise … even the skipper had lost his cabin to the Royals. In fact, the whole ship from stem to stern was in some sort of alterations of one kind or another. This*

*effectively meant that for the rest of my first day, I went on cleaning
duties. It was hard work, as our task was to polish the teak deck to clear
it of the tar that had been used to seal it when it had been laid.*

*My first evening onboard was spent listening to … the other lads (talk)
about life on* Repulse. *They all agreed that it was a fine place to be,
adding that the elder men onboard felt her to be the most efficient ship
in the Royal Navy and were rightly, very proud of her. After a few days
of cleaning work I had a welcome respite, being picked along with a
few others, to go to the dockyard stores and pick up fresh materials for
the refit.*

*… The situation with Germany was becoming much worse and all efforts
to defuse the situation were falling on deaf German ears. Because of
this, whenever I was off duty I heard one recurring statement from the
elder men onboard. Their main concern was that as we practiced for
hours on end each day to greet the Royals onto our ship in the manner
which they felt befitted them, the German sailors we would soon meet in
combat were more than likely on gunnery practice in the Baltic. I listened
intently to their comments and even as a young lad I could see they were
right. Our country already had a Royal Yacht, why wasn't it being used?
We were a warship but at that moment in time we looked more like a
cruise liner.*[3]

Another crewman was Royal Marine Frank Claxton who reported aboard *Repulse*
in November 1939. Claxton had left school at age fourteen, and, because times
were hard for his family, he took the first job that came his way: bicycle delivery
boy for a shoe shop. He slowly worked his way up from third assistant in the
shop to second and then first. He quit that job because he did not like being
confined indoors. He especially hated the 'groveling and sniveling' associated
with trying to sell shoes. He then got a job with a company that manufactured
canvas products that included tents and sails which he learned to set up for
the firm's clients. By now, he was 20. Rather than wait to be drafted he let
his experience with canvas and rope and the sense that 'Hitler needed to be

stopped' lead him to consider the Royal Navy. To his surprise, the recruiter told him that there were no slots available, but that if he joined the Royal Marines, he would certainly be able to go to sea. Despite the 12 year term of enlistment required, he still preferred the Marines to the Army and, after a brief deliberation, went ahead and enlisted.

Claxton went by rail from Plymouth where he had recently finished his training to join *Repulse* at Scapa Flow. During a long layover in London, he and several others who were also headed to Scapa decided to walk around to see a bit of the city. They were in a park near Parliament when the air raid sirens began to sound. A man walking nearby advised them to follow him to the nearest shelter. Being young and cocky, they laughingly and disrespectfully told him 'to bugger off'. The man went his way and, a few steps later, Claxton suddenly realised that he recognized him. The man was British Prime Minister Neville Chamberlain.[4]

Upon arrival aboard *Repulse,* Claxton was assigned to 'B' turret of the ship's 15-inch gun main battery. The entire gun, from turret to magazine, was manned by Marines and Claxton's station was the shell room deep below decks. It was cramped with shells that each weighed a ton. The shells were packed in amid the machinery used to lift and hoist them up to the guns. The deck was always wet with condensation and oily from the hydraulic and lubricating fluids required by the machinery. The entire compartment would creak when the ship was out to sea which initially made it 'absolutely frightening' for Claxton. As the ship was operating under wartime conditions the men spent every other day on watch: four hours on station with four hours off. Unless there was an actual encounter with the enemy, Claxton and the men with him in the shell room would spend their watch standing at their station just waiting for instructions. They passed the time playing cards or chatting among themselves about any number of topics. They often shared fond memories of civilian life, speculated about what each would do if the ship were to be sunk, and discussed plans on how to quickly get out of the shell room in emergencies. Once closed up in the shell room, they were not allowed to leave. If they needed to make a head call, or use the bathroom, they would do so into a bucket which they would carry out when their watch was over.[5]

## 'I Feel We Could Have Accomplished More'
## Routine, Monotony, and Disappointments

During the early months of the war, *Repulse* remained with the Home Fleet based at Scapa Flow which the crew, along with sailors from other ships, unanimously found to be inhospitable. According to Claxton, it was an unpleasant place with 'nothing there … no people … just a load of islands and the fleet'. Another *Repulse* crewman, Ted Matthews, who had come to *Repulse* by way of *Ganges* and the training cruiser HMS *Cornwall*, called it a 'godforsaken hole'.[6] A sailor from another ship wondered how anyone could possibly live there and recommended that it be left to the natives with whom he was equally unimpressed. Every fourth day at Scapa, the men would be given two hours ashore. Most would head directly to the Navy-run pub for their allotted two pints of beer.

While based at Scapa, *Repulse*'s primary mission was to remain ready for action against any Kriegsmarine capital units that might sortie towards open water. *Repulse* was also to remain prepared to interdict German merchant shipping. Whenever the ship sailed she did so as a convoy escort. *Repulse* helped to shepherd troop convoys to or from Canada or to Freetown in Africa and back. The majority of the men aboard *Repulse* felt that a combat ready asset such as their ship was being wasted on such duty. Morale remained high, but the common thread of sentiment about convoy duty aboard the battlecruiser was that it wore hard on the men and left nothing to show for their efforts. They had worked and trained hard to represent King and Country on the high seas. They chafed at being stuck in tasks that they felt were unbefitting of a battlecruiser.

With rationing in full effect at home, the food available to the fleet was usually canned, plain and unappealing. The memory of herrings in tomato sauce and baked beans for breakfast has endured with Royal Marine Claxton for over sixty years. According to Claxton, convoy duty, for all its monotony, did have some advantages. During 1939 and 1940, Claxton's primary impression of Canada, a regular stop on *Repulse*'s convoy routes, was that it scarcely seemed aware that there was a war going on. Whenever they anchored in a Canadian port, the men found food and other consumer goods, long since scarce or forgotten about in Britain, to be plentiful and inexpensive. The same applied to tropical Freetown where fresh and very exotic fruits and vegetables were abundant and inconsequential in cost. Many of the crew relished such overseas port calls that allowed them to eat better than if they had remained in home waters.

Convoys to Freetown also afforded the men some relief from the dreary and cold climate of Scapa. While they would start off with foul weather gear and heavy duffel coats, a few days steaming southward would provide such warmth and sunshine that tropical clothing, including short pants, would make up the uniform of the day. The return trip, however, would necessitate the breaking out of heavy gear once again.

*Repulse* stayed at Scapa with the Home Fleet through all of 1940 except for a brief sortie to Norway after the German invasion of that country in April. There were two primary naval actions at Narvik, but *Repulse* did not participate in either. The first engagement involved a Royal Navy force of five destroyers that entered the fjord sheltering Narvik to challenge the German force of 10 destroyers anchored there. The enemy destroyers, accompanied by several auxiliary vessels, were supporting the Wehrmacht troops that captured the port. The second battle took place on 13 April, three days after the first, when the British again entered the fjord in hopes of finishing off the German ships that had survived the first battle. *Repulse* was to have led a destroyer force into Ofotfjord, but the battleship *Warspite* had arrived on scene and, being the senior ship, took the battlecruiser's place. In addition to her seniority, the *Warspite's* heavy guns could elevate at higher angles than those of *Repulse*. *Warspite*, therefore, offered the tactical advantage of being able to fire on targets that might seek shelter behind any of the fjord's many heights. *Repulse* was relegated to steaming off shore, out of the way, so did not contribute to the action.

Their exclusion from the Second Battle of Narvik was especially bothersome to the crew and Ian Hay expressed feelings that were widely shared throughout *Repulse*,

> *I never experienced many greater disappointments than the ... orders we received. We were told to stand off at the mouth of the fjord and await the arrival of HMS* Warspite, *an older battleship. Apparently, she was carrying an Admiral and he wanted to supervise the action. It was upsetting to be so close to inflicting damage on the Germans and then having to back down. We later heard that our Captain protested but all was in vain. The*

*action was a success on our part and the destroyers did a thorough job on the Axis warships ... although I feel we could have accomplished as much and maybe more than the Warspite. After all our months of convoy duties we should have had a chance to show our mettle.*[7]

In late May 1941 intelligence picked up a major movement by the Germans. The battleship *Bismarck* was headed for open water. Her presence in the Atlantic shipping lanes could not be risked. Accordingly, *Repulse* was ordered to form up with other major Home Fleet units that included the battleship *King George V* and aircraft carrier *Victorious* for search, pursuit, and possible action against the German ship.

On 24 May, battleship *Prince of Wales* and battlecruiser *Hood* caught up with *Bismarck* in the Denmark Strait and the ships engaged in a brief but significant exchange of large caliber gunfire. *Hood* was sunk with all hands except three by a catastrophic explosion. *Prince of Wales*, newly commissioned, but having technical difficulties with her main battery, took several damaging hits and withdrew from the action.

HMS *Prince of Wales*

Reg Woods of *Repulse* had joined the Navy after working at Cammel Laird shipyard. His job at the yard had been to drill holes into plates that were to be riveted into the double bottom of *Prince of Wales* as she was being built. He recalled thinking that a ship of such size, strength, and sophisticated construction would surely be unsinkable. He was stationed on the after pom-pom, an eight-barreled automatic anti-aircraft gun, as *Repulse* pursued *Bismarck* at 28 knots through heavy seas. He was excited by the announcement made over the ship's tannoy that *Hood* and *Prince of Wales* would soon engage *Bismarck*. He remembered the complete silence that fell over *Repulse* when news of *Hood's* loss was received. The two battlecruisers had served as part of the same squadron and many aboard *Repulse* had good friends aboard the sunken *Hood*. Woods' mood shifted to one of apprehension about the possibility of action between his ship and the powerful German battleship.[8]

Stung by the sinking of *Hood* and fearful of incurring further losses among its battlecruisers, Home Fleet ordered *Repulse* to proceed cautiously. The thinly armoured ship was to approach no closer than 5,000 yards to *Bismarck* at any time. She was not to engage unless the German battleship was already under fire from *King George V*. *Repulse* ultimately left the actual combat to aircraft from carriers *Ark Royal* and *Victorious*, battleships *King George V* and *Rodney*, and several cruisers. For all her time at sea, *Repulse* was low on fuel so she turned back for port on the day after *Hood* had been sunk. According to crewman Matthews, the order for *Repulse* to avoid direct engagement with *Bismarck* was not popular with the crew,

*Everyone was totally devastated; we'd chased for days, and just as action with her appeared inevitable, we had to stand off.*[9]

## 'Bleating Like a Flock of Lost Sheep'
## There Was Time for Fun

While the monotony of the comings and goings from Scapa Flow in the maddeningly fruitless pursuit of action against the German navy wore on the men, there were still sufficient opportunities for them to keep their spirits up. Seaman Ted Matthews wrote of an incident that took place while *Repulse* was operating out of Scapa Flow,

*We'd been at Rosyth for a few days and were about to put to sea. Before we could leave we had to allow the battleship Rodney to enter harbour. As she had an Admiral on board this would mean that all our crew on deck would have to salute her* (this is a naval custom called 'rendering honours') … *At this point it (had been) stated that (a member of) Rodney's crew had been discovered on Flotta Island, Scapa … in a compromising position with one of a farmer's sheep. I couldn't say who first spread this rumor, but it was never to give her ship's company a minute's peace and this time was to be no different. As soon as we were ordered to salute, it started. Can you imagine some 1,300 matelots saluting the Admiral, whilst at the time bleating like a flock of lost sheep? The aftermath of this action was a reprimand for the whole ship's company. The skipper wasn't at all impressed and gave us some stick about it for some time afterwards. I still think nowadays that he must have found it funny once the dust had settled. The stigma never left the Rodney, but make no mistake there was no ship in the Navy that we had more respect for as a fighting unit. Their gunnery and efficiency were second to none, but I don't think they ate much lamb onboard.*[10]

### 'The Most Sincere Gesture from a Captain'
### Morale Lifted

The high speed pursuit of *Bismarck* which had consumed so much of *Repulse*'s fuel also caused her breakwater to be pushed back flat by the heavy seas. She was ordered to Newfoundland for refueling and repairs. Royal Marine Claxton unabashedly stated that it was just as well that *Repulse* did not linger to meet the German battleship. *Repulse*'s low fuel state had caused her to drastically reduce speed in order not to run dry in mid-ocean. Claxton was certain that *Bismarck* would have 'blown her out of the water'.[11] The marine's shipmate, Ted Matthews, recounted that,

*… We'd used up almost all our fuel reserves, this meant that we reduced speed to no more than 8 to 10 knots which left us wide open to attack from the abundance of U-boats known to haunt this area. From my point of*

*view, I found this more nerve wracking than when chasing the Bismarck. We had now lost our greatest defence over torpedo attack … speed … any increase at all would mean running dry in mid Atlantic. After an extremely tense period it was with great relief that we managed to reach land with no mishaps and everyone was able to relax properly for the first time in almost a week.*[12]

*Repulse* slowly steered for Conception Bay, Canada even as the now distant battle against *Bismarck* raged. If the crew's morale suffered from the ship's removal from yet another coveted combat situation, an action by the captain, once they reached shore, certainly helped temper such feelings. Matthews remembered,

*At this point I was privileged to witness the most sincere gesture from a Captain* (Captain 'Bill' Tennant, later Admiral Sir William George Tennant; MVO, CB, CBE, KCB. He was also recognised with awards from France, Greece and the United States) *to his subordinates I've ever heard of to this day. The harbour town of Conception Bay was living on the poverty line. It shouldn't have been the case as they had an abundance of that vital element in any mechanized war; iron ore … the British government, in their wisdom, decided not to buy this material from these people, some of whom were actually fighting in the war on our side …*

*Our skipper must have been fully aware of the plight of these people (and made) … to ease their situation which had the added effect of showing to his crew that he truly cared for their welfare. The area … was a great fishing community but nobody could afford to buy their salmon. He quickly remedied this point by purchasing, out of his own pocket, fresh salmon for the whole ship's complement … most of us came from poor backgrounds and at that time salmon was a delicacy; the cost must have been immense … he did it because he was someone special. I've only served under two officers, during my time in service, whom I have had total respect for. He is one … With this act of humanitarianism he'd both helped the people of the town, and also sent our morale through the roof.*[13]

*Repulse* was next assigned to convoy duty along the coast of Africa from Freetown to South Africa into the latter part of 1941. Despite all of their wartime responsibilities, the crew still managed to make time for some carefree playfulness. John Garner, a Royal Marine serving aboard the ship recalled that,

> *It was a very happy time on board as I think the climate* (off the African coast; especially in comparison to that of Scapa Flow and the North Atlantic), *to some extent, helped in making the crew put the war out of our thoughts. When we finally got to Saint Helena* (in the South Atlantic off the west central coast of Africa), *some of the lads played a great joke on a lot of the crew. At that time fishing had become a great past-time and those who weren't fishing had all gone into the swimming pool that had been set up on the foc'sl* (forward portion of the ship) *... after a while one of the men who had been fishing caught the most horrible looking fish I'd ever seen. It was a bloody massive red and white thing that was so ugly I was frightened being on the same ship with it. The next plan of action (was) to get the lads out of the swimming pool was to spread the word that this bloody thing was poisonous and the most obvious place for it was the swimming pool. This had the desired effect, I've never seen such panic; there were matelots* (shipmates) *everywhere screaming and bawling.*[14]

### 'We Are Going Off to Look For Trouble'
### Force Z and the Far East

By September 1941, the British were gravely worried about their position in the Far East. The strong Anglo-Japanese alliance with which Britain had opened the 20th century had gradually weakened until the British were forced to reconsider their overseas relationships. In the end, the power whose interests would be least likely to clash with those of Britain dictated a choice. London spurned Japan for the United States. British Far East interests could be found in India, Burma, Malaya (Malaysia), Hong Kong, and Singapore, but by 1940 Japan was bent on expansion. The Japanese, firmly entrenched in Manchuria, pushed further into China. When the Vichy French government conceded rights to Japan in French Indochina (Vietnam), the Japanese were quick to station army troops there.

Furthermore, French Indochinese air fields were opened to Japanese military aircraft, while Cam Ranh Bay offered forward basing to the Imperial Japanese Navy. Japanese military forces were now positioned less than 500 miles to the east or northeast of Siam (Thailand) and British controlled Malaya. Britain's government and military studied their options and reached the decision to make a show of force in the region.

*Repulse* and battleship *Prince of Wales* were ordered to the Far East just weeks prior to Japan's attack on the Americans at Pearl Harbor. *Repulse* made a brief stay in Durban, South Africa which earned the ship a visit from Prime Minister Jan Smuts. As the Prime Minister addressed the crew, he spoke to dispel any misconceptions that the Japanese, against whom *Repulse* would soon see action, were a race of myopic, undersized or inferior people. He added comments about the serious likelihood of war with Japan that he emphasized would be fought with courage, skill, and tenacity by well-trained and well-armed Japanese forces. This seemed to take many aboard *Repulse* aback as, unfamiliar with the world in general, they had been assuming that the widely circulated cartoon-like propaganda representations of their potential enemies were accurate. More by hearsay or by assumption, many Royal Navy sailors still felt that fighting the Japanese would 'be a piece of cake'. They were certain that Japan's armed forces were second rate and equipped with nothing better than antique airplanes and outdated ships.[15] The South African Prime Minister concluded with a foreboding comment which stayed hard with *Repulse*'s crew. He stated that he was sorry, but he knew with certainty that some of the men to whom he was presently speaking would not live to see the end of the war.

*Repulse* and *Prince of Wales* arrived in Ceylon in late November. There had been lengthy debates in Westminster as to how Singapore was to be defended and by what forces in case of war. First Sea Lord Sir Dudley Pound had wanted to send the bulk of the Royal Navy's battle forces, but he was over ruled by Prime Minister and former First Lord of the Admiralty Churchill. Churchill firmly believed that the appearance of just a few capital ships would suffice to deter any possible Japanese aggression. He was certain that, even should an assault against the city be launched, the ships' heavy guns would be more than adequate for its defense. Possibly making direct reference to the deployment of *Prince of* Wales to Singapore, Churchill stated that, 'A *KGV* class battleship exercises a vague general fear and menaces all points at once. It appears and disappears causing immediate reactions and perturbations on the other side.'[16]

The small British force, under the command of Admiral Sir Tom Phillips aboard *Prince of Wales,* was to have been accompanied by the new aircraft carrier *Indomitable.* The carrier had just entered service a month earlier, but while on her shakedown cruise she struck a reef and became suddenly unavailable. The loss of the air cover that the carrier's airwing could have provided to Phillip's force would shortly prove disastrous. Some of *Repulse*'s crew would remain bitter long afterward about what they felt was a sacrifice made through tactical (lack of air cover) as well as strategic (overall indefensibility of Singapore) misjudgments. *Repulse* and *Prince of Wales* departed Ceylon on 29 November for Singapore where they arrived three days later under the designation of Force Z.

Robert Fraser for whom Repulse was both a 'beautiful ship' and 'home' had left school at age fourteen to work as a 'trapper boy' at a mine near his home town. His job was to stand by to open doors for draft animals whenever they needed to go into or out of the tunnels. As unemployment was rampant in those days of economic depression, he could only work two or three times a week. Fraser was looking for security when he joined the Navy in 1939 at the age of nineteen. He was excited by the prospect of seeing action when he reported aboard *Repulse* in June 1941. His yearning for battle would come six months later. Until then, Fraser and his companions went about their shipboard work. They used their spare time to read in the ship's library, watch films in the on-board cinema or listen to the Marine band's frequent concerts. Fraser, in particular, looked forward to visiting all the ports of call along *Repulse*'s route to Singapore.

The former trapper boy enjoyed his visit to Durban, South Africa where families with strong ties to Britain waited outside the navy base gates to take sailors home or about town. Fraser was met by a couple whose son had been killed in action aboard a Royal Navy ship in the Mediterranean. He remembered that they drove him around and invited him to their home where they treated him as if he were their own son. When *Repulse* anchored at Mombasa in eastern Africa, Fraser marveled at how much he could buy on his navy pay. He bought a pair of pajamas for his sweetheart whom he would marry after the war. He was thrilled by the reception that the British ships were given on entering Singapore.

People lined the docks cheering and waving flags as the ship steamed by. Ashore, he felt as if he were a part of a fairytale storybook. He marveled at seeing rickshaws and exotic peoples. He thought Singapore was 'grand'. When news came on 7 December that Japan had attacked Pearl Harbor, Fraser was 'disgusted'. He understood that 'war is war' but still felt that the Japanese, by attacking without warning, 'were not playing the game'. He and his shipmates were particularly put out to discover that a good portion of the American fleet upon which Britain was counting for support was now sunk.[17]

Since November 1941, or even earlier, both the British and the Americans had been certain that Japanese military activities around the South China Sea would lead to war. They remained unclear, however, as to when, where, and how the war would exactly begin. Just two days before Pearl Harbor, Admiral Phillips flew to Manila where he met with US Army commander General Douglas MacArthur and Admiral Thomas C. Hart, Commander-in-Chief United States Asiatic Fleet. The three men agreed that Singapore would be impossible to defend against the type of well-planned Japanese attack that was being anticipated. They concurred that Force Z should relocate to Manila, but lack of air cover would prevent such a move for the time being. Admiral Hart offered to send a number of destroyers to help strengthen the British naval presence at Singapore. General MacArthur indicated that American B-17 long range bombers would be available to attack Japanese air bases in Indochina. Before anything could be finalized, a report was received that a large Japanese convoy had sailed from Cam Ranh Bay. Admiral Phillips departed after just one day in the Philippines.[18]

Among the Japanese preparations made prior to war was their naval command's sending of additional attack aircraft to French Indochina. The planes included new torpedo bombers to complement the existing force of high altitude level bombers already stationed there. All of the pilots belonging to the three Japanese naval aviation groups stationed at or near Saigon had been specially chosen for their experience and flying proficiency. The pilots practiced specific tactics to be used in attacks against surface ships underway at sea with live weapons. They developed precise strike doctrines based on low altitude torpedo attacks. Practice had shown that aircraft flying slowly just off the sea's surface aided the proper running of torpedoes and resulted in a better than one in two probability of obtaining a hit against a target. By flying low to the water, the aircraft were also better protected from shipboard anti-aircraft fire because defensive guns would not be able to shoot at low enough angles to hit them. Statements by gunners from *Repulse* would later confirm this.[19]

As word of the Pearl Harbor attack came through to Singapore, the Japanese were making simultaneous landings in the Philippines, Hong Kong, Borneo, Siam, British Malaya, and Guam. Any possibility of American air power coming to the aid of the British was quickly and suddenly removed by Japan's destruction of most of the B-17 force at its base in the Philippines. On the day after the attack on Pearl Harbor, the Japanese made multiple amphibious assaults along the Malay coast. Although the Siamese positions fell quickly, British ground forces kept up a vigorous rearguard resistance at Kota Bharu.

Admiral Phillips decided that all available Royal Navy units at Singapore should form up for an attack against the Japanese amphibious forces. The specific target was to be the Japanese landing and supply ships at Kota Bharu. The Royal Navy force hoped to arrive undetected in order to catch the Japanese by surprise. *Prince of Wales, Repulse,* the British destroyers *Express, Electra,* and *Tenedos,* and one Royal Australian Navy destroyer, *HMAS Vampire* steamed out of Singapore on the afternoon of 08 December. As *Repulse* made preparations to get underway, Captain Tennant addressed the crew:

HMAS *Vampire*

*We are going off to look for trouble. I expect we shall find it. We may run up against submarines or destroyers, aircraft or surface ships.*

Tennant provided the following outline of planned action:

1.  *We are going to carry out a sweep to our Northward to see what we can pick up. We must be on our toes.*
2.  *For two months past the ship has felt that she has been deprived of her fair share of hitting the enemy …*
3.  *There is every possibility that things are going to change completely.*
4.  *There is every possibility that we shall get a good deal of bombing in harbour.*
5.  *I know the old ship will give a good account of herself; we have trained hard for this day. May each one of us, without exception, keep calm and if and when action comes that is very important.*
6.  *Lastly, to all of you, whatsoever happens do not deflect from your job say when high-angle guns are engaging a high flying aircraft and all eyes are in the sky, none of the short range guns on the disengaged side should be looking at the engagement, but should be standing by for a low dive-bombing or torpedo bombing attack coming from the other side. Similarly in a surface action at night, provided the disengaged guns look out on the disengaged side they may be able to repel a destroyer attack that might otherwise damage the ship.*
7.  *For all of us, concentrate on the job. Keep calm.*
8.  *Lifesaving gear is to be worn or carried or is to be immediately to hand not because I think anything is going to happen to the ship; she is much too lucky, but if anything happens you have your life saving gear handy. That is all you have to think about in regards to yourself. You are then absolutely free to think about your duty to the ship.*[20]

It is not entirely clear if the above was stated over the ship's address system or if it was distributed in written form. Robert Fraser, the former mine trapper boy, stated, 'I read Captain Tennant's note on the board.'[21] *Repulse* steamed out of port to misty and rainy conditions that were encouraging for Force Z's hoped-for surprise attack. The British force steamed northwest of Singapore and around the Anambas Islands. In clearing weather, early in the morning, the destroyer *Vampire* signalled that she had sighted an enemy plane. Despite being in range of Japanese land-based aircraft, Phillips pushed on. At a position 150 miles south of Indochina and 250 miles east of Malaya, the force spotted three Japanese reconnaissance planes. With no remaining hope of achieving surprise, Phillips ordered a turn to head back to Singapore.

### 'Enemy Bombers Approaching. Height 21,000 Feet'
### *Repulse* in Action

HMS *Repulse*, a Renown-class battle cruiser of the Royal Navy built during WWI

Around midnight of the 9–10th, as it continued on its southwesterly course, Force Z was again diverted. The Royal Navy ships altered course on reports that there were ongoing Japanese landings at Kuantan which lay about midway between Kota Bharu and Singapore. Although the reports proved false, Phillips lingered in the area to investigate. He sent the destroyer *Express* close inshore, but no Japanese ships or activity were detected. Just a few hours before dawn on the 10th, a Japanese submarine sighted Force Z. The British position was given and an eighty-eight plane strike was launched from the Japanese air bases in and near Saigon.

The destroyer *Tenedos,* which had been detached from the force to head back to Singapore, caught the attention of the Japanese air groups first. She signaled her plight and Force Z was put on the highest alert. *Tenedos* would survive, but her signal was the first word Force Z had of an impending strike against it. *Repulse* soon came under attack and received a bomb hit that did not much affect her integrity or combat effectiveness. The attack has been well recorded by former crewmembers. Stationed on the aft anti-aircraft gun director, Seaman Ted Matthews remembered,

> ... *Our height finder ... had the planes in his sights; reporting to the transmitting station, 'Enemy bombers approaching. Height 21,000 feet.' Within moments they'd passed from the starboard side of the ship to port. At that time I couldn't see their bombs but everyone was certain they'd been despatched. Not surprisingly, it didn't take long for the results of their action to be felt ... we started getting explosions (on) either side of the ship – covering Repulse in heavy spray. Suddenly there was a tremendous detonation ... we'd been hit. They caught us on the port hangar* (for storage and maintenance on the ship's scout/spotter planes and just aft of the second funnel) *and almost immediately our position* (likely the aft H/A – high angle gun – director) *was covered in steam as a pipe had been ruptured by the explosion. I remember being shocked at the accuracy of the attack; it was far more precise than anything we'd previously encountered with the German Air Force.*[22]

As a civilian Steward Derek Jones had been working in domestic service as a footman when the master of the house was called up by the Army. Jones then followed his older brother's example of enlisting in the Royal Navy. Whenever *Repulse* was in action, Jones would forgo his steward's duties to serve as an ammunition bearer. He remembered that,

> *I was locked in my delivery room* (a station between the ship's magazines and guns that served for ammunition transfer) *when I heard the explosion and to some extent felt its force as it had gone off in the compartment next to ours, actually blowing a hole in our deck head. The smell was terrible and there was quite a severe fire burning. This was extremely worrying*

*as we couldn't get a message below for them to stop sending up more cordite* (powder charges for gun shells). *It just kept mounting up in our compartment. We couldn't send it up to the guns as at that time they were out of action. If one single lick of flame had entered our compartment, we would have been blown to bits.*

*…Our crew then got sent down below to move injured men to the sickbay. Some of their wounds, through burns, were horrific and I was shocked to see how many lads had been killed. After helping for as long as needed, we were sent to a small compartment just above the four-inch magazine to recover as we'd been inhaling smoke for quite some time.*[23]

The first wave of the attack had passed. About twenty minutes later, however, another group of Japanese planes appeared and split their attention between *Prince of Wales* and *Repulse.* These were all torpedo planes. Out of a total of seventeen attackers, eight made their low level runs against *Repulse.* While *Prince of Wales* was hit and suffered heavy damage, *Repulse* maneuvered and defended herself well enough to avoid all of the torpedoes launched at her.

Former shipyard worker Reg Woods recalled of the second attack,

*… I still remember that even after (the) first attack, it didn't shake our confidence … Suddenly I saw a low flying formation of planes coming towards us. I estimated their height was in the region of 100 feet or so. They certainly didn't look like the Swordfish our air force flew.*[24] *The speed they were travelling at made them look more like* (far newer and faster) *Spitfires. Almost immediately our ships, which had been steaming in close formation, took separate evasive actions, our skipper then began throwing Repulse around more like a minesweeper than a battlecruiser.*

*To our amazement these were torpedo planes and as they turned away from us we could see the tracks of their torpedoes plain as day in the water. Moving at what seemed like incredible speed straight towards the ship, just as contact seemed almost inevitable, we combed their tracks* (the ship was turned head on into the oncoming torpedoes to minimise the size of their target). *It was a superbly executed manoeuvre by Captain Tennant. This further cemented my belief in him being the finest skipper in the British Navy. Immediately after this onslaught a further alarm sounded followed by bomb splashes all around the ship. The Japanese had coordinated a high-level bombing to coincide with the torpedo attack … We tried to engage the low level planes but at that time had no real success.*[25]

Lack of air cover and the sheer number of enemy aircraft doomed both British ships. *Prince of Wales* took numerous hits and was seriously damaged by about noon, some forty minutes after the first attack. *Repulse* came under a renewed strike in which the Japanese planes split formation to attack the ship from both sides. The following crew statements about the final attack on *Repulse* serve to give a broad view of what that action must have been like.

According to Seaman Matthews,

*… I could see that Prince of Wales was in severe trouble, she appeared to be steaming in circles and I hadn't heard any of her 5.25s* (secondary battery guns being used for air defence) *fire for some time* (a torpedo had hit one of her propeller shafts and electrical power had been lost). *Several groups of planes came in for a further low level attack and we all knew that this could only mean more dicing with more torpedoes. The vibration and speed of Repulse was truly unbelievable, our skipper had us falling over everywhere in his attempt to comb the incoming torpedoes … I began to notice that the bombers were starting to fly directly overhead after they'd dropped their torpedoes. It was as if they were taunting us. I could even see the pilots' faces quite clearly.*

*Repulse had moved in a sort of protecting circle around Prince of Wales. I suppose it was an attempt to draw some of the enemy fire from her (or possibly lend anti-aircraft gun cover) as the situation for her crew must have been terrible. They were sitting ducks … I can't remember how many torpedoes we'd dodged when suddenly I felt a tremendous explosion on the port side amidships. They'd found their target and we'd definitely been hit. I remember wondering if we'd sink as I'd never been onboard any ship that even had a slight collision before, never mind been hit by a torpedo. I needn't have worried, Repulse wasn't going to give in that easily, she seemed to shake herself down and keep going. The fight wasn't over. The Japanese were going to have to try harder than that.*[26]

Reg Woods described his actions and thoughts while working one of the ships octuple pompoms,

*… Our gun was the scene of some degree of chaos. The ammunition in the pompoms was beginning to jam and foul up with frightening regularity; reason being the cartridges were separating whilst in the firing mechanism of the gun barrels. We thought this was due to the ammunition becoming too hot and the different metals in the shells having different rates of expansion causing them to literally fall apart. At one point we had 7 out of 8 barrels out of action. The thing that made it even more frightening was that the Japanese on the sides of the planes with machine guns would be directing a lot of their fire on our position so as to knock our gun out of action. To add further danger to the situation, we were all totally covered in cordite from the shells that had fouled the gun; one stray bullet would have been curtains for our crew … With hindsight, I must have been living purely on adrenaline … Possibly my strongest recollection which still fills me with pride … years later … is that even though we were attacked by planes we never thought existed … our backs firmly up against the wall, I never saw one of the lads shirk his commitment to the ship or his mates. It's obvious in any type of dangerous situation, if men of this caliber surround you the fear factor is greatly reduced.*[27]

Marine John Garner was a part of the after triple barreled 4-inch gun crew that claimed credit for downing one of the attackers. He recalled,

*As with all gun crews the pace of the action was frantic and never ending. Planes seemed to be attacking from all angles and the noise was unbelievable. I still remember one that our crew managed to nail. They came from the port side to the starboard quarter after launching their*

*torpedo … we'd just loaded up all three barrels, and immediately laid the gun onto them and, wallop. They got hit with all three shells; the plane just exploded in a massive ball of flames and fell into the sea. There were no survivors. It did our morale good to inflict some damage on them as we'd taken quite a hammering up to this point.*[28]

Many crewmen whose normal jobs were not directly related to defending the ship against air attacks were pressed into service as ammunition bearers. Ian Hay was, by now, dashing back and forth between gun mounts and ready ammunition spaces. He rushed along with many others to pick up shells to deliver, one at a time, by hand to the gunners. Hay said,

*… the run back along the exposed area of deck was to become terrifying. It had by now claimed the lives of three of our delivery party, all by machine gun fire. I lost count how many times we went down for further ammunition. It was like playing some crazy game of dare. Once you handed your shell to the loader you had no chance to speak to each other. There would have been no point. Everyone was terrified but we all did our work without exception. It was just after the first torpedo hit that I saw a sight that's haunted me to this day. We were on the way to feed the gun crew of S1, when the shout came up … 'Get down!' We dived into the gun well as a hail of bullets tore into the boat deck. Immediately afterwards I heard men screaming and shouting. It was obvious some had been caught by the machine gunners. I got up to see Bob (Hewlett) in pain, but still giving orders, he'd been shot in the arm but thankfully survived. Then he screamed, 'Don't just stand there, get some ammunition, star shells, anything, into the breeches'.*[29] *I could then see the carnage. Most of the gun crew had been killed or injured. A matter of minutes later there was another tremendous jolt, on the starboard side, roughly where we were located, so we felt the full brunt of this torpedo. I now knew deep down the Japanese wouldn't let us escape …*[30]

In all, *Repulse* was bracketed and hit by four torpedoes. She began to flood and her list quickly became severe. Knowing that the situation had become hopeless aboard the ship, the order to prepare to abandon was given. The battlecruiser's captain described the end of the action as follows,

> *Men were now pouring up on deck. They had all been warned 24 hours before to carry or wear their life saving apparatus. When the ship had a 30 degrees list to port, I looked over the starboard side of the bridge and saw … two or three hundred men collecting on the starboard side. I never saw the slightest sign of panic or ill-discipline. I told them from the bridge how well they had fought the ship and wished them good luck. The ship hung for at least a minute and a half to two minutes with a list of about 60 degrees to 70 degrees to port and then rolled over.*[31]

Reginald Jeffries of Derby had excelled in math at school. He later apprenticed in engineering in which he earned his certificate prior to joining the Navy in 1938. Although times were hard because work was not always available or steady, he got a job with Rolls-Royce in his home town. He worked on aircraft engines designed for the Spitfire fighter plane. He later transferred to the Admiralty torpedo factory at Weymouth when his family moved south so his mother, who suffered ill health, could enjoy a warmer climate. Ironically, some of the torpedoes being produced in Britain during the pre-war years were sold to the Japanese Navy. Jeffries took a motorcycle trip around Europe in the summer of 1938 and became keenly aware that war was on its way. After joining the Navy his aptitude was noticed and he was given training that quickly earned him advancement to ordnance petty officer.

During the attack on *Repulse* Jeffries was responsible for antiaircraft gunnery in the after portion of the ship, but struggled with pom-poms that were overheated and jamming. He remembered that it was sunny, hot, and humid and that he sweated a great deal as he wrestled with *Repulse's* malfunctioning guns. He was able to see several downed Japanese planes with their pilots calmly sitting on the wings in hopes of rescue. Some Japanese planes strafed the ship, but the grief they caused would be far less than that brought about by the torpedoes that were to strike her. Jeffries was showered with water thrown up by the torpedo hits and soundly jarred by the impacts that seemed to lift the ship out of the water.

When it became clear that the ship would soon have to be abandoned, Jeffries moved about the upper decks to assist wounded and disabled men with their lifebelts. The flotation belts were rubber rings that he inflated by blowing into them. He secured the inflated rings to their users by means of straps that went over their shoulders. He then lined these men up along the edge of the deck so that they could be gently pushed over the side when the order came. By the time he was done, water had already reached the roof of the after 15-inch turret. Jeffries jumped overboard into a sticky and tarry pool of fuel oil. He flipped off his steel helmet and slipped out of some of his anti-flash gear, but he could barely inflate his own life belt because his lips had gotten slick with oil.

Jeffries swam over to a group of survivors and, seeing the three escorting destroyers nearby, tried to remain calm while awaiting rescue. The group sang songs, among them 'Roll Out The Barrel,' and called encouragement to other groups that were swimming or drifting by. Jeffries reassured himself that there would be no problem with sharks as the explosions and concussions caused by bombs and torpedoes would certainly have run them all off.

The ordnance petty officer watched as *Repulse* rolled over. He saw men moving about the ship's upturned red-painted bottom. He could see some of the holes made in the hull by torpedoes and watched as men were blown out and clear of them by the tremendous release of the air pressure that had built up as the ship's internal spaces filled with water. Seeing the ship's propellers still slowly turning, Jeffries had to avert his eyes from the sight of survivors clinging to the ship's rails and rigging as she went stern up. *Repulse's* battle ensign still hung from the mainmast as she disappeared under the water.

Looking up, Jeffries saw a Japanese plane slowly circle over the destroyer *Electra*. He could read the international Morse being flashed by the pilot's signal lamp. The message asked the British to cease fire, pick up survivors, and clear the area. After spending about an hour in the water, *Electra's* whaleboat came by and picked up Jeffries. He remembered the frustration of trying to revive shipmates when he was finally aboard *Electra*. He could only tug at their arms or push on their chests in a primitive effort at CPR. None of his efforts helped. *Electra* made it back to Singapore and Jeffries, like all the other *Repulse* survivors picked up by the destroyer, could not thank the crew enough. Exhausted, they staggered down the gangway to the pier where the galley staff of the cruiser

*Exeter*, just months away from her own doom, had prepared hot soup and tots of rum for them.[32]

## 'I Knew Something Bad Had Happened'
## Aftermath

Several days later at Singapore things went on as if nothing had happened. Jeffries was given charge of a party of sailors, each armed with a rifle and a small quantity of ammunition. The men were instructed to go to a nearby base warehouse where they would find crates of Bofors anti-aircraft guns. Jeffries was to unpack and assemble them. Despite his training and experience with naval weaponry, he had never before seen this type of gun. He did not know how they went together. The job was urgent however, as the Japanese were on the way. Air raids had already been taking place. Jeffries and his party scrounged around until they found an assembly manual. They also came across an army engineer who was willing to help. Together, they eventually managed to assemble the weapons, but none had come equipped with sighting mechanisms. Jeffries found a workshop in which he managed to produce enough makeshift sights to fit onto all the guns. Just as he and his men were getting set to try a little gunnery practice, a military vehicle stopped by and informed them that they were all to be sent back to Britain.

Since the survivors had been issued a small amount of spending money, Jeffries went to a nearby cable office. He paid for a message to be wired to his parents to let them know that he was safe. Months later, when he knocked on the door of his family home, he met up with his cable. It was delivered that same day to inform everyone that Jeffries was alive and well.[33]

Marine Claxton had been knocked overboard of *Repulse* by a sudden lurch, and when he popped to the surface all he could see was the ship towering above him. He 'swam and swam and swam' in order to get away from her and to avoid either being crushed or sucked down when she went under. The ship was still making way, however, and by the time she sank, Claxton was clear of her. He floated amidst other survivors, bodies, and dead fish until, after four or five hours, he was able to pull himself onto *Electra's* deck by the cargo net hung for that very purpose over the destroyer's side. He made shore aboard the destroyer, was tended to, and returned to duty after several days.

As a Royal Marine, Claxton was expected to join other ground troops from the shore garrison or from among the survivors of *Repulse* and *Prince of Wales* to help defend Singapore. He was issued a rifle, bayonet, and ammunition and sent to stand guard outside a headquarters building containing military documents. He performed the role of sentry through a month of nights during which he was plagued by mosquitoes and a host of other 'creepy crawlies'. He never saw any sign of the enemy. Soon afterwards, as the Japanese began to draw closer, he was ordered to assist with the evacuation of British civilians. He did not feel that it was fair that these persons to whom the war had not caused any injury or suffering should get such preferential treatment. He dutifully did as ordered, but the small ship aboard which he was finally very belatedly evacuated was captured at sea by the Japanese. Claxton was to spend the rest of the war as a Prisoner of War.[34]

About 50 per cent of *Repulse's* original crew was ultimately rescued from the water. Total losses for the Royal Navy that day were 327 men from *Prince of Wales* including Admiral Phillips, and 513 from *Repulse*. When Churchill was informed of the losses he stated,

> *As I turned over and twisted in bed the full horror of the news sank in on me. There were no British or American capital ships in the Indian Ocean or the Pacific except the American survivors of Pearl Harbor, who were hastening back to California. Over all this vast expanse of water Japan was supreme, and we, everywhere, were weak and naked.*[35]

Back home, there were numerous loved ones of those lost who may well have also turned and twisted in bed at the horror of the news. Jean Gordon McClean, the sister of Reginald Gordon, a *Repulse* crewman who did not survive, recalled from the time when she was still very young,

> *I lived in a little country place called Carntall situated a few miles from Belfast … I … remember my eldest brother joining the Navy. I just remember seeing him home on leave once, in his sailor suit, as I called it. He was in the HMS* Repulse *which was sunk off Malaya by a Japanese … air torpedo*

*attack. One day as I recall a neighbor came to our school to take my other brother, two sisters and me home. When we got there, my Mum was crying. Our house seemed to be full of friends and neighbours. I knew something bad had happened, but I just didn't understand what was wrong. My Mum had just heard the* Repulse *had been sunk, and my brother was missing and presumed drowned. He was only nineteen years old. Our Auntie took us aside and told us to try to be good for Mummy. My Dad was in the Army so she was bringing us up on her own. I remember our home was very sad and quiet for a long time after that.*[36]

On 11 December 1941, the day after the action, an article, 'Blow Staggers London,' appeared in *The New York Times* about the loss of *Repulse* and *Prince of Wales*. It concluded by stating, 'Britain's grim determination to win through to a victorious finish, which was strengthened when the United States declared war on Japan, remains unswerving ...'

ENDNOTES

1.  Imperial War Museum. Sound recording archive. 8663. Smith, Richard Geoffrey. 1984.

2.  Imperial War Museum. Sound recording archive. 8267 Fraser, Robert William. 1984.

3.  forcez-survivors.org.uk. Ian Hay's anecdote is just a small part of his story that is found on the website of the Force Z Survivor's Association. A number Repulse's crew members are featured on the site under a section called 'Sailor's Tales.' Accessed November 2013.

4.  Imperial War Museum. Sound recording archive. 20134. Claxton, Frank Allen. 2000.

5.  Imperial War Museum. 20134.

6.  forcez-survivors.org.uk. 'Sailor's Tales, Ted Matthews.' Accessed November 2013.

7.  forcez-survivors.org.uk .'Sailor's Tales, Ian Hay.'

8.  forcez-survivors.org.uk. 'Sailor's Tales, Reg Woods.' Accessed November 2013.

9.  forcez-survivors.org.uk. 'Sailor's Tales, Ted Matthews.'

10.  forcez-survivors.org.uk. 'Sailor's Tales, Ted Matthews.'

11.  Imperial War Museum. 20134 (Claxton).

12.  forcez-survivors.org.uk. 'Sailor's Tales, Ted Matthews.'

13.  forcez-survivors.org.uk. 'Sailor's Tales, Ted Matthews.'

14.  forcez-survivors.org.uk. 'Sailor's Tales, John Garner.' Accessed December 2013.

15.  Imperial War Museum. 8267 (Fraser).

16.  _____ 'Attack on Force Z.' historylearningsite.co.uk. Web. Accessed December 2013.

17.  Imperial War Museum. 8267 (Fraser).

18.  Morison, Samuel Eliot. *History of United States Naval Operations in World War II, Vol. III.* 1948. pp. 156–157. Despite its imposing name, the American naval forces under Admiral Hart were far inferior to those of the Japanese. Three cruisers, one of them of WWI vintage, 13 older destroyers, 13 submarines, six gunboats, and a mix of lighter combatants, repair ships, and tenders were spread throughout the Philippines and the East Indies (Indonesia). By contrast, the Japanese forces collected for the Philippine invasion alone included two battleships, seven heavy cruisers, four light cruisers, 35 destroyers, and a host of smaller combatants and auxiliaries.

19.  forcez-survivors.org.uk. 'Pilot's Eye View.' Accessed December 2013.

20.  forcez-survivors.org.uk. 'Sailor's Tales.' Accessed December 2013.

21.  Imperial War Museum. 8267.

22.  forcez-survivors.org.uk. 'Sailor's Tales, Ted Matthews.'

23.  forcez-survivors.org.uk. 'Sailor's Tales, Derek Jones.'

24.  According to Force Z Survivor Association member comments, ship air defense drills had been practiced with the slow flying Swordfish in the role of attackers. This left many of the Repulse's gun crews surprised at and unprepared for the speed and agility of Japanese combat aircraft.

25.  forcez-survivors.org.uk. 'Sailor's Tales, Reg Woods.'

26.  forcez-survivors.org.uk. 'Sailor's Tales, Ted Matthews.'

27.  forcez-survivors.org.uk. 'Sailor's Tales, Reg Woods.'

28.  forcez-survivors.org.uk. 'Sailor's Tales, John Garner.'

29.  This is a testament to the determination and leadership among the crew. Star shells were a sort of flare used for illumination at night. They were inappropriate for anti-aircraft purposes, but the men of Repulse were clearly going to fight the enemy with everything and anything they could.

30.  forcez-survivors.org.uk. 'Sailor's Tales, Ian Hay.'

31.  Mason, Geoffrey. 'HMS Repulse – Renown Class 15-in Battlecruiser.' naval-history.net. Accessed November 2013.

32.  Imperial War Museum. Sound recording archive. 7480. Jeffries, Reginald Horace. 1984.

33.  Imperial War Museum. 7480.

34.  Imperial War Museum. 20134 (Claxton).

35.  _____ 'Attack on Force Z.'

36.  McClean, Jean Gordon. 'My Brother Reggie.' WW2 *People's War.* Article ID A 2686043. 2004.

# TEN
# MALTA UNDER SIEGE

The Royal Navy during WWII under the bombed bastions of the entrance to Grand Harbour, Valletta, Malta. An escort carrier arrives with the deck loaded with Supermarine Seafire IIIs.

Granted to Britain by the 1814 Treaty of Paris, Malta had been used ever since as a Royal Navy base. The island, located practically in the middle of the Mediterranean, was an ideal place from which to exert control, if not dominance, over that sea. In the mid-1930s, however, as England was planning for a war in which Italy would be a probable foe, the British decided to withdraw its fleet from Malta. They had concluded that the island's proximity to Sicily's military air bases made it indefensible. The Mediterranean Fleet left Valletta's fine harbor and well developed docking and yard facilities for the safety of a new base at Alexandria.

By 1940, faced with looming Axis threats to Egypt, the Suez Canal, the Middle Eastern oil supply, and British access to India and the Far East, the

British reversed their thinking about Malta. They returned, albeit slowly and piecemeal, to build up air and submarine strength on the island. The most notable submarine force based at Malta was the 10th Submarine Flotilla that consisted of the small 'U'-class submarines with each boat manned by a crew of thirty men. The specific mission of British air and sea forces in Malta was to disrupt Axis shipping bound for the German and Italian ground forces in North Africa. On 11 June 1940, the day after Mussolini's declaration of war against Britain, the Italian Air Force began to bomb Malta. Over the next two years, Malta would endure some of the most intense air attacks launched against any target during World War II. As the war hit full stride, the attrition rate for British warplanes based on Malta reached as high as 80 per cent. Continuous replacements were provided by flying planes to the island off of aircraft carriers.

### 'The Well Known Dreaded Sound of Falling Bombs'
### The Attacks begin

There was little respite from the fury of the interminable air raids against Malta. Day after day people huddled in underground shelters. When they emerged it was to sights of utter destruction. A former British Army air defense gunner gives a view of what it was like for those on the ground.

*The rays of the ... sun, slowly setting beneath the horizon of the blue sea, lit the heavens with a gay display of colours. It was a marvelous, inspiring sight, tranquil and peaceful, after the mid-afternoon bombardment ... But it did not last very long ... looking down from the bluff, to the airfield below, the wreckage of planes and hangars littered the field, and the few remaining serviceable aircraft lay at the far end of the landing strip, which was packed with bomb craters ... Behind us on the hills could be seen the blocks of hospital buildings, and among them the ruins of former wards ... one could see the domes and rooftops of (the town of) Rabat which, so far, had escaped any heavy demolition ... what was to be the next target, we could only guess ... (Then) came the soul rending impact of the siren, giving its ghostly warning to all, civilians and troops. Farm people in the fields below gazed aloft, no doubt wondering if they could finish their labour before the raid developed. Some stayed, others more cautious, made their way to the rocky shelters burrowed into the hillside … Suddenly Fort Tarja opened up with its 4.5's* (anti-aircraft guns), *a shattering salvo. High in the heavens, hardly discernible in the quickening dusk, rode six silver shapes making swiftly for the* (airfield), *faster they came, ignoring the bursts of flak around them, the leading plane swerved and waggled its wings as if in answer to an order. Down they came, headed for the far end of the dispersal area, a roar of engines shook the countryside, then there came the well-known dreaded whine of falling bombs. To our surprise, they were all incendiaries, and for what purpose we did not know, for nothing of an inflammable nature lay in their path. The 88s* (German twin-engine warplanes) *kept up fairly high* (but we) *poured a curtain of steel up at them. They made off in the direction of Rabat, still maintaining their formation, good pilots, they. As they slowly faded away in the distance, the gunfire … subsided until all was peaceful again except for the fierce glare of the incendiaries that were still burning …* (A) *few more minutes silence, and then faintly at first, gradually getting louder, the 'Throb-throb' of the engines could be heard slowly increasing in volume until it felt as though the heavens would split …* (we) *saw formation on formation, hundreds of planes sweeping the island … the sky was light with Ack-Ack, flare, tracers, and flaming onions as the guns took up the challenge …* (the planes) *broke formation, and in terrifying dives swept for* (their targets) *… the roar and vibration of the engines was suddenly drowned by the scream and whine of falling bombs, hundreds of them, like silver streaks they hurtled downwards … the earth shook and trembled, smoke billowed upwards, at times obscuring our vision, at times our ears felt as if they would burst … more and more planes swept in from the sea … they circled round and round, bombing and gunning. Everywhere fires raged … thunderous roars shook the earth … strike after strike … pan after pan of ammunition we used … we blazed away for forty minutes until our ammo was expended … The Luftwaffe … paid the price, planes were losing height, crippled by flak, to fall … to the ground. Machine guns waiting … no quarter asked, none given. Bailers* (downed enemy fliers) *were shot. They had attacked the hospital.*[1]

## 'I Later Found Out That Only One Man Survived'
## Success Followed by Misfortune

In late 1940 and early 1941, Italian troops in Libya struck eastward and entered British controlled Egypt. The long desert distances caused an exhaustion of supplies and fuel that stopped the Italians, however. When the British counterattacked, they drove their foe 500 miles back into western Libya. Hitler ordered the German army to the rescue. General Irwin Rommel landed in Tripoli to begin an immediate counterattack of his own. The Germans drove the British all the way back across the Egyptian border. Many British units had stopped at Tobruk, in Libya, to sort themselves out. They managed to set up such a strong defensive perimeter around the city that, although he kept Tobruk under siege, Rommel chose to bypass it as he pushed eastward to the Egyptian border.

In October 1941, the Admiralty decided to reintroduce a strong Royal Navy presence to Malta through the formation of Force K. Home Fleet cruisers *Aurora* and *Penelope* were teamed with Force H destroyers *Lance* and *Lively* from Gibraltar to be stationed at Valletta. Force K was to act as a striking force against Axis shipping bound for the resupply of Rommel's Afrika Korps. In early

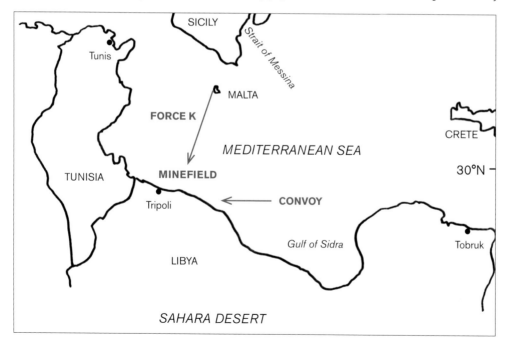

This map shows the route taken by Force K on 18 December 1941

November, the British ships at Malta sighted an enemy convoy headed for North Africa. They executed a surprise night attack in which they sank all seven Axis merchant ships along with a destroyer of the escort. The following day, a Royal Navy submarine torpedoed and sank another of the convoy's destroyers that had stopped to pick up survivors of the earlier attack. The loss of the convoy put a severe crimp on Rommel's operational capabilities against Tobruk and other key points to the east in Egypt.

Force K managed a second successful attack against ships headed for Rommel in late November. The British sank two supply ships laden with fuel and, at that point in time, 60 per cent of the supplies bound for North Africa were being destroyed.[2] Meanwhile, the Admiralty sent two more cruisers, *Neptune* and *Ajax*, along with two more destroyers, to bolster the strength of Force K. Soon afterward, in December, *Penelope*, *Aurora*, *Lively* and *Lance* attacked and sank another two ships headed for Rommel: a freighter and a tanker.

Force K suffered devastating misfortune as 1941 drew to a close, however. Royal Marine John Robert Porter, a member of *Aurora*'s B turret gun crew, described the incident.

*(One) run I recall was after we were joined by the … cruiser HMS* Neptune *… We were again told of another German or Italian convoy coming from Italy and we were to leave Malta with* Neptune *in charge to intercept it. Unfortunately, we missed the convoy and ended up only eight or nine miles off the port of Tripoli. We only then  realised that we had strayed into a minefield when we heard over the tannoy at about two in the morning that we were in a 'tense position' … ten minutes later we heard a tremendous explosion. Once we  realised that it wasn't us, we heard someone shout that* Neptune *had struck a mine and sunk … of a ship's company of over a thousand men, I later found out that only one man survived. After that our captain … addressed us very calmly and told us we were still in the mine field. He sent the destroyer* Kandahar, *which was with us, to pick up any survivors but (from* Neptune*), five minutes later, she too struck a mine. Then, there was a further explosion and this time it was our turn. The bows were blown off the ship but, fortunately, no one was killed. We could now do only about nine knots and we had to get out of the mine*

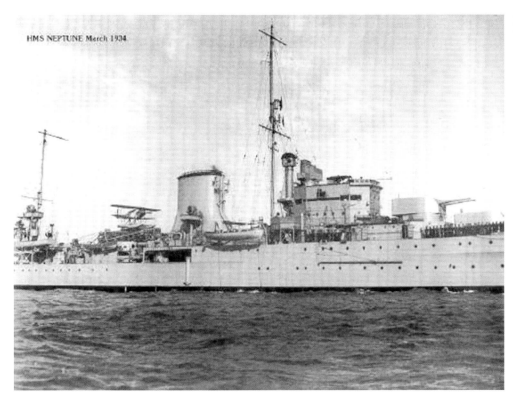

HMS NEPTUNE March 1934.

HMS *Neptune*

*field and back to Malta before dawn as we would have been a sitting duck for the Luftwaffe in daylight. Fortunately, we did get back before daybreak, but the ship was so badly damaged that it would not put to sea again until the end of March 1942 … and she spent the rest of her time (in) Malta in the dry dock.*[3]

The destroyer *Kandahar* was damaged beyond salvage. Her crew was carefully transferred to the destroyer *Jaguar. Jaguar* then sank the abandoned ship by torpedo. The cruiser *Penelope* also suffered mine damage but it was slight. *Aurora* underwent repairs in Malta to make her seaworthy. When the work was complete after three months, she steamed home to England.

If life for crewmen aboard a ship tied up for yard repairs can be routine or boring, it was anything but that for those dry docked at Malta. Gun crews were kept active for daily Axis bombing attacks. Personnel, whose jobs did not entail gunnery against attacking aircraft or specific repair functions, would be scrambled into nearby shelters carved into the island's rocky cliffs. Other crew members might be sent off to perform duties, as needed, around the island. Marine Gunner Porter remembered his days on Malta after the return of the mine damaged *Aurora*.

HMS *Aurora*

*The 6-inch guns were generally used only against surface ships, so while Aurora was in dry dock, the six inch ammunition was taken off the ship leaving only the 4-inch guns to be manned for use against attacking aircraft. In the event of an air raid, therefore, we 6-inch gun crews were of no use to the ship and the ruling was that anyone not on duty as a watch keeper should leave her and go into the underground shelters in the rocks around the harbor. These shelters were only yards from the ship and … I wouldn't go into them. I think (I) thought it was too sissy to do so, so instead, when off duty (I) stayed on deck while the blitzes were on and had a grandstand view. You'd see twenty or thirty aircraft at a time coming over (and) diving like birds.*

*I do remember one particular occasion, however, when having heard the call, 'all men to blitz stations,' and seen everyone either manning guns or leaving the ship, I decided to have a little sleep by the turret as it was a nice warm day. Unfortunately, our sergeant-major was on top of the turret firing at the Stukas with an Oerlikon gun. When he noticed me, he shouted out, 'Marine Porter, you get in that shelter! That's your duty!' while all the time firing at the enemy planes. I've never seen such coolness and went into the shelter feeling very sheepish.*

*During the time that the ship was laid up, I used to go ashore as much as possible. You could get a little bread and breakfast hotel for sixpence a night. One particular night, I stayed at a hotel on the seafront of Valletta called 'The First and Last'. Up to then the sea front hadn't been bombed. As far as I can recall, I was the only marine from Aurora ashore that night and I fell soundly asleep. When I awoke the following morning, I found that my hotel and two other buildings were the only ones still standing on the sea front. All the others had been blitzed and were just rubble.*[4]

Following the sinking of *Neptune* and *Kandahar* and the damage sustained by *Aurora* and *Penelope*, Force K was disbanded.

## 'The Guns and Turrets Were Pockmarked by Splinters'
### *Penelope's* Ordeal

HMS *Penelope*

After the damage *Penelope* sustained in the minefield off Tripoli in late 1941 was repaired at Malta, the light cruiser returned to duty in the Mediterranean. She served on escort duty for convoys between Malta and Alexandria during the first months of 1942. Having sustained cumulative damage from air attacks, she was finally returned to the drydock at Malta in late March. The shipyard was situated at French Creek, near the city of Senglea, which along with the adjacent Cospicua and Vittoriosa, was one of the Three Cities of Malta. As did practically all Royal Navy ships confined to Maltese dock facilities, *Penelope* wore out many of her gun barrels providing anti-aircraft defense for the harbor as well as for herself. She spent an extended time in the yard to have repairs made to the additional damage she suffered from air attacks even as she was being tended to for her original damage. The heaviest concentration of air attacks endured by Malta took place at the time *Penelope* was docked there. A description of the ship's condition and experiences while in the yard was provided by a correspondent writing for the *Sunday Express*.

> *The scene was Easter Sunday morning* (1942) *in Malta Dockyard. Hitler's Luftwaffe was trying to pulverize the island into subjection. In one of the docks was the cruiser HMS* Penelope. *She had been bombed for days on end, she was shrouded in the light dust of Malta, near misses had made thousands of holes in her, dozens of wooden plugs jutted from her sides where the holes had been filled.*

> *The guns and turrets were pockmarked by splinters. The quarterdeck was like a rock garden, littered with pieces of the dockyard flung up by explosions. Captain A.D. Nicholl, DSO,* Penelope's *commanding officer, clambered on to the after gun turret and, to cheer his tired but willing gunners he led them in song. Standing in the smoke and dust of the last raid and waiting for the next one to start, they sang, 'Get Them in Your Sights' … The song, as one of the officers explained, 'was as abusive as the occasion permitted' … Her story really begins on March 26, after a convoy had been brought into Malta and the Luftwaffe began their ferocious attacks. Soon after lunch on March 26th massive attacks came from formations of Junkers 88s and 87s.* Penelope *sent off parties to help extinguish the fires on other ships.*

*Three hours later another wave of bombers put a bomb down aft of the ship and the jetty. Penelope was holed by this one. Another stick of bombs hit the jetty and one of the close range guns vanished. Next on Friday, the 27th Penelope was moved into dry dock for repairs while the air raids continued. Men who had been working all day in the ship went off through the blitz at night to help unload merchantmen before their cargoes were damaged … Constant heavy raids were causing serious interruption to dockyard work and the solution was for the ship's staff of shipwrights and artificers to co-operate with the dockyard in the work. They … work(ed) day and night through the raids … The captain went ashore and borrowed six Army welders … Next day there were more massed attacks (and when) the oil fuel in the harbor became ignited … men were detached from the ship to help the Malta fire brigade extinguish it.*[5]

Through all the air strikes, crew and yard workers laboured on to get *Penelope* seaworthy. The Germans did not let a single day go by without attacks. They had apparently made *Penelope* their highest priority target. The battle to save the ship went back and forth over two weeks.

*On Friday April 3rd Malta was raided almost continuously from dawn to dusk … All the electrical wiring rigged up in the dock was destroyed and had to be replaced … Saturday, April 4th the bombing continued throughout the day, one bomb near missed, another hit the port after gangway, peppered the port side, holed a propeller shaft, and started a fire … On Easter Monday the German planes did not arrive until early evening. The respite enabled the repairs to the ship to be hurriedly finished … More than 200 bombers came over that evening and there was no doubt that they were all going for Penelope and nothing else … Wednesday, April 8th … (All) had been through so much to save their ship and they were worried sick lest they lost the last trick. They all realised that if they did not get the ship to sea that night they would probably lose her.*[6]

Seventeen-year-old Stoker Eric Beasley was off duty and taking a break from the heat of below decks. He was lying on deck when a bomb hit the jetty adjacent to *Penelope*. He was flung into the air, suffering a fracture to the knee when he landed. He was sent to a hospital ashore that was staffed by British doctors and nurses. The day after his arrival, the hospital was bombed and he was evacuated to a second hospital which was also bombed. The medical staff took what they could from the rubble and transferred all patients to a shelter dug out of a cliff side. Beasley recalled that there was a shortage of fuel so that water for drinking or medical use could not be properly boiled. The desperate consumption of untreated water led to high rates of dysentery among the island's general population. Malnutrition was also rampant, but the young stoker remembered that the Maltese he met remained largely cheerful and supportive of the British.[7]

Communications rating Robin Hopson-Hill was one of *Penelope's* crewmen detached from the ship to perform duties elsewhere on Malta. He was sent to a wireless transmitting station that was used to communicate with Royal Navy submarines at sea. The station was bombed regularly but Hopson-Hill remained fairly safe as the facility, like so many others in Malta, was an underground one. He recalled that each of the German Stukas was equipped with a siren that shrieked loudly as the bombers dived towards a target. He confirmed that the sound's intended purpose of intimidating those under attack was thoroughly achieved. Air raids could not be made in darkness so, at night, the beleaguered sailors would head to a part of Valletta called 'the Gut' for whatever release they could find among its bars, dance halls, and cafés. He remembered a place called the 'Egyptian Queen' where beer flowed freely, men danced on table tops, and the local ladies were always willing to share in and contribute to the fun. At daylight, however, all would return to the fearsome endurance of incessant aerial bombardments.[8]

Finally, on a night in early April, *Penelope* fueled and weighed anchor to steam out of Valletta at her best possible speed for Gibraltar. She was attacked throughout the following day. The ship was near missed by bombs and torpedoes alike. Her ammunition supply was used down to a final sixty rounds. Except for a single mount none of her guns could any longer fire. The ship had a list to starboard and she was down by the head. Men were below decks bailing by hand in up to six feet of water. Other crewmen took loose fittings from the upper decks and tossed them overboard to lighten the ship in order to reduce her chances of going under. Finally, the ship, her crew cheering, made it to Gibraltar. *Penelope* steered to her anchorage by alternating turns with her engine. *Penelope* was safe at last. She would live on to fight another day.

### 'It Was All Much More Glamorous Than Driving a Bus' A Fighter Pilot on Malta

Following her exploits of against the *Bismarck*, aircraft carrier *Ark Royal* returned to Gibraltar on 29 May 1941 to serve in the Mediterranean throughout the summer months. She participated in the screening of Malta bound convoys, attacks on Italian military targets ashore, and the delivery of planes to Malta. Reinforcement aircraft destined for the island were often ferried unassembled from England aboard merchant vessels. They would be put together at Gibraltar prior to delivery to Malta via fly-off from an aircraft carrier in what were called 'club runs'. Sometimes fully assembled planes were carried from England for transfer to the aircraft carrier. They would be manhandled across a rough wooden bridge set up between the delivering ship and the carrier as the two ships lay anchored stern to stern. *Ark Royal* would then steam out to sea to launch the planes to Malta. In order to reduce enemy threats to *Ark Royal* and the other carriers making such deliveries, external fuel tanks were attached to the planes. The ships would then be able to remain safely beyond the range Italian or German air attacks.

RAF pilot Hugh Parry migrated from England to South Africa because he did not know what to do with himself after finishing school at the age of seventeen. He got a job as a surveyor and played a good game of tennis in his spare time. His talent for the game earned him a raise and a transfer to Rhodesia to do the same sort of work while also representing his firm on the courts. When the war began, he felt enough of a combination of patriotism and a sense of adventure to gain passage back to England so that he could join the RAF. He did not know anything about airplanes, but wanted 'just to be a pilot, nothing else'. If he could not do that he '… would have accepted a navigator's job'. Once back in England, he persisted through a complicated process of going from place to place and talking with person after person until he was finally accepted into the RAF. He became a fighter pilot because he '… had read about the Red Baron and all the big aces … (and) it was all much more glamorous than driving a bus …' In a grading system where trainees were rated as exceptional, above average, average, or below average, Parry was consistently marked as average.

After training Parry was assigned to 601 Squadron that was equipped with Spitfires. When his squadron received orders to Malta Parry was clearly aware of the high casualty rate among pilots there. He would have preferred just about any other assignment. 601 was put aboard the American carrier USS *Wasp* that was on loan to the shorthanded Royal Navy. The ship and squadron put to sea with an 'enormous escort' that, according to Parry's admittedly less than perfect memory, included '… two either battlecruisers or battleships … light cruisers … and twenty-four destroyers'.[9]

According to Parry, the American carrier was more suitable than the British ones then available for transporting the Spitfires. Unlike those with which Royal Navy carriers were equipped, *Wasp*'s elevators were large enough to handle Spitfires that did not have folding wings. Parry's chief complaint about the US Navy was that it was 'dry'. He and his fellow RAF pilots were forced to mix aspirin tablets with Coca Cola in order to attain a similar effect to the Royal Navy's rum ration. Playing cards, Parry won a good deal of money from a fellow pilot who told him that he wanted to wait until they arrived on Malta before paying. All were aware that there was a very good chance that he would be wasting his money if Parry were to be shot down. Parry and 601 took off from *Wasp* 35 miles north of Algiers and, staying at wave top altitude, flew the 795 miles to Malta by way of Cape Bon, North Africa. The fliers maintained radio silence because the Luftwaffe had a base on nearby Pantelleria Island that could otherwise detect their presence. In spite of this, Parry could not help but get on his radio to request permission to fire on a slow moving Italian bi-plane that he had sighted. Permission was denied but, just to put a good scare into the Italian pilot, the entire squadron made it a point to fly directly over him.

As soon as the squadron landed, the pilots were told to quickly get out of their planes which were expeditiously refueled and immediately sent back aloft. The experienced RAF personnel on Malta knew that the Germans were aware of the reinforcement flight and either they or the Italians would soon be overhead to attack it. The British were generally relaxed when the Italians appeared because they knew that the Regia Aeronautica was not particularly bold. The

USS *Wasp*

USS *Wasp* with a
Spitfire on board

Italian preference for holding formation for high altitude bomb delivery usually resulted in great inaccuracy. The Germans were another matter. They used a two-engine multi-role aircraft, the JU-88, and the Stuka dive bomber to achieve highly consistent and devastating hits on RAF planes on the ground. It did not help that there was a persistent shortage of anti-aircraft gun batteries on Malta. True to form in the case of Parry's just landed 601, the Germans arrived within minutes to bomb and strafe the airfield. 601's Spitfires were long gone, however. Still, the attrition rate among British planes based on Malta was extremely high. Parry estimated that of a total of about 100 planes delivered by *Wasp,* losses to ground attacks, aerial combat, and other causes quickly reduced the number to just about twenty. Parry admitted to being personally terrified in view of the high odds against him and the other Malta-based pilots.

Axis air attacks on supply convoys approaching Malta and on the island itself were equally intense. Italian and German planes were constantly present and seemingly could go anywhere they pleased. The occasional German pilot who crashed or parachuted onto the island would be immediately set upon by the locals and viciously attacked. But for British military intervention, the pilots would have, according to Parry, been torn apart. The locals seemed to hate the Italians even worse than they did the Germans. Parry correctly surmised that the island's residents seethed at the betrayal by fellow Catholics who were contributing so much to the destruction of property, near starvation conditions and casualties among the populace. For a while Axis pilots who ditched or parachuted into the water would be picked up by a German flying boat. The British, however, had no such means of at-sea rescue and many RAF airmen who went into the water off Malta were lost. The German flying boat would sometimes pick up downed British fliers. These men would, more likely than not, be interrogated thoroughly before being sent on to a POW camp. The British on Malta warned the Luftwaffe that the rescue plane was fair game for attack even though it displayed red crosses on its wings and could pull RAF men from the water. When the Germans ignored the warnings, the plane was shot down. No subsequent German flying boats intent on rescue missions appeared again.

Like everyone else on Malta, the RAF pilots' allotted rations were very scanty. Diets were high in carbohydrates with one of the staples being a type of hardtack that Parry and his companions referred to as 'dog biscuits'. Parry, who became a POW after leaving Malta, recalled that he got more to eat as a prisoner in Germany than he did as a free man on Malta. Parry and his fellow airmen routinely lamented the lack of beer or any other form of alcohol. The closest such beverage available was a local wine that the men could purchase at one of the few local bars. At its best, it was characterised as 'vinegar'. There were opportunities at these same bars, and at one or two of the local hotels, for the men to find female companionship. The women were not always comfortable with what they were doing but, they were willing to exchange favours for food: especially chocolate or cigarettes.

Aside from furtive liaisons in certain bars, there was little contact between military and civilians in the very conservative Maltese society. Some pilots employed locals to help keep their on-base quarters neat and clean. The Maltese houseboys and British got on reasonably well, although theft of small items from among a pilot's property was not unknown. Given the conditions on the island, it was not unusual for a Maltese to abscond with everything if the pilot he worked for were to be shot down.

Most people on the island suffered equally during the siege, but there were a few, including members of the Maltese nobility, who were scarcely deprived. Among the privileged were the Marquis of Scicluna and his family. On the occasion of his daughter Marie Corrine's eighteenth birthday and coming out celebration, the Marquis invited the men of 601 Squadron to his palace. The men went mostly for the food and the alcohol of which they knew there was to plenty. They were astounded by the wealth contained in the house. It even had an extensive model railroad layout housed on the upper floor under a glass skylight. The Marquis invited Parry to play with it which the pilot delightedly did. He stood in the elevated control booth to electronically maneuver and construct trains by coupling and uncoupling cars as if on a real railroad.

When one of 601's pilots claimed that he had become engaged to a particular young woman of high social standing, the power and control of the wealthy and noble families of Malta was quickly demonstrated. The woman's professionally and socially prestigious father had been Malta's attorney general until 1941. The very day after the announcement, the British flier was called to RAF headquarters and presented with orders for an immediate transfer from the island. The woman in question was married in 1942 into a family of long tenured nobility.[10]

### 'There Were Worrying Reports on the Food Shortage'
### Life During the Siege

The heavy toll on supply ships carrying food, fuel, plus other essential stores to Malta came very close to bringing about starvation and the island's surrender. Norman Reginald Gill, a member of the Royal Army Medical Corps, and George Hart, an army bandsman, were both stationed on Malta and spoke in separate interviews about their experiences there. Rita D. Salmon nee Gauci wrote a book titled, *Memories of an English Childhood in Malta* that offers a view of the war on Malta through the eyes of a young girl.

Gill arrived on Malta in late July 1941. He, along with other Royal Army Medical Corps staff and RAF ground crew members, had been carried there by a convoy ship. He spoke about the defeat of an Italian surface navy attack on ships anchored in Valletta's Grand Harbour just a few days after his arrival.

*So here we were in Malta … We'd heard about (it) … It had had a terrific battering since Italy came into the war, several hundred raids and lots of fatalities they said. The signs of damage were all there … the three cities as they were called, Cospicua, Vittoriosa and Senglea, housed the dockyard workers and had been terribly battered. The area all around the Grand Harbour was a tremendous mess, and the Naval Hospital at Bighi had been put out of action (which) was probably the reason why it was considered necessary to reinforce the medical personnel on the island.*

*We were happy to survive (the) Mediterranean convoy (that brought us) but we weren't happy to have landed in Malta which showed such devastation. Of course, much worse was to come later … the second night – about two o'clock in the morning – we were awoken by the most terrific row as every gun on the island appeared to be firing, including guns we hadn't heard before. We were quite familiar, after two days, with anti-aircraft guns but long-range guns were firing, too. We had a 230mm – 9.2-inch – battery about 2 km. away from the hospital and when those opened up the whole hospital seemed to shake. This went on for quite a time and the whole island was lit up by flashes of shellfire which appeared to be going out to sea. We*

*all thought the Italian fleet was standing off the coast of Malta preparing to*
*blast the place. This was something we always feared … After an hour or so*
*it all died down and we heard on the Maltese radio the next day that some*
*20 Italian motor torpedo boats had attempted to sink the convoy in Grand*
*Harbor … every gun within range on the island had opened up and their*
*(defeat) was, of course, a tremendous morale booster for the Maltese forces.*[11]

Rita Salmon's father was in the Maltese Army. She, her mother, and siblings
had arrived on Malta in 1938 while she was still quite young. The family lived
in a modest house of two bedrooms, a cook room, and a WC. The house was
enlarged when the Axis bombing attacks began. Inspired by the local farmers'
use of natural rock caves, the father dug out a rock-side in which he placed
bunks for sleeping. The shelter-dormitory was lit by wick oil lamps and the
children, once ordered in, were not to go back outside without permission.

Writing her book many years afterward, Salmon, and by then using her
husband's name of Gauci, made mention of 'Victory Kitchens'. These were
community kitchens first established in January 1942 by government decree
in an effort to minimize wastage and to equalize food distribution throughout
the island. Within six months, as the island faced increasingly meager food
supplies, there were forty-two such kitchens. Food was collected from farmers
and other food producing communities to be used by the kitchens. Citizens
were required to sign up to receive food cooked at the kitchens which they
would, in take-out fashion, bring home. In exchange, they had to give up a
portion of their tinned meat, preserved fish, and fats rations to the kitchens. The
meals they received were prepared from items that were both on and off of the
rationed commodities lists.

There was a popular 'Victory Kitchen Song' whose lyrics in English were:

*Baked pasta in trays and people in array at the Victory Kitchens.*
*Minestra and sardines, pasta and beans at the Victory Kitchens.*
*What a treat on New Years Day!*
*They made us eat sardines at the Victory Kitchens.*
*Their legs are so fat, they eat so much grub.*
*The girls at the Victory Kitchens.*

*Their hair set all wavy to flirt with the boys in the navy.*
*The girls at the Victory Kitchens.*
*The kitchen staff was not slow to retaliate by saying we served you goat's*
*     meat that you had to eat from the Victory Kitchens.*[12]

Gauci recalled the constant food shortages on Malta.

*Our water came from a well and had to be boiled and there was also a tap*
*some distance away with the slogan, 'waste not; want not' engraved (on it)*
*… as the war progressed and food got shorter we were in rather a difficult*
*position. The local farmers lived off the land and we could buy food from*
*them or from the local village shop. But as the food got shorter the farms had*
*all the produce confiscated for the Victory Kitchen. We were friends with the*
*entire village and they helped all they could. Mum would make them cakes*
*whenever any flour was available and knit in exchange for fruit or eggs. I*
*would go round to the villages to families (that had) a baby and goats. In*
*return for rocking the baby in a hammock I would get a cup of goat's milk.*
*My father had an arrangement with the cookhouse (at his army base) that he*
*could have whatever rations were available to him for the week and he would*
*bring it home. Mum would eke it out for the five of us. Father's typical ration*
*was a tin of corned beef, a tin of herrings in tomato sauce (and) perhaps*
*army biscuits which were … hard tack. He would also barter for food (as) the*
*farmers were desperate for machine oil for the pumps in the fields.*

*The food situation was getting very bad … the ration initially was a loaf*
*of bread, three ounces of fat, 1¾ ounce of cheese, 1¼ ounce of coffee,*
*three pints of milk, three pounds of tomatoes, 1½ pounds of potatoes,*
*and eight gallons of water. No sugar, pasta, tea, oil, butter, soap, meat or*
*fish. This was, of course, if you were near enough to a town with a supply.*
*I remember walking three miles once for a small loaf of bread. All the*
*confiscated food was given to the Victory Kitchens to be made into soup.*
*We visited an aunt (once) and I went with her for a bowl of soup. It was*
*very meagre and had very little in it. It looked like clear soup to me. Aunt*
*said it would be good for me!*[13]

Gauci's narrative depicts a good relationship between the military personnel and the civilians on Malta. Despite their own hardships, it appears that soldiers, sailors, and airmen would take time and pains to offer small favours and kindness to those living on the besieged island.

> *One Christmas ten soldiers from the camp at Ghain Tuffiegha came to our home with their dinners and Mum shared it out between us all ... That year, 1942, I had a book given to me called,* The Jungle Man And His Animals *by Carveth Wells. I didn't know the soldier but his name was Sgt. Wells. I know I had to write and say thank you. I also had a dolls house my dad brought home that one of the soldiers had made. All the doors and drawers opened ... The camp cobbler made us hob-nailed sandals and Mum knitted us rope-soled sandals. We rather liked the hob-nailed sandals as they made a lovely loud noise ... During one very big raid on the army camp several of the soldiers were killed. At that time I was covered in scabies and had to go to the camp Doctor, who had to soak the bandages off my arms and legs (Mum had to boil the bandages), then he would cover the sores with sulphar (sic) ointment, made with lard, which we had to supply ... There was also a naval rest camp at Ghain Tuffiegha. The sailors were off the battle ships and I remember all were in a very sad state of shock. They were very kind to us and would come to see Mum and tell her all about what had happened to them. They would bring a bar of soap or chocolate if they had any.*[14]

Army medic Gill also remembered the scarcity of food, lack of nutrition, and drastic weight loss.

> *There were worrying reports on the food shortage. Certainly our rations were pretty terrible and all veterans will remember the hunger. The water we drank was heavily chlorinated. There was no butter, cheese, eggs, milk. In fact, it would be easier to say what there was. Corned beef, dry biscuits, and Chinese pilchards* (sardines). *At least they* (the tins) *had Chinese writing on the front ... That was all there was ... (One of the cooks) would curry, he would fritter, he would boil, he would fry bully beef. He would*

*soften the biscuits and make some sort of mishmash of biscuits and corned beef with a few pilchards worked into the mixture and, for those of us as hungry as we were, it was very acceptable … (In August 1942) the supply situation, however, got worse and worse and we were told that our rations would be cut again. We were really hungry. I had weighed almost 70 kg but by the end of 1942 I was down to 50 kg … I think that we were all just skeletons. If you've been subjected to starvation for a long period, a key rule is never talk about food. We all thought about it, but if anyone said, 'wouldn't it be nice if we had steak and chips', they were immediately jumped on.*

*The other thing from a morale point of view was the irregular mail. It was a terribly difficult journey for an unescorted transport plane to make and a lot were shot down. A lot of sea mail was also lost on ships sunk trying to get to Malta … There was a submarine flotilla which managed to survive in Malta and they would bring vital supplies; aviation fuel, some ammunition, and some mail. When I did receive letters, it was sometimes three at a time but I did appreciate this contact with home.*[15]

Marine Musician George Hart was sent to Malta in 1938 as a bandsman but, when war was declared in 1939, he was handed a rifle and turned into an ordinary soldier. He spent the first year of the war in relatively quiet fashion helping to string barbed wire and place sand bags around the island. Once Italy declared war, things changed. Action came quickly in the form of regular bombing raids.

Hart stated that the British and the Maltese did not tend to mix, although there were some marriages between Maltese women and British service personnel. He thought that the men were lonely and the women were seeking a way off the island. Aside from farming, Malta had no industry or business. The island did not appear to offer much in the way of a future for its young people. According to Hart, courtship on Malta could not have been very exciting for any of his fellow servicemen. The Maltese remained very conservative in their ways and would only allow their daughters to go out with British men under close scrutiny of at least one chaperone. For the rest of the men who missed female companionship, there was a section of Valletta called the 'Gut' which was along the narrow thoroughfare of Strait Street. It was lined with bars and clubs where sailors could go for a little music, drinking, or dancing. Hart recalled that each club had its own little band and a small contingent of girls who would dance with the male clients. The companionship, he reiterated, was limited to dancing. Some veterans might have recalled differently, but, according to Hart, there was nothing that even resembled a brothel on the island. 'The chances for vice were slim.'

As many other Malta veterans have stated, Hart did not think of the Regia Aeronautica as particularly effective. He felt that the Germans were much better fliers, equipped with larger and louder bombs, and far more accurate than their Italian counterparts. Still, he did not think that the loss of life was particularly heavy on Malta as the shelters dug into the hillsides offered very effective protection. Buildings, however, were made of soft sandstone and collapsed rather easily to leave a very large mess. Along with everyone else, Hart's chief discomfort was that of hunger. He managed to raise some chickens, but they were good only for their eggs as they were too scrawny to have made good eating.[16]

ENDNOTES

1.  erniesdaughter (contributor). 'Sunset.' BBC WW2 *People's War*. Article ID A 4452734. 2005.

2.  _____'Malta and Force K.' HistoryLearningSite.co.uk. 2011 Web. Accessed June 2014.

3.  Porter, John Robert. 'HMS *Aurora*.' Wartimememoriesproject.com. Web. Accessed June 2014.

4.  Porter.

5.  Smart, Norman. 'This is the Immortal Story of HMS *Penelope*.' world-war.co.uk. Web. Accessed June 2014. Originally published in the *English Sunday Press*, 24 May 1942.

6.  Smart.

7.  Imperial War Museum. Sound recoring archive. 11255. Beasley, Eric. 1990.

8.  Imperial War Museum. Sound recording archive. 21657. Hopson-Hill, Robin Knowling. n.d.

9.  Imperial War Museum. Sound recording archive. 8985. Parry, Hugh Lawrence. 1985.

10.  Imperial War Museum. 8985.

11.  Gill, Reginald. 'The Siege of Malta, Part One.' BBC WW2 *People's War*. Article ID A 2902132. 2004.

12.  _____'Maltese Food in the War – Victory Kitchens.' ilovefood.com.mt. Web. Accessed February 2014.

13.  Salmon, Rita D. 'Memories of an English Childhood in Malta, Chapter 2.' BBC WW2 *People's War*. Article ID A 4453517. 2005.

14.  Salmon, Rita D. 'Memories of an English Childhood in Malta, Chapter 3.' BBC WW2 *People's War*. Article ID A 4452823. 2005.

15.  Gill, Reginald. 'The Siege of Malta, Part Two.' BBC WW2 *People's War*. Article ID A 2902222. 2004.

16.  Imperial War Museum. Sound recording archive. 10454. Hart, Dennis. 1988.

# ELEVEN
# SHOCK OF THE RISING SUN

Following her exploits against *Graf Spee* in 1939 heavy cruiser *Exeter* was decommissioned for a lengthy refit. The ship recommissioned and returned to duty with a new crew in March 1941. It was against the backdrop of ever rising Japanese power and ambitions in Asia that *Exeter* was sent to Colombo in October. In December she was part of a troop convoy bound for Singapore when Japan attacked Pearl Harbor and declared war against the United States and Britain. *Exeter* and the Singapore convoy were attacked by Japanese dive bombers and torpedo planes, but the cruiser was not once hit. Her captain took it upon himself to lie down on the flat of his back in order to better see his attackers. His precise orders to the helm for evasive steering kept *Exeter* from harm. The gunnery department also used the tactic of firing the ship's main battery of 8-inch guns at low flying torpedo planes. Instead of hoping to hit an oncoming plane, the gunfire was directed at a spot in the water ahead of the attacker. A heavy curtain of spray would be raised by the shell's impact to either throw a pilot off course or misdirect an otherwise properly aimed torpedo.

The first two months of the Pacific war were busy and successful ones for the Japanese Imperial Navy. Following 'Top Secret Operational Order No. 1,' it was intent on having Britain and the Dutch driven from the East Indies and America ousted from the Philippines. By mid-February 1942, Japan had either managed, or was well on the way to the following goals: the destruction of the American Fleet at Pearl Harbor, the invasion of Siam, and the conquest of the Philippines, British Malaya, Singapore, Borneo, Sumatra, and Java. In addition to the fulfillment of her self-declared hegemonic destiny, Japan sought to establish a defensive barrier against any future American counterattack from the east. Tokyo expected that control of the region's natural resources of oil, timber, rubber and minerals would lead Japan to quick victory.[1]

The Allied response was to do whatever it could to halt the Japanese advance in the East Indies. They formed themselves into the nominally unified American, British, Dutch, and Australian, or ABDA command. Unfortunately, their military resources in the region were few in number, scattered, and operationally unfamiliar with one another. In February *Exeter* steamed south to Java where she joined ABDA. The command's largest warships were *Exeter* and the American heavy cruiser, USS *Houston* which were backed by seven light cruisers, about 20 destroyers, a handful of submarines, and half dozen auxiliary ships. ABDA had no aircraft carriers and the availability of land-based air support was practically non-existent. Meanwhile, Japan's forces in the area included some of her most modern and powerful ships: two battleships, 13 heavy cruisers, five light cruisers, two small aircraft carriers, four of the large aircraft carriers that had raided Pearl Harbor, and numerous destroyers. The warships were accompanied by an invasion force consisting of many troop transports and heavily laden supply ships.[2]

## 'We Went Into Action'
### HMS *Exeter* and the Battle of the Java Sea

As ABDA was coming together, the Japanese launched an air attack against the port at Darwin in efforts to cut the sea link between Java and Australia.

An aerial view of
HMS *Exeter*

Oil rich Dutch Borneo had already fallen as had Bali off the eastern tip of Java. The next Japanese targets were the ports of Batavia (Jakarta) and Surabaya on Java's northern coast. Late that month, an ABDA cruiser-destroyer force under command of Dutch Admiral Karel Doorman was ordered out of Surabaya to meet the oncoming Japanese invasion force. Doorman had overall command of *Exeter* and USS *Houston*, Australian light cruiser HMAS *Perth*, Dutch light cruisers HNMS *Java* and *de Ruyter*, and nine destroyers of mixed national origins. The Japanese force was about 50 miles north of Doorman's position. The Imperial Navy steamed southward with two heavy cruisers, two light cruisers, fourteen destroyers, and many heavily loaded troop transports and supply ships.

Admiral Doorman requested air cover but, unsurprisingly, was informed that there could be none. When the ABDA ships sighted the Japanese force on the horizon, Doorman's ships were disposed in two columns: one of cruisers and the other of the destroyers. *Exeter* was the second in the line of five cruisers which sped ahead to meet the enemy. The two Japanese heavy cruisers opened fire first and the Japanese light cruiser, serving as a destroyer flotilla leader, brought her column of destroyers into action against that of the ABDA force. The Japanese light cruiser opened fire and immediately straddled a British destroyer. The opposing cruiser columns had been steaming on a parallel track, but the Japanese executed a turn to port that could have placed them perpendicular to the ABDA column. This would have allowed the Japanese to steam by the head of the column of ABDA ships to consume them with raking fire from all guns. The ABDA cruisers would have only been able to answer with their forward guns. Admiral Doorman took the advantage away from the Japanese, however, by making his own turn to port to bring his column back on parallel track with theirs. *Exeter* and *Houston* fired at their enemies.

Thomas Adams joined the Navy when he was fifteen after seeing a former schoolmate who had joined earlier home on leave. He asked his friend if he could try on his uniform and, when he did, he was very taken with the way he looked. Just a week later, he had a uniform of his own. He began service as a boy seaman. He was thirty-two years old with over fifteen years in the Navy as a gunner and gunnery instructor when he reported aboard *Exeter* when she recommissioned. He remembered the battle with the Japanese.

*We left Surabaya on February 27th to intercept what a Dutch reconnaissance aircraft had reported as a convoy of merchant ships. When eventually we encountered them, we found that it was a very strong force of warships … We went into action led by the Dutch cruiser and the Dutch Admiral … who steamed into attack in line ahead. He opened fire at a range of about 24,000 yards when the maximum range of his guns was about 18,000 … we fought an action where all the shot from the Dutch cruisers was falling short so that the target was obscured from our controls. I was enclosed in the turret … we were informed by control of roughly what was happening. And then after about an hour we received a hit on S2 4-inch gun … that was the second of our antiaircraft guns on the starboard side which was manned by the Royal Marines. The shell which landed there went through the deck and down by pure bad fortune for us, good luck for the Japanese, it went down through the hatchway into the boiler room, and exploded in the boiler room bursting the main steam pipe in B boiler room. That meant that we lost all power; our dynamos were off the board and as all our main armament was operated electrically we were out of action … we were forced to reduce speed to six knots and* (Australian light cruiser) Perth *and* (American heavy cruiser) Houston *made a smoke screen and allowed us to escape out of the line and we limped back to Surabaya. We were to discover afterwards that the whole of our fleet was either sunk or dispersed … One English destroyer, the* Encounter, *and one American destroyer, the* Pope, *came back (with us)….*[3]

Even though the hit on *Exeter* did not actually explode as Adams stated, it nonetheless caused the ship to lose speed. In order to avoid being rammed from behind by *Houston*, *Exeter* turned sharply to port. This was interpreted by *Houston* as a maneuver to follow, which she did. The next two ships in line, *Perth* and *Java*, did likewise, and the ABDA line was now hopelessly out of formation.

Doorman ordered a destroyer attack to cover the broken line and to allow *Exeter* time to clear to safety, but the action was ineffective. The British destroyer *Electra* was sunk. Shortly afterward, another British destroyer, *Jupiter*, exploded and was lost when she hit what was probably a Dutch mine. Formation with the four as yet undamaged cruisers and a destroyer was eventually regained, but the Japanese launched a torpedo attack which sank the two Dutch cruisers. Before his ship went down, Admiral Doorman ordered *Houston* and *Perth* to turn for Batavia, but the Japanese caught up with them in the Sunda Strait and they were overwhelmed. The surviving ABDA destroyers straggled back to port, but the allies' overall effort had been thoroughly futile. But for several hits on a single destroyer, the Japanese suffered no damage. The invasion convoy remained intact and was not at all delayed from its mission.[4]

### 'Abandon Ship!'
### The End for *Exeter*

*Exeter* made port at Surabaya just before midnight of 27 February. The crew made what repairs they could, offloaded the seriously wounded, and buried the dead. As night gave way to light, Japanese aircraft appeared and made frequent attacks

HMS *Exeter* under
attack

which *Exeter* managed to hold off with heavy fire from her 4-inch guns. When darkness fell on the 28th, *Exeter*, accompanied by her destroyer companions USS *Pope* and HMS *Encounter,* departed with the intention of making a break eastward to Colombo.[5]

Even as she was underway, *Exeter's* engineering department worked with urgency on her damaged boilers. They had gotten the cruiser up to 23 knots when a lookout spotted the masts of two ships on the horizon. These were the Japanese heavy cruisers *Nachi* and *Haguro*. Nearby were two more hostile heavy cruisers, *Ashigara* and *Myoko* along with two destroyers. The Japanese opened fire first. *Pope* and *Encounter* made smoke to screen *Exeter*. *Exeter* returned fire, but electrical problems with her fire control systems caused her shells to fall off target. The Japanese were being spotted for by a plane overhead and their gunners immediately straddled the British cruiser. *Exeter* turned towards a rain squall in hopes that it could conceal her well enough to allow for an escape. Her main battery engaged the Japanese cruisers while her secondary battery, *Pope,* and *Encounter* dueled with the Japanese destroyers. *Exeter* also launched torpedoes at her tormentors, but she soon suffered a crippling hit to another of her boiler rooms. The ship's electrical power went off so that none of her guns were able to fire. *Encounter* was soon hit and sunk. *Pope* would outlast her two companions only to succumb to dive bombers just a few hours later. Gunner Adams recalled the action.

*We steamed through Saturday night and at first light on Sunday morning (1 March), sighted Japanese warships. Once again, I went to action stations in my turret … we engaged the first of the enemy … it was about 0900 on Sunday morning and we continued in action then until 1130 during which time A turret, of which I was captain … my position as gunnery instructor … had fired some 600 rounds of 8-inch ammunition at the Japanese, to what effect I wouldn't like to say. I've read the Japanese account of it and we had only scored two hits according to them, but my talks with our gunnery officer … led me to believe that we did far better than that … once again the Japs had one lucky hit and that burst the main steam pipe in the other boiler room. We were then completely helpless … gradually coming to a stop … so the next thing I heard was over our tannoy system … was 'Abandon ship! Sink the ship!' I was flabbergasted because at no time had I ever even dreamed we weren't going to get out of it … the last thing that I thought was that my ship was going to get sunk, but that was a fact, and the captain ordered us to sink the ship … (We) proceeded to abandon ship. I … and some others attempted to get one of the whalers out … but I found myself in the water … I was swimming around … and eventually found some of the others in the water. The Japanese [6.] were very close to us and they were beginning to pick up survivors … they picked up some and then steamed away and we were left there.[7.]*

### 'It Seemed a Policy to Humiliate Us'
### Prisoners

*Exeter* went down after her seacocks had been opened and explosive charges had been set in some of her propulsion spaces. Her captain could not risk that the enemy might salvage her for his own uses. The following day, a number of Japanese destroyers reappeared and took all the remaining survivors they could find. Those pulled from the water included men from *Pope, Encounter,* and *Exeter.* Although saved from the sea, none of the survivors were treated with any particular kindness. Most of the men who later spoke about the experience told of being left to sit on the open decks of the Japanese destroyers and of being hit when they could not move quickly enough to satisfy their captors. *Exeter* survivor, Cecil Rowse, who was a supply rating in his early twenties at the time, wrote a letter home that was made public by his wife in September 1945. A portion of the letter describes Rowse's first days with the Japanese.

*We drifted round all night and all next day, until four o'clock the following afternoon, when a Jap destroyer came into view and finally hauled us out of the water. Out of the original sixteen* (in Rowse's group), *two had died during the night – one had been wounded in the stomach by shrapnel from exploding shells while in the water, and the other had swallowed a lot of oil … It was difficult to hoist my hind quarters out of the water and when I did, I found that my legs were so thoroughly water logged that I could not stand. This inability did not go well with 'Churchill's funny little yellow men' who proceeded to plant a few hefty kicks in the ribs just by way of a greeting … However, I got planted on the forecastle of the ship with about 100 others who had been picked up previously. While sitting here I noticed that our guards were going round taking the rings, watches, etc. off of the fellows …* (Rowse then deliberately threw his watch overboard) *… this action was observed by one of the guards who gave me a wallop over the head with a rifle butt and laid me out … We were issued with two ship's hard biscuits through the evening and some water … We arrived at Makassar* (northeast of Java) *on March 10th where we were marched about three miles bare footed over red hot roads in the middle of the day. We must have presented a lovely sight, with the captain in the front rank and us trailing behind, looking very bedraggled with oil covering us … We had received no clothes as yet (and) some of the fellows were negative trousers. It seemed to be the policy of the Japs to humiliate us as much as possible … for this I can never forgive them.*[8]

Gunnery Instructor Adams was eventually picked up to spend a full day on a

Japanese destroyer. He and his companions were taken to a captured Dutch hospital ship that was still staffed by Dutch personnel. After a week during which the wounded were cared for aboard the ship, the prisoners were transferred to the same Makassar camp that held Cecil Rowse. Adams' group was placed into what had previously been a horse stable. The men were placed eight to a stall. The Japanese recognized that Adams was a senior rating so they assigned him to act as a kitchen supervisor. He took to the task and made certain that food rations were fairly and evenly distributed to his fellow prisoners. The typical food doled out was rice that had been cooked into a soft porridge accompanied by coffee for breakfast. Cooked rice and some greens made up the afternoon meal and, in the evening, there was a miniscule meat ration that often amounted to little more than a greasy liquid. Eventually, many prisoners would find or make items that they could barter through the fence with native Indonesians for a little extra food.

### 'A Handful of Rice and a Dried Fish Head'
### Life in the Camps

Another *Exeter* crewman, Ordnance Artificer Doug Grant, was eighteen when he was originally to have been posted to Glasgow in his native Scotland. It was a duty station that he did not relish.

> ... I told the lieutenant in charge – 'you can't send me there, sir. I joined the Navy to get away from the damn place.' And I was lucky. There was a young fellow who had just got married and was being assigned to Colombo to await posting. So I swapped with him. He went to Glasgow and I went to Colombo and was eventually assigned to Exeter.[9]

Grant was working in Y turret as his ship vainly fought for survival. One of the shell hoists to the turret had gotten jammed. He worked for what he felt was hours trying to free it so that its gun would be able to fire. He managed to free the jam, but was so exhausted by the effort that all he could do for a time afterwards was to lie atop a pile of shells that had accumulated in the turret. He could barely move. It was from that position that he heard the order to abandon ship. Not being a swimmer, Grant carefully inflated his life belt before jumping into the water after a Carley float. The ship was still making way forward as the Japanese continued to shoot at it. Grant was picked up several hours later to begin a three and a half year ordeal as a Japanese prisoner of war. Entries from Grant's preserved diary provide a look at what life was like for some of *Exeter*'s men in prison camp.

> *March 9, 1942. Arrived off Makassar. Not much of a place to look at ... Not bad as prison camps go. It was a native military camp before the Dutch ran to the hills ... where sixteen native soldiers lived, eighty (prisoners) live now ... one thing in its favour ... it's all stone floors so we'll be able to keep it fairly clean ... at 6 pm we got two biscuits each, the first we've had since 8 am and that consisted of about an eighth part of a biscuit and a watery cup of coffee so we didn't hesitate digging into the hardtack ... Turned in on the stone deck and I don't mind telling you it's bloody cold and on top of that we are practically eaten alive by mosquitoes.*[10]

Some of the prisoners were paid a small salary for being put to work. Others were able to sell their meager possessions to the locals for a few cents. Because food was scarce, the money would usually be spent on the purchase of extra rations from natives near the camp. Much of Grant's diary contains entries that are centered on themes that are common to the memories of practically all of his fellow POWs: the scarcity of food and constant hunger.

> *Half a bun for breakfast this morning ... At 5 pm we get our next meal ... a handful of rice and a dried fish head ... It's the most awful looking thing I've ever seen ... it stinks like hell and the flies have been crawling all over it ... but as I'm semi-starving it tasted delicious ... Some prisoners are even boiling up grass to try to make soup and some are catching sparrows. You have to have about ten of them before you can taste anything. I sold my (navy issue) shorts for 35 cents. I bought four eggs and three small native buns. ... Sold my breakfast this morning for 25 cents ... Went working party and had a swell time in the grass cutting party. At stand easy the Jap guards opened up a case of ship's biscuits and gave us three each. When*

*dinner time came I was able to buy five cents worth of banana fritters* (from local residents who were not prisoners) *before the lorry came with dinner (consisting) of rice, greens and an egg – then the Japs brought down what had been left of their meal … I got a whopping big ladle filled with meat and greens and by God it was lovely. The finest thing I tasted since I left the ship.* [11]

Grant, as did many other prisoners, worried that his family would not know what had become of him. He did not want them to worry or to think that he might be dead. In most cases it would not be until the end of the war before the ones left behind would know for certain how their sailors had fared. On the home front the sister, then a mere child, of an *Exeter* sailor recalled her family's ordeal following the ship's loss.

*I was only three years old when the war started … My brother, Raymond, worked for the electricity company at the time but, knowing that he would get called up, enlisted in the Royal Navy … The first and last time I saw Raymond in his Navy uniform was at Christmas 1940 when he was home on leave. He made a very impressive sight for a four year old! On 1st March 1942 my brother's ship … was … sunk in the Java Sea. My family was sent an awful telegram saying that he was 'missing, presumed dead' … Some months later, another telegram arrived telling us that, in fact, Raymond was alive and living in a Japanese prisoner of war camp. We had no way of knowing what conditions were like in these camps and this gave us renewed hope … There was no more news until March 1945, when a further telegram arrived to tell us that Raymond had died. Now aged nine I screamed 'blue murder' when I heard the news and I was scared to sleep at nights. My other brother kept it all inside and my mother convinced herself that the telegram must be wrong and Raymond was still alive. There was no counselling available for anyone. A little while after the war, Dick Best, a (friend) of my brother's on HMS* Exeter *and in the camp came to (our home). He remained in contact with the family until he died in 1992 and I still have contact with his wife … As a child, I was asked whether I felt any animosity towards the Japanese because of my brother's death. At the time, my innocence led me to assert that I was not aware that any animosity should be felt or a grudge borne. However, when after my mother's death, Dick told me how Raymond had died horribly at the hands of his captors, my feelings welled up. I have a strong Christian faith, however, and through prayer and reconciliation I was able to forgive and move on.*[12]

The British prisoners were mixed in with those of other nationalities; notably Dutch and American. As they were all in the same situation, they tended to get on well together. They spent many hours talking to one another about the life and culture of their respective countries. Prisoners were organised into work parties that would spend early morning until about 6 pm at manual labour of various types. The Japanese allowed the men to organise themselves as they saw fit. The British developed a system in which every man would be able to rotate through a series of types of work in an equitable fashion. There was little, if anything, be it food, clothing, or medication that the Japanese would provide for the prisoners. Whenever possible the men would steal from the Japanese.

*… stealing wasn't theft as we know it now. It was stealing from the Japanese which was part of the war effort. We just stole anything and everything … Food, principally, if we could steal anything to eat, that was the main thing, but otherwise we stole anything we could use to barter with the natives for food … a working party one day, while they were unloading a ship, discovered a case of Gillette razor blades which they promptly confiscated and hid away until they could get them into camp … the Japanese never knew who took the razor blades but (they) were so sure it was us … (so) they issued an order for everyone to shave.*[13]

Discipline was strict and punishment for even the most minor infractions against Japanese established rules was harsh. Any failing on the part of a prisoner was usually treated with a sound beating. A man would be stood up and hit across the buttocks with a baseball bat. A 'light' sentence was forty blows, but 200 were not unusual. There was also the withholding of food. On the other hand, good behaviour or work well performed was sometimes rewarded with extra rations. Escape, while instilled by all branches of the military as an obligation of the fighting man, was not a realistic option. The prisoners understood that they were white men on an island of brown skinned natives. There would be no place to go or hide if they were to leave the confines of their camp. The closest friendly territory was in Australia, 600 miles away over water.

Although practically all of the Japanese guards were cruel, harsh, or, at best, indifferent there were some exceptions. Gunner Adams and some of his fellow prisoners were at work clearing a patch of jungle when one of the guards who had occasionally done little favours for them offered the prisoners a surprise. According to Adams,

> … one day (the guard who had been kind) gave us a present … a yak, the Asian beast of burden. (It was) one that had gone past its useful working life … he brought this old yak into the camp and presented it to me. I promptly said, 'Well, shoot it.' He said that he'd never killed anything in his life. I said, 'Lend me your gun.' He gave me his gun … and I fired one round at it and I hit it fair and square between the eyes and the poor old yak just grunted and looked at me and didn't flinch. I said, 'Well give me one more shot.' He gave me another shot and I fired and put another hole about an inch and half below the first one … the yak then went down on its front knees and spouted a little bit of blood out its nostrils … still very much alive … (the guard then) told me to take shelter behind some bamboo poles … in case the yak should charge me … I asked for one more shot, and with the third shot I killed the yak. The outcome of this was that we had so much meat we couldn't eat it all. We lived like fighting cocks for a week or so … and I suppose it did quite a bit in keeping us alive.[14]

## 'A Colossal Sheet of Flame Shot Into the Air'
## The Atomic Bomb at Nagasaki

After some time, a group of prisoners, Ordnance Artificer Grant among them, was sent to Japan to be used as labourers in a dockyard near Nagasaki. They would stay there until the war's end. Grant witnessed to the dropping of the second American atomic bomb.

*At 11 o'clock (on 09 August 1945), I was standing at the workbench when, from behind the hill in the direction of Nagasaki, a colossal sheet of flame shot into the air ... followed almost immediately by the most terrific explosion ... (it was) like the flash of a million photographer's light bulbs at one time ... (most thought) a concentration of oil tanks had been hit (by air raid) that caused the terrific sheet of flame, the heat of which we felt even though we were seven or eight miles away ... I myself thought that they had struck a cordite dump because the flame was so intensely blinding ... (Later) boatloads of injured severely burned (arriving) ... hundreds of wooden caskets being made by girls for the dead ... pretty grim ... we have heard that between fifty and sixty thousand were killed in the explosion.*

Grant and the other prisoners were freed shortly after the Japanese surrender. His diary entry for 25 August states,

*My 23rd birthday today and I have the best present I have ever received: FREEDOM! This will be my fourth birthday in prison camp ... the next one I will be having Mom's famous treacle pudding and, oh boy, am I looking forward to that!*

As glad as he was to be free and to have the war over, Grant made an undated entry to his diary in which he expressed some of his thoughts and feelings about the atomic bomb.

*After a couple of days of medical and radiation checks we finally left our prison. I am sure it will affect the lives of all of us imprisoned there, both physically and mentally for the remainder of our lives ... After our release from camp we were taken into Nagasaki (to) witness the awful destruction ... Unbelievable ... There are no words to describe that terrible scene. I will always wonder if we will ever be able to justify using such a terrible weapon against innocent civilians or even a cruel enemy such as the Japanese were.*

Even in 2009, Grant maintained concerns that the atomic bombing of Nagasaki represented an unnecessary and excessive use of military power.

*I can understand Hiroshima. It was first and it did end the war for which*
*I must be eternally grateful. But, Nagasaki? I really don't think that can*
*ever be justified. The war was over with Hiroshima. That was enough.*[15]

### 'I Can Never Forget … and I Can Never Forgive'

As the war dragged into its final year, the men held at Makassar began to die at higher rates than before. They had been weakened, injured, and made ill by the grind of manual labour, lack of food, shortage of medical care, and unhealthy climate. There were several doctors among the prisoners, but with no medication or medical instruments, there was little that they could do. Malaria and dysentery were two of the most common causes of death. At one point, the Japanese attempted to contain malarial outbreaks by assigning each man to a daily quota of seventy mosquitoes killed. They were issued strips of sticky paper on which to place any mosquitoes that they caught. Typically, any man who failed to meet his quota would be beaten. The men countered by breaking the mosquitoes into two or more pieces since the guards would usually count any part of one, no matter how large or small as a whole mosquito. As might be expected, the measure did nothing to contain the disease. Men continued to falter and die.

In the waning days of the war, there were frequent American air raids. Food supplies, even for the Japanese, dwindled. One day, a bomb struck a nearby pig farm. There were so many animals killed that the guards could even afford to bring carcasses to the prisoners. Many, because they were already suffering from intestinal disorders, became violently ill from overeating. Some even died. The uncertainty of future food sources and the persistent hunger compelled the men to bury what they could not immediately eat for later consumption. This ultimately caused as much harm as good.

The American airstrikes suddenly ceased without resumption for several weeks. The men, who had never gotten any news better than that created by rumor, surmised that the war might be nearly over. When the Japanese divided them into three groups of relatively healthy, partially ambulatory, and non-ambulatory men, the prisoners knew that the end had to be near. Some could communicate with their guards who told them that those prisoners who could not walk would be shot when the Americans landed. The others would be carried into the hills, possibly as hostages for bargaining. This did not happen as, before long, the Americans located the camp. They landed in large flying boats and removed the men from *Pope* along with all other American prisoners. Soon afterwards, Australian commandos entered the camp to liberate the British and Dutch prisoners.

He was sixty years old when Thomas Adams spoke of his post war condition:

> *I was invalided out of the service (in 1946) ... with very bad eyesight ... I was left with ... very limited use of my limbs ... I've got no feeling at all in my fingertips or on my face ... and then I had so much dysentery that ... I still have an awful lot of bowel trouble. However, there are a lot worse off than me ... (As for my feelings towards the Japanese) ... well, I bought a record player, and when I went into the shop to buy that, I told the assistant that I would buy any record player he had so long as it had no Japanese parts in it ... no matter what anybody says ... I can never forget and it is a certainty that I can never forgive ... We have to accept that life has to go on but don't ask me to be any part of it ... If I saw (any Japanese) laying on the ground, he'd lay there; I wouldn't pick him up and I wouldn't expect him to pick me up.[16]*

About fifty men were killed in *Exeter*'s two gun battles against the Japanese. Of the approximately 650 men who took to the water as their ship sank, 152 would die as POWs. On the home front, news about the loss of *Renown* and *Prince of Wales* in December 1941, the fall of Hong Kong and Singapore, and American disasters at Pearl Harbor and in the Philippines had overshadowed reports about events in the Java Sea. However unknown or unheralded the actions of the men and their ship might have been, it is nonetheless clear that despite the overwhelming futility of *Exeter*'s final mission, her crew did not falter.

ENDNOTES

1.  Morison, Samuel Eliot. *History of United States Naval Operations in World War II,* Vol. II. Little, Brown & Co. 1948. P9. 80–81.

2.  Morison. pp. 271–276.

3.  Imperial War Museum. Sound recording archive. 5206. Adams, Thomas John. 1981.

4.  Morison. pp. 353–358.

5.  Tonks, Randall A. *HMS Exeter, Heavy Cruiser 1929–1941.* Profile Publications Ltd. 1971. pp. 15–17.

6.  According to Morison, pp. 333–334 and 371–373, the Japanese ships were probably the destroyers *Akebono* and *Ikazuchi* of the Java Invasion Support Group that also included heavy cruisers *Myoko* and *Ashigra.*

7.  Imperial War Museum. 5206 (Adams).

8.  COFEPOW (Children of Far East Prisoners of War). 'Cecil Rowse's Story.' cofepow.prg.uk. Web. Accessed June 2014.

9.  Royal Navy Memories. 'Prisoner of War and a Lucky Man.' royalnavymemories.co.uk. Web. Accessed June 2014.

10.  Royal Navy Memories.

11.  Royal Navy Memories.

12.  _____ 'My Brother Raymond and HMS Exeter.' BBC WW2 *People's War.* Article ID A 5899323. 2005.

13.  Imperial War Museum. 5206 (Adams).

14.  Imperial War Museum. 5206.

15.  Royal Navy Memories.

16.  Imperial War Museum. 5206 (Adams).

# TWELVE
# CONVOYS FOR MALTA

In mid-1942, the situation on Malta was alarming in the extreme. Supplies of food, water, medicine, and practically all the necessities for life were about exhausted. Aircraft, fuel, ammunition, in fact all the military supplies necessary for the island's defense had become either scarce or completely unavailable.

In June two urgent convoys were simultaneously organised for Malta's relief. One, named Operation Vigorous, originated from Alexandria in the east. Departing on the 11th the convoy was persistently and heavily attacked from the air. After several days of constant fighting the escort, for all its maneuvering and anti-aircraft gunfire, ran so low on fuel and ammunition that the convoy was ordered to turn back.

The other convoy, named Operation Harpoon, sailed from Gibraltar in the west. Harpoon was composed of eleven merchant vessels and their naval escorts. One of the most vital cargos belonged to the tanker SS *Kentucky* that was on loan to Britain from Texaco, The Texas Oil Company. The convoy's escort included two aircraft carriers, a battleship, four cruisers, sixteen destroyers, and some smaller warships.

Like Vigorous, Harpoon faced immediate and determined attacks. Italy's air force and surface navy exacted heavy losses. *Kentucky* and all of her precious fuel oil, three freighters, a Polish destroyer, and the *Tribal* class destroyer, HMS *Bedouin* were all sunk. Of all the relief ships originally collected for Harpoon and Vigorous only two of Harpoon's freighters ever reached Malta. Of those two surviving vessels one was holed so badly that a part of her cargo was lost due to water damage.

## 'Engage the Leading Destroyer'
## HMS *Bedouin* and Operation Harpoon

HMS *Bedouin* in low visibility camouflage for operations around Narvik (1940) Model 1:700

*Bedouin's* last battle began on the morning of 15 June 1942. The destroyer and several other escorts were stationed several miles ahead of the convoy to keep a watch for enemy ships. *Bedouin's* crew, alert and on edge, spotted what was assumed to be a hostile ship. *Bedouin* quickly opened fire. As *Bedouin* was shooting, some doubt arose about the target. Some on board thought it was nothing more than a rock. Firing continued until the carefully watched target was identified as friendly. Cease fire was immediately ordered. The story was related by *Bedouin's* gunnery officer, Sherard Manners.

*At about 01.30 someone on the bridge shouted, 'Alarm dead ahead' ... (and) ... sure enough there was a dark ship-size shadow. Guns were loaded and we were all ready. Then it struck me that the shape wasn't moving. I shouted to the bridge, 'I think it's a rock.' No sooner said than Partridge next astern put her searchlight on – and there was a destroyer. A short, very sharp gun battle followed. I had been so busy trying to identify the target that my first salvo of four shells went whistling off into Tunisia. For what seemed like a couple of minutes the target was covered in flames and sparks – then suddenly came a cry, 'Christ. It's one of ours' and sure enough there was the silhouette of a British destroyer. It was all too true. We ceased fire and generally calmed down. It was in fact the hulk of the* Havoc, *which had run aground at high speed on 06 April, 1942 … we knew nothing about this and no-one had warned us about her. I don't suppose it did much harm except possibly giving up our position.*[1]

Shortly afterwards *Bedouin* sighted a strong force of Italian cruisers and destroyers. As she turned to rush the enemy, the other British destroyers of the convoy escort followed. An abrupt and intense gun battle ensued in which *Bedouin* was hit several times by enemy shells. When her propulsive machinery was damaged, the ship stopped dead in the water. The crew was preparing to fire torpedoes when the Italians turned away. The destroyer *Partridge* was tasked to tow *Bedouin* back to port. Italian aircraft soon appeared and *Partridge* cast the lines off in order to defend herself. Still without power, *Bedouin* could not fire her guns or maneuver. She took an air dropped torpedo hit, flooded, and sank. Most of the crew managed to get off, and practically all who went into the water were soon picked up by an Italian hospital ship. The British were well treated and transferred to a prison camp where they remained until after the Italian surrender. They then fell under control of the Germans. Most were transferred to POW camps in Germany for the remainder of the war.

Although grateful to the Italians for picking him up and treating him well, Manners maintained a poor opinion of their military prowess in his postwar comments.

*It was a poor effort by the Italian Admiral. He had considerable superiority, but as usual the Italians had no stomach for a fight and the (Italian) squadron turned away to the northeast. It is difficult to imagine a British Admiral acting similarly – the convoy should have been annihilated and the destroyers, too.*[2]

*Bedouin's* captain, Cmdr. B.G. Scurfield, survived the sinking. He wrote a letter home to his wife from an Italian POW camp about his ship's final action. The letter mentioned many of the ship's crew by name.

HMS *Bedouin*

*I knew what we had to do and the cost was not to be counted – the Italians must be driven off. It was no time for fancy manoeuvres – it was to my mind merely a question of going bald-headed for the enemy and trying to do him as much harm as possible by gun and torpedo. Otherwise it was within his power to destroy us and then the convoy at his pleasure.*

*I knew too that the other destroyers would follow me and know what I was about, whether they had signals from me or no … I could do no more about it, except give (Gunnery Officer) Manners a target and do my best to avoid punishment for as long as possible.*

*The (Italian) cruisers opened fire almost at once and the first salvoes fell astern of Bedouin. Their spread was good – too good perhaps – at that range – and the shooting seemed to be unpleasantly accurate. Perhaps this is always the impression when one is the target!*

*My time was taken up by the time honoured dodge of steering for the last splash. I had often heard of it being done and found it exhilarating.*[3] *It worked, too, for some time. A little before 06.30 Manners reckoned that we were within range, so I told him to engage the leading destroyer, and we opened fire at 17,400 yards. Ten minutes later the enemy altered another twenty degrees away and we shifted our fire to the leading cruiser at 12,400 yards. By this time we were starting to get hit. Tinny crashes succeeded one another to such a tune that I began to wonder how much the ship could stand. Though I did not realise it at the time, one of the first things to go was the mast, and with it the wireless* (radio).

*I knew the bridge had been hit; the compass repeater was shaken out of its gimbals and I had water and paint flakes dashed at me, but the splendid Bedouin was forging ahead and closing the gap minute by minute. Montgomery was passing news to the plot and Moller was standing by to fire torpedoes – wounded himself and with his assistant lying dead beside him. Skinner, though I didn't know it, was lying at the back of the bridge mortally wounded in the throat; Yeoman Archer and most of the signalmen and 'rudolf' men on the flag deck were either dead or wounded.*[4]

*All I knew was that the coxswain was calmly doing his job at the wheel and that the ship was responding splendidly. We appeared to be straddling* (shells were observed to be landing close aboard and on either side of the target) *the enemy and must have been hitting, but observation of fall of shot was difficult and it was not possible to allocate targets.*

*At about 0650 the director* (structure above the bridge in which personnel sighted and calculated gunfire solutions) *was hit. The layer was killed outright and Parker, who was keeping the rate, mortally wounded; Manners and the sight setter escaped unscathed and so did the cross-leveler, though he was blown clear out of the tower.*

*The ship had received more punishment than I knew and I felt in my bones that she would not be able to go much further. So I told Moller to go down and fire the torpedoes and when the range had come down to 5,000 yards – tracer was being fired at us by the enemy's close range weapons – turned the ship to starboard. During the turn we were hit several times, but the*

*torpedoes were fired when the sights came on. After swinging past the*
*firing course the ship came to a standstill.*[5]

The captain was killed late in the war in what appears to have been a friendly
fire incident. He was in a group of prisoners being marched along a road by its
German guards when they were strafed by Allied planes.

### 'The War Seemed Very Remote'
### Prisoners of War

Gunnery Officer Manners recalled watching *Bedouin* sink by the stern as he and
some 230 other crewmen floated in the sea. They had not been in the water
long when an Italian floatplane painted white and marked with red crosses
landed near a small group of survivors. The plane took the men aboard and
flew off. The pilot may have signaled the position of *Bedouin*'s crew for, just as
it began to get dark and cold, a fully lighted Italian hospital ship came along to
take everyone on board. As the men were being loaded onto the ship they were
suddenly attacked by Italian dive bombers who, fortunately, missed the target.
Long after the war Manners had an opportunity to speak with one of the bomber
pilots who told him that his orders were to proceed to the position where Italian
reconnaissance had determined *Bedouin* to be and bomb her. The pilot radioed
that there was no enemy destroyer and he could only see the hospital ship.
Surprisingly, he was ordered to attack anyhow. It is possible that the attackers
missed on purpose. As the ship approached the Italian island of Pantelleria not
far from Sicily, it was fired on by shore batteries but, again, escaped damage.

The British sailors were fed and cared for as needed aboard the hospital ship.
They landed at Pantelleria for later transport to the Italian mainland where
the officers were separated from the enlisted men. The POW camp for officers
to which Manners was sent had been set up in an old monastery. It housed
approximately 300 men most of whom were army officers taken prisoner in the
North African deserts. Manners described life as a prisoner of the Italians.

*Accommodation was quite adequate, washing facilities and food also. Red*
*Cross parcels came with fair regularity. The earlier prisoners had worked up*

*a good black-market, using cigarettes from the Red Cross parcels as currency … Accommodation was in the old monks' cells – each of these had a couple of rooms and a small garden about 12 × 5 yards at the back. Some ten officers would occupy each cell … The weather was pleasantly warm in the spring and summer but jolly cool in the winter. However, the old beams in the roof made excellent, if unofficial, burning … There was plenty to do to occupy one's mind. There was a small library furnished by the Red Cross; one could take part in plays, musical concerts; learn almost any subject under the sun. We also had a soccer pitch and exercise yard next to the monastery. We were joined regularly by newer prisoners but never overcrowded. The war seemed very remote. Each time a new lot of POWs arrived, they would give lectures to bring us up to date with war news.*[6]

The prisoners were allowed to send letters about once every two weeks. After six weeks Manners began to receive mail and regular packages from home. It was comforting to him, as it was for all the others, to know that his family knew that he was alive and reasonably well. At the time of his capture, England's fortunes were uncertain, but as time passed and newly arriving prisoners brought news, Manners was able to surmise that the war would end favourably.

According to one of his surviving grandchildren, Terrence Doyle had attained the minimum enlistment age of fifteen years and three months when he joined the Navy in 1939. He arrived aboard *Bedouin* in September 1941. His early experiences with the ship were relatively routine ones as the destroyer and her crew trained primarily in anti-submarine exercises. As a seventeen-year-old from a close-knit family and away from home for the first time, Doyle recalled often feeling lonely. He spent a gloomy Christmas 1941 for which there was no shipboard celebration. Doyle turned eighteen just a week before the action in which *Bedouin* was sunk.

Doyle recalled that time slowed as he watched the Italian torpedo plane that ultimately sank *Bedouin* approach. He saw the plane get hit and come crashing down towards the ship. Still living in slow motion, his next sensations were of falling to the deck and then slowly rolling over with the ship. He could not regain his footing as he and the ship kept rolling until he was in the water. Earlier from aboard *Bedouin* the water had looked calm, warm, and even inviting. Now that he was actually in it the cold made Doyle feel as if he were being cut all over his body by sharp knives. Near dusk, as weariness set in and his mind became less clear, he worried that if he were not picked up soon he would surely die. He saw a ship coming towards him, but all he could think of was how cold the water felt. He was not aware that rescuers had gotten hold of him until he suddenly felt warm air hit him as he was pulled from the water. His next thought was that there could be nothing that would ever be able to hurt him again.

Doyle and the other enlisted men were split off from *Bedouin*'s officers and transported by rail to a prison camp at Castelvetrano, Sicily. There he was asked to fill out a card to be mailed to his family. The contents simply stated that he was 'being treated well'. Although he would have begged to differ, he was at least satisfied that his family would know that he was alive. Later, he was always deliberate to write only positive letters home as he did not want anyone to worry. Letters that he received usually had large sections blacked out by British censors. This caused Doyle to think that his family might have been writing disparaging things about his captors that were removed in efforts to protect him from possible retaliatory mistreatment. His worst time as a captive may have occurred on a day when the prisoners were allowed to play soccer. When the ball was inadvertently kicked beyond the confines of the camp, one of Doyle's friends asked and received permission to retrieve it. A guard who may not have gotten the word shot and killed him. Doyle, angered and frustrated, began to throw rocks at the guards who, fortunately, remained restrained. Once subdued, Doyle was given two weeks solitary confinement as punishment.

When the Allies landed in Sicily in July 1943, the prisoners were moved to a camp on the Italian mainland where Doyle gradually learned to speak Italian. His primary recollections, however, were of the many days of feeling hungry. The typical daily prison camp rations included six ounces of bread along with a carefully measured half pint of macaroni soup. The prisoners were given a small ration of meat on rare occasions. The only vegetables they got were whatever happened to be mixed into the daily soup. Unfortunately, things were to get worse after the Italian capitulation in September when the prisoners were taken in hand by the Germans. They were moved to an auxiliary camp of Auschwitz called Blechammer. There, along with the others from *Bedouin,* Doyle was given a medical exam to determine what type of work would suit him. He was assigned fairly menial work that was a daily three mile walk from the camp. His assigned jobs included painting, bunker repair and grave digging. He was able to see through a fence to observe Jewish prisoners receiving treatment that was far more harsh than his own. While he had been issued boots, he saw that Jewish prisoners marched and worked barefoot whatever the weather or climate. As the war began to go badly for Germany, the *Bedouin* prisoners were moved again by forced foot march to a very overcrowded camp. It had been built for 10,000 but housed 80,000. The camp was called Moosburg where Doyle's weight dropped by 'eight stone' or 112 pounds. He recalled that one day, as he trudged to work under guard an old woman clandestinely slipped him a caraway seed cake. He was very careful to conceal it until he could later eat it without being noticed. When American troops arrived to liberate the camps, Doyle had been a captive for three years. He was examined, cared for, and sent home. In June 1945, while in his family's living room in West Bromwich, the mail delivered the card he had sent from the liberated Moosburg camp the month before. It simply stated, 'Terence Doyle. Number TX 177385: I am safe and well.'[7]

## 'Malta looks to us for help. We shall not fail them'
## Operation Pedestal

At the beginning of August 1942 Messages from Malta were dire. Incidences of disease that included polio and dysentery were on the rise. There were no medicines with which to relieve the sick. The entire population had been reduced to starvation rations. It was estimated that food supplies would be gone by mid-month. Beyond that time, it was thought that sustenance would have to come through the slaughter of the island's remaining goats and horses. Such a measure was expected to be capable of extending Malta's food supplies for no more than an additional five to ten days. A last-ditch convoy called Operation Pedestal was assembled at Gibraltar with hopes of staving off the looming abandonment or surrender of the island.

A total of fourteen merchant vessels, among them another large American tanker on loan from Texaco, SS *Ohio*, set out on 9 August 1942. It was escorted by four aircraft carriers, two battleships, seven cruisers and thirty-two destroyers. The convoy had barely entered its second day at sea when the

German submarine *U-73*, based at La Spezia, Italy spotted one of the carriers, HMS *Eagle,* near Mallorca. The submarine scored with four torpedoes that very quickly caused *Eagle* to develop a sharp list to port. Slightly down by the head,

HMS *Eagle*

the edge of the carrier's flight deck touched the water. Several convoy escorts rushed over to conduct rescue operations, but 160 men out of a crew of 927 were lost. All of the carrier's aircraft went down with the ship. George Amyes, a survivor of the sinking, remembered,

> … *The* Eagle *shuddered with four distinct lurches. For some reason I thought that we had hit a school of whales! The deck tilted under my feet … and as the ship began to list I realised we were in serious trouble. … Frightened voices shouted and men began to stream up from the lower decks … bodies were already floundering in the water below. And the wake of the Eagle had developed a distinct curve as the vessel pulled out of line. The rhythmic throb of the main engines died away and the ship slewed further around rapidly keeling over. … I never did hear the order to abandon ship but when I saw marines jumping from the flight deck,*

*hurtling past the gundeck, and hitting the rising torpedo blister as the ship keeled over I really did begin to get worried. Less than two minutes had passed, and the marines who had smashed themselves to jelly when they jumped had already slithered away leaving behind a blood soaked trail of slime. … I clambered between the rails, and suddenly I was sitting on the torpedo blister. Two ratings were already there, terrified, they could not swim. An officer slid between the two ratings and shouted, 'now is your time to learn,' and with a rating beneath each arm he dived into the sea. I never saw them again. … (after entering the water) … I saw other frightened faces and suddenly I did not feel quite so lonely. … The sea suddenly boiled; an unbelievable crushing pressure stunned my senses, and I spun around the water like a toy … Something bumped into me from behind, it was 'Stripey,' … but something was wrong. His face was discolored, his eyes staring, and he was flopping uncontrollably in the water. I grabbed for him and my hand slid down his torso and suddenly there was nothing but mush. … Panic stricken I pushed him away and felt my stomach heaving uncontrollably. We drifted apart.*[8]

Amyes had inflated his rubber life belt but, weighted down with oil soaked clothing, struggled considerably. He could not remove his clothing because he would have had to remove his lifebelt first. He was also fearful of being stung by jellyfish that he believed were abundant in that part of the Mediterranean. He managed to secure a second life belt from a dead sailor. He was eventually hauled aboard a tugboat with much difficulty by rope. Although sickened by oily seawater that he had swallowed, and nearly exhausted by his ordeal, Amyes and the other survivors aboard the tug were ordered to transfer to a destroyer that had come alongside. He had to swing himself off the deck of the tug, grab at the scrambling net hanging from the destroyer's rails, and climb up to her deck. He saw numerous others fall between the two vessels. He recalled,

*… I was given twenty-four hours to clean the clothing I was wearing – clean myself of oil, slime, blood and filth; and draw* (from available naval supplies) *a minimum of essential clothing; in my case one pair of deck shoes – pass the medical officer – and if we could breathe we were declared*

*fit for duty – report to administration, and be assigned to our new station. Seventy-two hours after being (sunk) … I was hard at work on the old but faithful aircraft carrier,* Argus.[9]

## 'Mine, Bomb, or Torpedo …'
## HMS *Rodney* and Operation Pedestal

HMS *Rodney*

Battleship *Rodney* was teamed up with her sister ship, *Nelson*, four aircraft carriers (one of which was the ill-fated HMS *Eagle*), and three cruisers to form Force Z, the distant escort for the Pedestal convoy. Force Z was assigned to stay with the merchant ships and the near escort until they all arrived at the Strait of Sicily between Tunisia and Sicily. From that point, the task of protecting the convoy from surface attack by the Italian Navy would be completed, and Force Z would turn back to Gibraltar. The convoy would proceed to Malta under the eyes and guns of the near escort and Malta-based air cover.

William L. Meyers was a member of the Fleet Air Arm and a petty officer trained in the maintenance and operations of shipboard Walrus scout aircraft. Meyers recalled the days about a year prior to Operation Pedestal when he had first reported for duty aboard *Rodney*.

> *My first days on board were spent trying to find my way around and marveling at the massive size of everything. The aircraft was mounted on the top of a turret manned, as tradition demanded, by the Royal Marines. They invited me into the turret and what an experience that was. Three massive guns and three sets of operating mechanisms, no automation, everything controlled by hand. Breech open, up from below would come the massive shell weighing one ton, into the breech followed by the cordite, breech closed, gun ready. Each gun weighed 100 tons ... For me those early days were a series of firsts. The first time aboard a seagoing ship and getting acquainted with the stomach churning motions. My first time in a hammock. I have never claimed to be a gymnast and my clumsy efforts to swing myself up into that canvas bag suspended from the deck head were a source of much amusement to my messmates.*[10]

Fearful that it could become a fire hazard during combat, Rodney's captain ordered the Walrus to be deactivated for Operation Pedestal. Without an airplane to care for, Petty Officer Myers was temporarily left with no duties. He was assigned to a gun crew but, being unoccupied on deck during much of the time, he had a good view of the action that began soon after the convoy raised anchor.

> *As I recall we left Scapa in early August 1942, once again in company with our sister ship Nelson and headed south being joined by other ships both merchant and naval as we proceeded. As was common practice in those days we had no idea of our destination ... and, as always, in the absence of positive information rumor ran riot. The Far East seemed to be a popular choice until we reached the 36th parallel when it was left hand down and hey ho for the Straits of Gibraltar. There was much excitement at the thought of a run ashore at Gib. But it was not to be – in the middle of the night of 10th August we belted through the Straits in the forlorn hope of not being spotted by enemy watchers on either side ... There can be no disputing the fact that if you have to go to war at sea then the Mediterranean is the ideal place. The water is almost invariably calm and*

*of civilized temperature and the sky, when not obscured by shell bursts and enemy aircraft, is invariably clear and blue.*

*With Gibraltar well behind us the Skipper addressed the ship's company. He confirmed that the destination of the convoy was Malta, told us that if the convoy did not get through then Malta would undoubtedly have to surrender … spelt out the potential danger and advised that the next few days would be very interesting … We did not have to wait long for the 'interest' to develop. About an hour later (the captain) was on the 'blower' again with the comment, 'looks as if the* (aircraft carrier) Eagle *has been torpedoed off our port quarter.' We all rushed to the upper deck and there was Eagle, flight deck already touching the water, and a few minutes later she vanished from view. Apart from the sorrow of losing a great ship we had also lost a third of our air cover. Fortunately, most of the crew had been rescued by the escorting destroyers but the enemy submarine had escaped. Shortly after that we went to action stations where, apart from a few brief lulls, we remained for the next three days. Our first action was to defuel the Walrus much to the relief of the Royal Marines manning X Turret who did not relish the thought of gallons of high octane aviation spirits pouring through their air vents. To keep us (Fleet Air Arm personnel) busy we became part of the 4.7-inch (anti-aircraft) ammunition supply … every shell had to be manhandled from the magazine to the gun deck. Almost the same as in Nelson's day except that now the cannonball and the powder were all in the same container. Each shell weighed 75 pounds but after a few hours it felt like 75 hundred weight.*[11]

Myers reproduced information from a book written by his ship's chaplain. It described a series of frantic events that took place in a span of just twelve minutes during one of the air attacks on the convoy.

*Mine, bomb, or torpedo explodes astern … (cruiser)* Manchester *opens fire (*Manchester *would be hit by a torpedo launched from an Italian patrol boat and sink as a result on 13 August) … destroyers open fire port side … nine torpedo bombers coming in outside screen … 16-inch guns open fire*

*to port ... torpedoes dropped port bow ... six torpedo bombers of port beam*
*... torpedo bomber shot down by fighter ...*[12]

The use of Rodney's 16-inch guns against incoming aircraft attests to the ferocity
of the attack and the desperation of the defenders. The basic idea for employing
large caliber guns against aerial attack was to either have their shells burst in
the air to release clouds of heavy shrapnel or to fire into the sea. A heavy shell
striking the ocean would throw up a heavy curtain of water that might force the
attacking planes off course or even to cause them to crash against it.

As the convoy struggled to get through to Malta, Meyers recalled,

*Whenever possible I made my way to the upper deck to observe the*
*operations of our two remaining carriers,* Indomitable *and* Victorious.
*With the convoy under constant air attack from dawn to dusk there was*
*continual flight deck activity. It must be remembered that fresh aircrew*
*manned each succeeding wave of enemy aircraft, whereas our small band*
*of pilots was continuously in action. I watched the aircraft land ... and*
*taxi to the forward lift where (they would be) lowered into the hangar.*
*I could imagine the action as it moved back through the hangar being*
*refueled, rearmed, and repaired while the pilot was debriefed, having a*
*cup of coffee, and a pee ... and by the time the aircraft reached the after lift*
*he was ready to go again. It was possibly the most concentrated period of*
*action for the Fleet Air Arm. Very comparable to the Battle of Britain but*
*with the added hazards of a moving airfield, having to fly through friendly*
*flak to reach it, and flying aircraft inferior in performance to those of the*
*enemy ... the performance of those young naval aviators is deserving of the*
*highest praise. I had many friends on both (carriers) ... (I) must admit to*
*some embarrassment at the comparatively easy passage I was having but*
*at the same time must admit to being very grateful for the security provided*
*by Rodney's 14-inches of armour plating.*

*It was during one such bout of reverie that disaster struck the Indomitable.*
*Two large bombs (got) through the flight deck (and) within seconds the ship*
*was engulfed in flame and smoke. Through it all the ack-ack (anti-aircraft)*

*barrage was maintained – a remarkable and courageous performance, but the ship was now out of action as an aircraft carrier. With many of Indomitable's aircraft airborne and only one deck available (Victorious) there was a landing problem. 'Vic' already had a full complement of aircraft plus some from Eagle so space was at a premium and we were forced to witness the very sad sight of aircraft landing, crew evacuating, and then the deck party manhandling the aircraft ... into the sea in order to make room for the next to land.*

*As we approached the area known as the Skerki Narrows (Bomb Alley to the sailors), between Sicily and Cape Bon* (North Africa) *the heavy units had to withdraw leaving the convoy in the care of the escorting cruisers and destroyers with air cover from Malta ... We were escorting the damaged Indomitable back to Gibraltar ... (it was) a typical Mediterranean evening, the sea flat calm, the sun still high in a clear blue sky, and the silence was bliss after the deafening clamor of the previous few days. Suddenly we could feel the ship losing speed, the flag was lowered to half-mast, and our attention was drawn to* Indomitable. *From the stern of the ship we could see bundles toppling into the sea as* 'Indom' *buried her dead.*[13]

## 'There Was Absolute Mayhem'
## HMS *Eskimo* and the Relief of Malta

HMS *Eskimo* was a *Tribal* class destroyer and a sister ship of HMS *Bedouin* that had been lost during Operation Harpoon. *Eskimo's* actions during Operation Pedestal were described by John Manners, first lieutenant (executive officer or second in command) aboard the destroyer from 1942 to 1945.

*By the middle of July things were stirring and the next operation turned out to be a large and heavily escorted convoy to Malta ... it was the biggest and most important of the war called Pedestal. It consisted of fourteen merchant ships (and) (T)hey all had a mixed cargo with the exception of the SS Ohio*[14] *which was most important of all with its cargo of fuel ... there was a good deal of excitement and we knew that something big was in*

HMS *Eskimo*

*the offing. As always we were topped up with fuel and food, and we were ready for action … It was thought that Malta could (only) hold out until September so the next Russian convoy was postponed much to Stalin's displeasure as there were hardly any escorts left at Scapa Flow.*

*On the night of 10 August the convoy passed through the Straits of Gibraltar in a light fog and the destroyers put into Gibraltar … to fuel … With Algéciras only five miles across the bay … it was almost certain that the Germans knew about the convoy, indeed it had been thought that there were security leaks already.*

*Bearing in mind that we had been at cruising stations for a week which meant continuously being on watches (every day) with four hours on and eight hours off, personnel were somewhat weary even before there was any action. In addition to being on watch, there were the normal household duties to keep the ship decently habitable as well as catching up on sleep, and feeding. Nobody took their clothes off apart from boots whilst sleeping. Around ones chest was tied the inflatable life belt which was kept partially inflated, or not, according to taste.*

*... Six hundred miles from Malta ... we were at defense stations, which meant that half of the ship's company was at action stations all the time working four hours buttoned up, and four hours off duty. However, when the frequent air attacks came, we went to action stations with every single man allocated a particular duty. I was first lieutenant and therefore second in command and it was the practice to be away from the bridge in case it was hit and all key personnel were put out of action. My station was on the four barreled pom-pom* (anti-aircraft gun mount). *Being away from the bridge meant that I was not completely aware of what was going on, though a running commentary was passed by telephone. At action stations everyone donned their tin hats and anti-flash gear consisting of a balaclava head covering and anti-flash gloves.*

*On 11 August tension was building up. There were various alarms of the presence of enemy aircraft but they were only shadowers (that) served to keep our fingers on the triggers. Coupled to this there were frequent alarms from submarines on the Asdic sets and the occasional sighting of torpedoes, none of which scored any hits. The whole convoy did numerous emergency turns, normally of 45 degrees to avoid these submarines, and, as the destroyer screen was zig-zagging all the time, maneuvering was not easy.*

*At last, in the evening, our radar detected a large enemy attack impending. Our aircraft* (from the screening aircraft carriers) *were flown off and no doubt unsettled the attacking force which consisted of thirty-six planes: a mix of JU88 high level bombers and Henkel 111 torpedo bombers with the latter flying in low and releasing their torpedoes rather far away. All ships opened fire with every gun and the sky was filled with short bursts and a number of the enemy were shot down, but more importantly, the convoy suffered no damage.*

*... By now (12 August), we were getting close to the enemy airfields, and around midday all hell broke loose. Firstly some black canisters were dropped by parachute ahead of the convoy by ten Italian aircraft. These were 'motobombs' a newly developed but untried weapon that was in*

*effect a circling torpedo. Yet another emergency turn was made, this time of 90 degrees, and there were no casualties. The whole day was spent at action stations with everybody getting increasingly weary. Coupled to the fact that the galley fires were drawn, feeding arrangements were either chaotic or non-existent.*

*… Eskimo was always on the starboard … of the screen, on the French North African side, whereas most of the attacks came from the port side which was nearest the enemy airfields. During the morning, a large number of Italian torpedo bombers said to be forty-two (in number) … kept circling the convoy at low altitude not daring to risk flying through the outer destroyer screen. They could easily have swamped our defenses, but declined to do so. After seemingly hours of trying, they dropped their torpedoes out of range and departed for home.*

*At the same time, there were various submarine contacts on the Asdic followed by the dropping of depth charges. With torpedo planes circling, high level bombers, dive bombers, parachute bombs, emergency turns, two aircraft carriers careering about either flying off (or) landing aircraft the scene was of organised confusion …*

*Then around midday twenty Junkers and eighty-seven dive bombers made their attacks. The sky seemed filled with planes as we were now within range of the long-range enemy fighters. (One merchant ship had her) speed reduced (by hits) and she dropped behind the convoy where she was repeatedly attacked and eventually sunk by torpedoes from (Italian planes). By this time we were within 300 miles of Malta.*

*In the evening 13 (Italian) torpedo bombers attacked in a half-hearted way and were deterred by a fierce barrage of fire, but one torpedo hit the stern of the destroyer Foresight rendering her immobile, and, she had to be sunk. By about six o'clock in the evening the sky became thick with aircraft obviously waiting for a coordinated attack. There were forty-two (that were mostly German Stuka dive bombers), 40 Italian torpedo bombers, and thirty-eight fighters … the enemy attacked, and there were planes everywhere, and all the ships were firing every gun, and in the middle of it all, it was evident that the aircraft carriers were the main target. Suddenly huge plumes of smoke appeared in the bows and stern of the* (aircraft carrier) Indomitable *as the Stukas dived down on her and hit her with two or three bombs. She turned towards us escorted by* (a cruiser) *and as she got close we could see a huge piece of her side plating hanging loose and a plume of black smoke rising from her stern, but she was not put out of action completely.*

*The time was seven o'clock in the evening … we were 250 miles from Malta which should have been sixteen hours of steaming with a time of arrival on the next* (13 August) *afternoon … Dusk was just beginning when, suddenly, the* (cruiser) Nigeria *was torpedoed followed almost immediately by the* (cruiser) Cairo, *and, a few minutes later, another torpedo struck the* (oil tanker) Ohio. *This was the work of one Italian submarine and her salvo of six torpedoes must have been either the most skillful or luckiest of the whole war. The* Cairo *sunk but* Nigeria *remained afloat and was able to limp back to Gibraltar …* Ohio *was stopped but stayed afloat and was later able to proceed at slow speed … With the advent of dusk, enemy torpedo bombers arrived and, with the merchant ships silhouetted against the evening sky, hits were registered on the* Empire Hope *which sank. The next was* Clan Ferguson *which blew up with no survivors and hits were registered on the* Brisbane Star *and* Santa Eliza *but both were able to carry on at reduced speed.*

*The convoy in the space of about half an hour, had suffered crippling losses. There was absolute mayhem. With enemy submarines in the vicinity, torpedo bombers attacking, ships blowing up, and everybody firing their guns for all they were worth, the situation was completely out of control … the depressing news came through that the Italian fleet was at sea … (S)ome ships fired star shells which illuminated some attacking E-boats* (torpedo craft somewhat like the well-known American PT boat) *and ships opened fire whenever they could.*

*With all the escorts twisting and turning causing the destroyers to heel over, no hits were scored on them. Soon afterwards (cruiser)* Kenya *was hit in the bow by a torpedo from an Italian submarine, but fortunately, she was able to continue at reduced speed back to Gibraltar ... Early on the morning of 13 August, the convoy ran into a number of Italian and German E-boats ... and the (cruiser)* Manchester *was hit and brought to a standstill with both boiler rooms flooded. We passed her in the* Eskimo *and, soon afterwards, passed the* Ohio *as well. The tanker continued steam very slowly forward.*

*Further attacks on the merchant ships were carried out by E-boats who damaged the* Rochester Castle, *and sank the* Glenorchy *and* Wairangi. *The* Almeira Lykes *was abandoned. So by dawn the convoy was in a very sorry state with ... only five merchant ships (left), but a sigh of relief went up when a fighter (plane) from Malta hoved into view ... (W)e were ordered back (with another destroyer) to pick up survivors. To pick (them) up we let down our scrambling nets, which had a mesh rather like a rope ladder We had two of these on each side. They were about fifteen feet long and reached down into the water. We picked up all we could find from the* Wairangi, Almeira Lykes *and* Manchester, *which had been abandoned and sunk. It was a lovely calm sunny day and we were able to pick up about 200 survivors.*[15]

*Eskimo* and the other destroyer that accompanied her in the rescue work were detached from the convoy so that they could return to the safety of Gibraltar with their decks loaded with survivors.

In addition to the loss of HMS *Eagle*, the Pedestal convoy suffered the sinkings of, two cruisers, one destroyer, and nine out of its original fifteen merchant ships. Extreme fuel shortages that kept most of the Italian Navy's large ships in port and the earlier diversion of a great portion of German air power to the Russian front prevented even greater losses to the convoy. The tanker *Ohio*, one of the convoy's most crucial ships, had been hit repeatedly and barely made it into the Grand Harbour at Valletta before settling to the bottom. She had been towed in and was kept upright by a destroyer pushing against each of her two sides. Her cargo of oil arrived intact and unspoiled as did the supplies aboard the five other surviving convoy ships.

As the convoy's remnants straggled into Grand Harbour, they were greeted by cheering people, blaring ship's sirens, and band music. Because it arrived on 15 August, the feast day St. Mary, Our Lady of the Assumption, the convoy was gratefully named the Santa Maria Convoy or, in Maltese, *Il-Knovoj ta Santa Marija*. The supplies delivered allowed Malta to survive and to continue serving as a viable base for military operations against the Axis in the central Mediterranean and in North Africa. Although still proficient and determined, the weakened Axis forces in the region could not prevent follow-up convoys from reaching Malta. The battle of attrition over Malta had turned in favour of Britain.

The arrival of Pedestal has been commemorated and celebrated throughout the years on Malta. Veterans of the convoy as well as Italian and German veterans have always been invited to participate. As time passes, the number of veterans who return to visit Malta steadily dwindles. In 2014, there were only fourteen veterans or widows of veterans who attended the Santa Maria Convoy's anniversary celebration.[16]

## ENDNOTES

1. Manners, Sherard. 'HMS *Bedouin*, 1942.' world-war.co.uk. Accessed November 2013.

2. Manners.

3. The US Navy referred to this tactic as 'chasing salvos.' The practice was to steer directly to the spot where the enemy's previous shells had landed. The assumption was that the shooter would deliberately correct his shot. In such a case all subsequent shots would land on any spot other than the one to which the intended target ship was headed.

4. The full identities of Montgomery and Moller could not be ascertained. Based on the Captain's descriptions of their actions it is possible that Montgomery was either Bedouin's first lieutenant (second in command) or navigator. Sometimes the responsibilities were shared by a single officer. Moller could have been the ship's assistant gunnery officer. Yeoman Archer would have been one of the enlisted men on the bridge. The reference to Archer does not offer any clue to his identity.

5. _____ '15th June 1942: HMS *Bedouin* Charges the Italian Fleet.' ww2today.com Web. Accessed August 2013.

6. Manners.

7. Beccihaste (contributor). 'The *Bedouin*.' BBC WW2 *People's War*. Article ID A 3324674. 2004. The submitted anecdote was annotated, 'Grand dad, this is for you. With much love xxx.'

8. Aymes, George. 'HMS *Eagle*.' BBC WW2 *People's War*. Article ID A 2654589. 2004.

9. Aymes.

10. Meyers, Lesley. 'HMS *Rodney* – My First Days at Sea.' BBC WW2 *People's War*. Article ID A 7738923. 2005.

11. Meyers, Lesley. 'HMS *Rodney* – Operation Pedestal.' BBC WW2 *People's War*. Article ID A7873004.

12. Meyers. Article ID A 7873004.

13. Meyers. Article ID A 7873004.

14. SS *Ohio*, like SS *Kentucky* which had been sunk during Operation Harpoon, was on loan to Britain from Texaco. The ship was able to carry 170,000 barrels of oil and was manned by an exclusively British crew.

15. Manners, John. 'HMS *Eskimo* 1942–1943.' Militaryrecord.org/Official. Accessed August 2013.

16. George Cross Island Association. Web. Accessed May 2014.

# THIRTEEN
# THE ROYAL NAVY IN THE PACIFIC

The British Pacific Fleet was formed in November 1944, with Sydney, Australia, being selected as its headquarters. The new fleet included the battleships *Howe* and *King George V*, four of the Navy's newer aircraft carriers, five cruisers, and fifteen destroyers. One of the cruisers was from New Zealand and a number of the destroyers were from the Royal Australian Navy.[1] Additionally, the Navy drew on resources from across the Commonwealth to put together a support fleet composed of repair ships, tankers, supply ships, hospital ships, ocean-going tugs, and floating dry docks.[2] The British were clear in stating that its Pacific Fleet would be fully self-sustaining and flexible to operational necessity. They were emphatic that the Royal Navy did not expect to play second fiddle to the US Navy. The creation and deployment of the fleet was vital to Britain as she sought to re-establish herself as a power player in the coming postwar world order. The British were eager to regain control of their pre-war Far Eastern colonial empire that included Hong Kong, Singapore, Malaysia, Burma, India, and Borneo.

As the fleet began to mobilise the British Combined Chiefs of Staff issued a report to Prime Minister Churchill and President Roosevelt that stated:

> *We have agreed that the British Fleet should participate in the main operations against Japan in the Pacific, with the understanding that this Fleet will be balanced and self-supporting. The method of employment of the British Fleet in these main operations in the Pacific will be decided from time to time in accordance with the prevailing circumstances.*[3]

### 'We Sailed South'
### HMS *King George V* with the British Pacific Fleet

HMS *King George V*

Able Seaman Hubert Hancox joined *KGV* just as she was completing a yard period at Liverpool in the summer of 1944. Hancox had been earlier forced to leave technical school in his home town of Worcester when his father who owned a small shoe repair business died. Hancox took over the shop for which he was given a deferment from military service as the family's sole breadwinner. In 1943, when his deferment was terminated, he chose to enlist in the Navy. His choice of service branch was based on having seen and been impressed by HMS *Hood* as a very small boy. After a period of working up by both *KGV* and her numerous new and inexperienced crewmen, the battleship sailed to become part of the newly formed British Pacific Fleet. Hancox, who was to stay with the ship for the next two years, recalled the rather roundabout passage from England to the Pacific.

*Early November (1944), we were ready to start our journey for the Far East, calling at Plymouth where everyone (in rotations) was given embarkation leave of three days and eight hours. As soon as (the last group) returned from leave, we made a hasty return to Scapa as it was thought the German battleship* Tirpitz *was about to make a dash into the Atlantic to attack convoys. We and other capital ships were to intercept and sink her as had happened with Bismarck. It was a false alarm and, late one Saturday night, we anchored off Greenock (near Glasgow). Early next morning we started to ammunition ship … before going to a late breakfast and changing into our best uniforms to welcome the King and Queen and two princesses aboard.[4] We formed up by divisions to be inspected by the King, followed by 'Hands to Dinner,' and changed again into working rig to continue taking on stores and ammunition. The Royal Party walked around the ship talking to some of the crew whilst we worked, then … left the ship. 'Splice the Mainbrace' was signaled from their launch (which meant) an extra tot of rum for each crew member. Soon afterwards, we sailed, calling at Gibraltar, en route for Malta where we stayed a week. Next we arrived at Alexandria (and) went out to a bombardment of the island Milos off the coast of Greece to destroy the heavy guns interfering with shipping in the narrow channel. After again returning to Alexandria, we soon passed through the Suez Canal, into the Red Sea, and the Indian Ocean. (We) arrived at Colombo briefly before moving around the coast of Ceylon to Trincomalee. This was a beautiful anchorage, surrounded on three sides by trees that (grow) down almost to the water line. This is where we spent Christmas day and it is also where I received the news that my son David had been born and both mother and baby were doing fine. The news was well celebrated in a suitable manner!*

*… (S)oon we were back at sea, but this time as escorts to the aircraft carriers whose planes were attacking the oil fields on Sumatra around Palenbang. Several times we had to abandon strikes as the weather was so bad the planes couldn't take off in the mountainous seas. Eventually … the attacks were carried out. Some of our planes did not return, but a few airmen were rescued from the sea, having either run out of fuel or being damaged by enemy action. The fleet was attacked by Japanese aircraft (that) were driven off by (shipboard anti-aircraft) fire and patrolling*

*(carrier-borne) fighters.*[5] *The same types of target were attacked for several days. Then, instead of returning to port in Ceylon, we sailed south … arriving at Freemantle to a true Australian welcome. Every man on board received a box of goodies, mostly things we hadn't seen for a while, like fruit and Cadbury's milk chocolate … A few days later we sailed around the coast to another rapturous welcome in Sydney which was to be our main base for a year.*[6]

### 'You'd Get an Air Raid Warning'
### *KGV* and Friend or Foe?

On arriving in the Pacific, *KGV* operated either with a shore bombardment group or with a British carrier task group. The primary targets in both instances were Japan's remaining resource infrastructure and any island based airfields that could impede the Anglo-American path towards the Japanese homeland. *KGV*'s first assignment with the British Pacific Fleet was to protect the British carriers as they launched strikes against Japanese controlled oil facilities in Sumatra. The Indonesian oil fields were producing upwards of 75 per cent of Japan's fuel needs. The continuous availability of the British carriers was to become vital as Kamikaze attacks were to completely knock several American fleet carriers out of action.

The closer the British and Americans got to Japan, the stiffer the resistance grew. The Kamikaze concept of desperate suicide attacks was not limited to the familiar air strikes, but included the use of small manned submersibles packed with explosives and called 'human torpedoes'. The Kamikaze role was even given to the super-battleship *Yamato* when the giant ship was sent forth on a one way mission to cause as much damage to the naval forces arrayed against Japan as she possibly could before running herself aground. The Royal Navy took every possible precaution against attacks by Japan's suicide forces. In training, every ship in the BPF was subjected to mock suicide attacks by Fleet Air Arm aircraft. When simulating the enemy British pilots sometimes even fired live ammunition at their targets.

John Lang began his naval career as a midshipman aboard the *Hood* in the late 1930s. By 1945 Lang was serving on *KGV*'s open bridge beside Vice-Admiral

Sir Bernard Rawlings who was second-in-command of the BPF. Not yet thirty years old at the time, Lang recalled several incidents in which unknown aircraft approached his ship.

*You'd get an air raid warning 'Red' and the possibility of Kamikaze strikes and you'd all get very tensed up waiting for things to happen. I remember (that) I saw two little tubby airplanes coming towards us and I told the Admiral to get flat on the deck as I thought we were going to get Kamikaze'd and two (American or Fleet Air Arm) Hellcats flew over and landed on one of the carriers and my face turned red and I said, 'Sorry, sir … better safe than sorry.' … Whenever there was an air raid warning 'Red' the staff used to disappear into the conning tower behind 11-inches of armour but the Admiral didn't think this was right … with so many other personnel out in the open at action stations, that he should go (inside), too. So he stayed out on the flag deck with his assistant which was J. Lang! (I was there) to sort of advise him of the air situation so I thought it my special responsibility to look after him. He was a very tall man and I am a very little man, so I got down to the deck quicker … a few hours later, I saw another pair of tubby airplanes approaching the KGV and I said, 'I think this is alright, sir. Two more Hellcats.' And immediately bbbbbrrrrrr! … little holes were drilled just above our heads on the funnel cases just behind us … and they gained a little height and dived into the carriers … (this was) off the Sakishima Gunto islands … The captain of the Indomitable was a Japanese interpreter and they discovered from the crash some … notes for Kamikaze pilots … (saying) 'If your engine stops, switch off and fly home,' or words to that effect.[7]*

On 29 May 1945, *KGV* fired the last big gun rounds of any Royal Navy battleship at war against enemy targets. Lying off shore from the Japanese city of Hamamatsu, *KGV* fired her main battery at targets that included ammunition manufacturing plants, the Nakajima aircraft factory, the Japanese Musical Instrument Company which was a producer of airplane propellers, and the Suzuki Motor Company.[8]

## 'We Can No Longer Win the War by Adhering to Conventional Methods' Japan's Special Attack Units

The enemy the BPF was to face had suffered heavily from losses of warships, aircraft, and key personnel. The Japanese were especially short of combat experienced pilots. For all that, Allied personnel understood that the Japanese still remained highly resourceful, desperate, dangerous, and deadly. Pushed back, Pacific island by Pacific island, to the edge of its home islands, Japan was preparing to do anything and everything possible to resist what it knew was to be an inevitable invasion. In October 1944, the Americans were well on their way to regaining hold of the Philippines. That month, Japan's Vice Admiral Takijiro Ohnishi, the designated commander of the First Air Fleet and his country's foremost expert in aerial warfare, convened a meeting in which he announced:

> ... (T)he First Air Fleet has been designated to ... render enemy carriers ineffective ... In my opinion this can be accomplished only by crash diving on the carrier flight decks with Zero fighters carrying 250 kilogram bombs.[9]

Admiral Ohnishi's predecessor made a journal entry dated 18 October 1944 in which he wrote:

> We can no longer win the war by adhering to conventional methods of warfare ... we must steel ourselves against weakness. If fighter pilots set an example by volunteering for special attack (Kamikaze) missions, other units will follow suit. These examples will in turn inspire surface (navy) forces and army forces ... we conclude that the enemy can be stopped and our country saved only by crash dive attacks on their ships.[10]

A Special Attack Unit, or Kamikaze, pilot's manual included the following advice:

- *Transcend life and death. When you eliminate all thoughts about life and death, you will be able to totally disregard your earthly life.*

- *In the case of an aircraft carrier (when attacking), aim at the elevators. Or if that is difficult, hit the flight deck at the ship's stern. For a low altitude horizontal attack, aim at the middle of a vessel, slightly higher than the waterline. If that is difficult … aim at the entrance of the airplane hangar or the bottom of the stack.*

- *At the very moment of impact do your best. Every deity and the spirits of your dead comrades are watching you intently … do not shut your eyes … many have crashed into the targets with wide open eyes. They will tell you what fun they had.*

- *Remember when diving into the enemy shout at the top of your lungs: 'Hissatsu!' ('Sink without fail!'). At that moment all the cherry blossoms at Yasukuni Shrine in Tokyo will smile brightly at you.*[11]

One of the BPF's missions was to strike at the Ryuku Island chain that extends in a long southwesterly arc from the tip of Kyushu, Japan's southernmost island. The arc of islands includes Okinawa and continues to the northernmost point of Formosa. The value of Okinawa to the Allies lay in the island's airfields and anchorages from which the expected invasion of Japan could be staged. Japan intended nothing other than to fight desperately to prevent that. Heavy anti-aircraft fire against Fleet Air Arm planes flying against Okinawa took its toll on British aircraft. While no target was immune to their attention, Kamikaze pilots made special efforts to target aircraft carriers. The aircraft carrier HMS *Victorious,* which had transferred to the BPF in February 1945, was hit by her first Kamikaze in April. Despite the fact that the hits absorbed by *Victorious* and her well-armoured counterparts always had to be considered seriously, American naval historian Samuel Eliot Morison's assertion was that …

*… a Kamikaze hitting a steel deck* (of a British carrier) *crumpled up like a scrambled egg and did relatively little damage, whilst one crashing the wooden flight deck of an American carrier usually penetrated to the hangar deck and raised hell below.*[12]

11 April 1945: USS *Enterprise* CV-6 after the Kamikaze attack

## 'They Were Very Difficult to Shoot Down'
### Kamikazes

In May the Japanese went full bore after the Allies off Okinawa. The famed USS *Enterprise* was simultaneously set upon by twenty-six Kamikazes of which the ship's defensive planes and anti-aircraft guns shot down all but one. The lone surviving Kamikaze crashed into the ship, penetrated the flight deck, and exploded deep below decks. *Enterprise* had to be withdrawn from combat operations and sent home for repairs. Not long afterwards, a second American carrier was so badly damaged that she too had to be withdrawn from combat operations. The British carriers would each have their turns.

*Formidable* took a Kamikaze hit that, while not causing much damage to the ship, exploded among aircraft on the flight deck. The hit caused fires and explosions that wrecked a great number of the parked planes. When her time came, *Indomitable* tried to protect herself by ducking under cloud cover for a spell, but persistent pursuit by the Japanese resulted in her being hit. Not two days, later *Victorious* was again hit, this time by two Kamikazes just minutes apart. The armoured British decks proved their value by preventing the type of extensive damage taken by the American carriers.

According to Raymond Barker of HMS *Victorious*, Japanese air attacks were often announced ahead of time by the appearance of an enemy scout plane. Flying out of defensive gun range, such planes served to report pertinent target information to incoming attackers. Defensive aircraft would be launched in order to engage the Kamikazes as far from the ship as possible, but there were practically always some who got through. As in the case of the American *Enterprise*, only one hit always had the potential to raise hell. Although the British sailors had been warned about Kamikazes, very few could get a sense of what they really were until they actually experienced their first attack. Then they were 'astounded,' 'shocked,' and 'amazed' that someone would want to deliberately kill himself for a cause. It seemed to defy all logic. An attacker, after all, would never know if he had been successful or not. Even if successful, there could never be any enjoyment of victory. Barker recalled that the first Kamikaze strike against *Victorious* involved seven planes. They appeared to be torpedo planes approaching to drop their weapons, but they suddenly gained altitude, wheeled, and began to dive. All of them were shot down, but until they were all gone, Barker could not avoid an intense feeling of helpless vulnerability. He felt that he could tolerate a conventional bomb attack reasonably well enough. To him, such cases were impersonal matters of an airplane going against a ship. Having to watch a Kamikaze bore in on him, however, made him think that the pilot was aiming precisely at none other than just him. For Barker, the sense that he was being personally attacked made the Japanese suicide attempts on his ship eerily unpleasant. In all, Barker witnessed three Kamikaze hits on *Victorious*. He said of them,

*They were very difficult to shoot down. Once you saw them wheel and start to dive you loosed every gun you had on them but it's a fact of life that a lot of gunnery is very inaccurate … most of it is … and whilst we shot some down, most of them that attacked the fleet got through … they caused damage but not the damage they caused on the American ships … we were different from the Americans insofar as we had an armoured flight deck; 3½ inches thick (of) armour plate ... the Americans had wooden flight decks under which was a ½ inch steel plate and when a Kamikaze hit their flight deck it went straight through and often into the hangar where other airplanes were either being bombed up or being fueled or whatever and tremendous explosions and conflagrations took place. When we were hit we had a hole ... 3 feet in circumference and we just put a steel plate over and some quick drying cement and our airplanes were back to flying in a quarter of an hour's time. The material effect (of Kamikaze hits) was very small but the morale sapping effect was in a different league ... and then they had a variation of that towards the end of the war when an airplane would drop, from twenty miles away, a bomb with a man attached to it and he had a little guidance system and he was rocket propelled ... he could chase you around. They were very unpredictable ... most of them got nowhere near the fleet; they crashed into the sea, they blew up in mid-air; all sorts of things happened to them. We never suffered a single hit from these. We called them 'Chase McCharlies'.*[13]

British carrier sailor Graham Oakes Evans described the Kamikaze strike against *Indomitable* of 4 May,

*... The ship performed evasion maneuvers as the first Kamikaze (of only three from a formation of 20) to break through the CAP closed in on the starboard side and somehow evaded the ship's ferocious flak barrage. The Kamikaze struck (our) flight deck about 10 yards astern of the island sending personnel diving for cover. The Kamikaze spewed burning petrol engulfing the flight deck in black acrid smoke. But surprisingly it did not explode as it bounced off the armoured flight deck and glided over the port side. It detonated upon impact with the ocean, throwing a huge sheet of water over the carrier ... There was no respite though as a second Kamikaze attacked. Miraculously our luck held as I watched the suicide plane pass just above the flight deck over our heads. It too exploded harmlessly as it hit the ocean alongside punctuated by another shower of water over the deck.*[14]

Walter Hagan, a crewman aboard another carrier, *Illustrious,* remembered a near miss aboard his ship,

> *The aircraft that was diving on to our deck on this particular occasion was hit by our anti-aircraft guns which diverted its dive slightly ... for its wing to hit the bridge in passing and dive into the sea alongside the island (superstructure). It exploded in the water and the remains of the aircraft were blown onto the flight deck, plus the pilot's skull, which was kept by the medical officer. Years later I met (him) ... at the Ophthalmic Hospital in Maidstone (and) asked him what had happened to the skull. He told me that he had given it to the C.O. of one of the squadrons on the ship.*[15]

Another British carrier crewman, Paddy Vincent, offered his thoughts and feelings about the Japanese suicide corps,

> *(At) Okinawa ... we became very familiar with the Kamikaze attacks. They were unusual! I don't recall being frightened – once committed to action you're too busy doing your job to feel miserable ... I had a grandstand view as a Kamikaze pilot strafed the* Indomitable *then crashed into the* Indefatigable.[16]

Vincent was wounded while on *Indefatigable.* When he was brought down from his battle station, he was dropped roughly onto the deck. His shipmates found shrapnel wounds in his arms and legs and a bullet hole in his chest. He kept the bullet inside him long after the war. Vincent added,

> *One of the most striking things about our war is that we were all kids – the average age of our ship's company was only twenty-one – half of us were aged just eighteen, nineteen, or twenty – and the Kamikaze pilots were just the same. We found out later that the Kamikaze pilots were the youngest in the Japanese Air Force. They were expendable – to be a Kamikaze would have been a waste of an experienced pilot.*
>
> *They were very difficult to stop – they would dive fast and change course unexpectedly. Altogether there were about 2000 Kamikaze attacks and*

*Formidable* on
fire following the
Kamikaze attack

*about a fifth of them got through – 402 of our ships were hit and half of
these were sunk or damaged beyond use.*[17]

Kamikaze attacks were further described by Douglas Parker who had been a
pilot and squadron commander aboard several aircraft carriers, among them
*Victorious* and *Formidable*.

*… we were vulnerable, as were the Americans operating against Okinawa,
to that dread thing called the Kamikaze dive bomber … and whilst we were
operating off Okinawa we in* Formidable *were hit with two Kamikazes
in rapid sequence. The first one literally bounced off the ship with not
too much damage but it thoroughly succeeded in making everyone aware
(of) what a menace it was trying to deal with these people who would fly
through the most vicious of antiaircraft fire imaginable … (they) would
fly literally down the barrels of Oerlikons and batteries of light AA guns*

*(that were arrayed) all around the flight deck of an aircraft carrier 'til they literally flew down the barrel of the gun and they would still keep going. It was quite depressing at times to see that ability to keep going ... while the pilot was killed or the wing was blown off of them the rest would continue as it had been originally continuing until it hit the ship ... some were literally breaking up in front of the gun barrel as they practically ran down them. This presented a problem, obviously, to the command because with the best will in the world it was very difficult to expect gun crews exposed in the catwalks, i.e. the decks alongside the flight deck of carriers out in the open fresh air, operating their guns to stay there firing when the aircraft was practically on the other end of their gun. It was very tempting for them to dive under the 3½ inch of Skoda armoured steel which was used in the construction of the flight deck because we had great faith that no matter what happened with the Kamikazes they would bounce off our armour plate. ... (but) they were very gallant men who literally did go on firing until they could see the whites of the pilot's eyes.*[18]

The British concept of fairness was so shaken by the Japanese suicide attacks that they themselves, at least on one occasion, violated the so-called rules of war. Norman Harrison, *Victorious'* Assistant Operations Officer, recalled that after the ship had been hit by a Kamikaze, he saw the plane, still fairly intact, land in the water. The pilot climbed out and was standing on the wing when every gun that could bear turned on him and fired. The tradition among sailors had always been clear that, friend or enemy, a man in the water was to be helped rather than hurt. *Victorious'* gunners left no trace of Japanese plane or pilot but later, many could not help but feel badly for what they had done.[19]

ENDNOTES

1.  Morison, Samuel Eliot. *History of United States Naval Operations in World War II,* Vol. XIV. Little, Brown & Co. 1960. pp. 102–107, 211–214, 247–250, and 262–266. Information on the British Pacific Fleet and its individual ship operations cited from Morison is contained in these referenced pages.

2.  Morison.

3.  Morison.

4.  The shipboard guests were King George VI, whose father was the ship's namesake, Queen Elizabeth, and Princesses Elizabeth (future queen) and Margaret.

5.  It was routine for carrier groups to have defensive aircraft continuously aloft to guard against an enemy air attack. The protective planes were called the Combat Air Patrol, or CAP.

6.  historycentre (contributor). 'HMS *King George V* – My Experiences.' BBC WW2 *People's War.* Article ID A 3186416. 2004.

7.  Imperial War Museum. Sound recording archive. 12503. Lang, John Robert. 1992.

8.  Mason, Geoffrey LCDR. 'HMS *King George V* – King George V Class 14-inch Gun Battleship.' Naval_history.net. Web. Accessed July 2014.

9.  Evans, David. *The Japanese Navy in World War II,* 2nd edition. Naval Institute Press. 1986. pp. 421–422.

10. Evans.

11. Axell, Albert and Kase, Hideki. 'Japan's Suicide Gods.' Excerpted in *The Guardian.* Web. Accessed February 2014.

12. Morison.

13. Imperial War Museum. Sound recording archive. 25209. Barker, Raymond. 2003. The manned bombs were called Jinrai, meaning 'sudden peal of thunder,' by the Japanese. The Americans referred to them as Baka, or 'stupid.'

14. Robin Marie (contributor). 'RNVR HMS *Wanderer* and HMS *Indomitable* (1941–1945), Part 4.' BBC WW2 *People's War.* Article ID A 9031493. 2006.

15. Kent County Council Libraries & Archives – Maidstone District (contributor). 'A Navigator in the Fleet Air Arm to May, 1945.' BBC WW2 *People's War.* Article ID A 7751063. 2005.

16. Lancshomeguard (contributor). 'Captain Paddy Vincent's War.' BBC WW2 *People's War.* Article ID A 4477737. 2005.

17. Lancshomeguard.

18. Imperial War Museum. Sound recording archive. 15533. Parker, Douglas. 1995.

19. Imperial War Museum Harrison, Norman. Sound recording archive. 28803. 2006.

# FOURTEEN
# WHEN SAILORS FELL

### 'The Ship Hasn't Been Announced as Sunk Yet'

Almost 66,000 Royal Navy personnel were killed or wounded in the course of World War II. Among those injured in the line of duty was Elijah Cheetham aboard the cruiser *Penelope*. The ship, just detached from shore bombardment duties off Salerno, was hit by torpedoes from a U-boat in February 1944. The cruiser went down quickly and nearly three quarters of her crew were killed. *Penelope*'s sinking was not immediately made public as attested to in a letter written to his mother by the eighteen-year-old Cheetham. The letter was mailed from Naples about two weeks after the incident. It addressed matters of wartime secrecy and security.

HMS *Penelope* at Malta harbour in June 1942 showing the damage that earned her the nickname HMS *Pepperpot*

*I'm terribly sorry I haven't written to you for the last fortnight, I have been rather ill in hospital. I am a survivor of HMS* Penelope *... There were 750 in the ship's company and only 200 were saved. Terrible isn't it? I am pleased to say that Stan Lake survived. I couldn't write to you separately. I have had to smuggle this into the country, the ship hasn't been announced as sunk yet. We are not allowed to mention that we survived. Paddy is going home so I have asked him to post this in England. It doesn't get censored there, but he insists on bringing this personally ... Please try not to worry too much about me. I'm OK now and, believe me, I'm willing to go back and give Jerry exactly what I received and more ... Cheerio and God Bless You All, Your Loving Son ... xxxxx* [1]

### 'Return to Sender on Admiralty Instructions'

The envelope of a letter written by a mother to her son was used to inform family members of his death. The letter was returned as undeliverable with a sticker on the envelope reading,

**Return to Sender on Admiralty Instructions.** *It is with deepest regret that you are informed that the addressee has died on Active Service.*[2]

The most common means by which families were notified of a wartime death was telegram. The wording of the messages was straightforward and unemotional. A preserved copy of one such telegram, sent in regards to a Royal Navy sailor's death states,

'DEEPLY REGRET TO REPORT THE DEATH OF YOUR SON (*name omitted*)
ON WAR SERVICE. LETTER FOLLOWS.' [3]

The promised letter mentioned in the telegram informing the mother about her son's death was ultimately delivered. The letter emphasised the importance of the duty being performed by the deceased, a crewman aboard the cruiser HMS *Arethusa,* at the time of his death. It also attempted to soothe the pain of loss with a brief description of the respectful manner in which the man's remains were placed at rest. A portion of the Admiralty's official account of the action which led to the death was included with the letter.

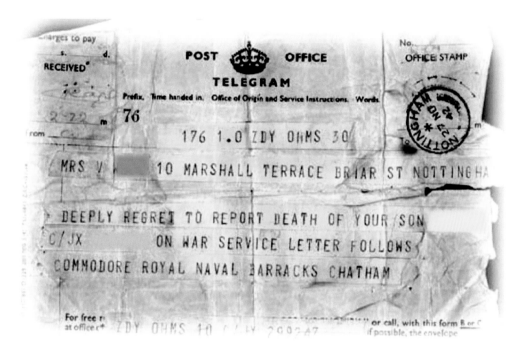

The official telegram by which wartime families were notified of a death

*On 18 November 1942, HMS* Arethusa *formed part of the escort of cruisers and destroyers taking an important convoy through the Eastern Mediterranean to Malta. It was important because Malta needed stores to enable her to fulfill the role allotted to her in the great general offensive operations which had opened with the British Eighth Army's advance from Alamein positions a few days previously. During the day the convoy was passing through that part of the Mediterranean between Cyrenaica and Crete known as 'Bomb Alley' and at dusk had reached a position about half way between Derna, on the hump of Cyrenaica, and Malta. Both the convoy and the escorts had been attacked during the day but neither had been damaged.*

*At the very end of twilight, in that difficult light when visibility favours aircraft rather than a ship, a strong formation of German Torpedo-Carrying Aircraft made a most determined attack upon the escort.*

*The* Arethusa *was attacked simultaneously from both sides and was able to avoid all but one of the torpedoes. This torpedo hit her and caused a violent explosion accompanied by a severe blast. The blast killed instantaneously all the men in the vicinity. Some not quite so close were badly burned by the flash and some of these unfortunately died later of their injuries. The next of kin of these men were informed that their kinsmen had died from burn injury, but it can now be stated with some certainty that all the remainder were killed at once by the tremendous blast and that they would not have suffered pain.*

*Their bodies were buried at sea, altogether three services were held, and they were taken by the Chaplain very beautifully and reverently.*

*A memorial service was held ashore later when the ship reached port and it was a most impressive service. Correspondence is now being exchanged with the Commodore of the Royal Naval Barracks at Chatham about a permanent memorial to these gallant men to be placed in the Barracks Church. It will probably form a part of the general memorial to all the men of the Chatham Division who lose or have lost their lives in this present war.*[4]

## 'And Gently Pressed the Bodies Until They Sank'
## Burial at Sea

When the combat damaged *Arethusa* returned to Alexandria the destroyer *Aldenham* was ordered alongside to pick up the bodies of about fifty of the men who had been killed. The destroyer's duty was to carry the bodies to a point about three miles offshore of Alexandria and to lower them into the sea. An *Aldenham* crewman described process.

(The canvas covered bodies on the dock were) *laid out in lines and attached to each one was a four-inch projectile. The bodies of the* Arethusa's *men (were) mostly Marines ... Without any fuss we tied up, and a section of the ship's guardrails removed on the starboard side against the jetty, and a wide board placed down on* Aldenham's *deck and made fast at the*

HMS *Arethusa*

The destroyer
*Aldenham*

*other end. Then commenced the job of sliding the bodies carefully down the ramp and stacking them high on deck, some under the boat davits, some against the torpedo tubes, and more aft towards the quarterdeck, leaving the port side clear for the conduction of the service.*

*The last body brought inboard, the board pulled back, the guardrails replaced, and then two padres came in (sic) board followed by a funeral firing party from* (cruiser) *HMS* Orion, *and lastly a very young Marine bugler.*

*With a signal from the bridge wires were cast off, and* Aldenham *slowly moved away to commence her journey to the open sea. At the same time the cruiser had cleared lower deck, the men standing quietly facing outboard, caps removed in a last farewell gesture to their fallen comrades. Suddenly the peace of the afternoon was shattered by the shrill blast of a bosun's call from high up on the cruiser's bridge.*

*The 'still'. Everybody at attention and not a sound except the* Aldenham's *screws churning up the water. Then the 'carry on,' as the ship turned away crossing the harbour to the open sea, ensign at half-mast … Slowly we cleared the boom and out into the blue calm of the Mediterranean, the sun settling away in the western sky throwing long rays across the placid water … The ship's engines shut down and slowly we came to a standstill, and with that the C. of E.* (Church of England) *Padre stood up on the torpedo tubes platform and commenced this solemn service for burial at sea, his voice sadly droning on, the ship's company gathered around with heads bent, the sea breezes playing little tricks on hair and collars. Then it was the R.C.* (Roman Catholic) *service. Emotionally and bravely, the Padre carried on this sad service until at the conclusion he closed his prayer book with a definite movement. This was the cue for the funeral firing party. At a command from their officer they raised their rifles to the firing position. Then one volley and another and another until the end with the order, 'present arms'. A pause and the Marine bugler sprang to attention, his bugle ready at his lips. Loud and clear across that still water – the 'Last Post'. Slowly the notes died away and the one minutes silence. Everybody and everything dead quiet, even the sea breezes and the birds seemed to pause in stillness at this very heart rending moment. Then it was over as if a spell had been broken and men who had volunteered commenced their gruesome task of committing the dead to the deep.*

*The guardrails were slipped and a suitable board positioned and in pairs the corpses were tilted over the side. Half way through this task some of the bodies were floating having not been sufficiently weighted and both padres became very agitated but their fears were soon allayed when (several of the crew) produced a couple of very long boat hooks and gently pressed the bodies under until they sank.*[5]

## 'After That I Didn't Sleep Very Well'
## Preparing Bodies

HMS *Abercrombie*

In August 1943 Leading Seaman Patrick Fitz's ship, the monitor HMS *Abercrombie*, struck a mine while shelling targets at Salerno. The ship was placed out of action and Fitz along with many of his shipmates were sent ashore to various duties in Italy. One day, he was asked by the petty officer in charge of his particular detail if he knew how to sew. When he replied affirmatively, Fitz was then asked if he would be willing to volunteer for a job. He innocently agreed and was informed that,

*… (there was) a nasty job to do in the morning … (the petty officer in charge) said, 'we've got 16 bodies down at the morgue off a minesweeper that was sunk some weeks ago and the bodies have just been recovered … (and) they're not in a very nice state … and we've got to go down to prepare to sew them up (into canvas bags for burial at sea)' … so I said, 'well, I'll certainly give you a hand'. So the next morning … we went down to the morgue and we went into this room and there was all these bodies lying there and they were all covered in sheets but because they'd been picked up from where they'd been in the sea they were all in rather grotesque positions … and we took with us a large bolt of canvas and we spent all that day and part of the next day sewing these poor souls up and we then took them to a minesweeper … and I took a small (honor) guard of sailors and we fired a salute over them and we buried them out (at sea). I have to admit that when that was all done for several weeks after that I didn't sleep very well.*

*We had another occasion that another minesweeper was sunk and … the bodies … we had to sew again … but they actually had been in hospital and they were covered in sheets and so we were able to not have so much of a horrific job as when we done the previous one. They used to say that Giuseppe Garibaldi … the Italian (national hero) … he is buried in a little island called Caprera (off Sardinia) … it's a very small island (and) you can walk to it over a little causeway … and they've got his tomb there in a large building … and the rumor is that if anyone goes to visit it, he's then troubled with bad luck. And I found out that the crew(s) of both those minesweepers … or some of them … had actually visited Garibaldi's tomb. If there's any truth in this, I don't know.*[6]

### 'Sold Before the Mast'- Personal Effects

Several months prior to the formation of the British Pacific Fleet in 1944, HMS *Victorious* was ordered to join the Eastern Fleet at Ceylon. From July through October the aircraft carrier participated in air attacks against heavily defended Japanese oil and rail facilities in Indonesia. Even though the attacks devastated their targets, British aircraft losses were high. Individual missions often resulted in a 15–20 per cent aircraft attrition rate.

Pilots or officers who were killed had their personal effects sent home but, if the deceased were a rating such as an observer or a telegraphist/air-gunner, his effects would be taken on deck and auctioned off, or 'sold before the mast'. The items to be sold generally included such things as clothing, playing cards, pens, reading material, cigarettes and cigarette lighters. The sales proceeds would be sent to the man's widow or mother. If a man had been especially popular, or if the crew knew that his family was needy, they would be deliberate in bidding everything up. In one case where it was known that a man's widowed mother was practically destitute, the bids netted her £350, a sum that in those days was enough to buy a house. In another case where it was widely known that a wife had been cheating on a man who was killed, there were no bids at all and the effects were placed over the side.[7]

ENDNOTES

1.  'Able Seaman Elijah Cheetham, HMS *Penelope*.' The Wartime Memories Project. wartimememoriesproject.com. Web. Accessed June 2014.

2.  _____'HMS *Arethusa*.' hms-arethusa.co.uk. Web. Accessed June 2014. The artifact, along with similar others, is reproduced on the website and can be viewed under the link 'Memorabilia.'

3.  _____'HMS *Arethusa*.'

4.  _____'HMS *Arethusa*.'

5.  Mason, F. A. The Last Destroyer. Excerpted in 'HMS *Arethusa*.' hms-arethusa.co.uk. Web. Accessed June 2014.

6.  Imperial War Museum. Sound recording archive. 21284. Fitz, Patrick Walter. 2001.

7.  Imperial War Museum. Sound recording archive. 25209. Barker, Raymond. 2003.

# FIFTEEN
# THE WRENS WERE IN IT, TOO

One of the key branches of the Royal Navy during World War II was the Women's Royal Navy Service. The branch bore the abbreviation of WRNS but its personnel were popularly referred to as 'Wrens'. Most of the women were volunteers, but as the war progressed and its demands became acute, some were called up. By 1944 there were 74,000 Wrens aged nineteen to forty-three, some of them mothers and others of them widows of the war.

The jobs assigned to Wrens quickly began to include responsibilities that were originally considered to be beyond the capabilities of women. Besides clerical or kitchen work, Wrens became drivers, radar operators, communications specialists, meteorologists and crypto analysts. The women who worked in cryptology often did so at the Government Code and Cypher School at Bletchley Park. The School was the heart of British intelligence where some of the most important enemy codes were broken. Wrens were also instrumental in the planning of naval operations that included the D-Day landings at Normandy. Although Wrens were not assigned to sea duty, more than a few operated yard craft in fleet support roles at the Navy's various bases at home and abroad. Over the course of the war 303 Wrens were killed in service.

### 'I Am Proud to Have Served With Them'

Although the stories of former Wren Olive (Swift) Partridge are those of but one woman, her words reflect the experiences of many of the women who volunteered to serve in the Royal Navy. Partridge's memories attest to the fact that the Wrens did far more than answer the call of a popular wartime recruiting poster encouraging women to 'free up a spot for a man aboard a ship'.

*In 1941, aged nineteen, I volunteered for the Women's Royal Navy Service. I was accepted because I was healthy and well-educated, as in World War II standards were high, and I am proud to have served with them.*

*I did my training at Mill Hill, near London. It was indeed a testing time. We did a lot to keep fit and we were taught how to protect ourselves in an emergency ... and what to do in a gas attack which was a threat throughout the war but, to my knowledge, never actually happened. The marching was the hardest part ... the feet suffered in the heavy laced up shoes.*

*We were allowed to choose our future job and I cheerfully volunteered for maintenance work ... I thought it would make a change from office work. In due course, five of us set off by train to Great Yarmouth. A more uninspiring sight can't be imagined (than us) in our ill-fitting uniforms and our safari-type hats. Soon, I am glad to say, we were issued with the up-to-date hat, complete with band bearing the name of our base, HMS Midge.*[1]

*We were billeted in a large former guest house, but found that it was bombed, so we were taken to a hotel near the sea front (which was) lovely. Most of the civilians were evacuated but we had a large number of service personnel (including) Wrens, the WAAF, and the ATS,*[2] *not to mention the frequent visits from American servicemen stationed at nearby Norwich. We were issued with bell bottom trousers, a boiler suit, and oil skins so we did wonder what we were getting into … We soon found out. The five of us were marched down to the harbor … where flotillas of motor gun boats and motor torpedo boats were moored … MGBs and MTBs, for short. There we were taken aboard and down the hatch into the engine room. I don't know which of us was more astonished, the engine crew or us. The general reaction was possibly, 'Oh, my God.' The engines were hot, having just returned from sea, and the sailors were stripped to the waist. Daphne, a general's daughter who had led a sheltered life, took one look and beat it back up the ladder. She went to Signals, a lovely girl, and we became great friends and cabin mates.*

*I never regretted my decision to stick with it. We were taught to change plugs, strip down gear boxes and distributor heads, and anything else needed to help* (any of the) *three Hall Scott or Packard American engines* (installed on the boats) *ready for action. We went out to sea on trials when the* (repair or maintenance) *job(s)* (were) *finished and stood on the deck, side by side with the men, as we sailed out of the harbor. A mutual feeling of friendship and great respect grew up between sailors and Wrens which lasted the whole four and a half years. We worked, danced, partied, and laughed together. We also experienced great sorrow when any of the boats were missing or damaged. I remember one in particular, No. 313, which limped home with a great hole where the engine room had been. The entire engine room crew had been killed.*

*I worked with a petty officer most of the time and, after the war, we were married. We saw a lot more action before that, though. We were regularly shot at by low flying German planes as we marched down to the base to work. We ran for cover, they weren't very good shots, nobody was hit. I must say, though, the bombing was devastating … a lot of service quarters were razed to the ground, including our own. I was sleeping in a top bunk but, found myself blasted from my bed, lying on the floor at the far end of the room amongst a lot of rubble and glass … There were seven of us in the cabin, and … nobody panicked … we had great faith in our naval friends … they dug us out alright … if they hadn't got a spade, they dug with their hands. Fire broke out and, being short of fire engines, we formed a chain and passed buckets of water along … We found many of our friends injured or in shock and (they) had to be sent home. Worst of all, seven Wrens and our officer were killed, but war is no time for brooding, and we survivors attended a memorial service for our dead comrades and went back to work.*

*… When VE Day came, we were immediately given passes to go ashore … my fiancé was stationed on the Isle of Wight at that time, and I went across on the ferry, but he was coming this way, so we missed each other. I ended up dancing and singing round Piccadilly Circus with thousands of people celebrating. VJ Day quickly followed and we had truly won the Second Great War along with our gallant allies. With pride, I think we could all say, 'Well Done.'* [3]

Two other Wrens, Margaret Boothroyd and her friend Laura Mountney met on the very first day of training and went on to serve together for the duration of their enlistments. The two women were assigned to ANCXF, the Allied Naval Combined Expeditionary Force at Southwick where they worked in communications during the planning and execution of the D-Day invasion. Operating teletype machines that had been connected to the beach heads by means of underwater cross channel cables, the young women handled important and secret messages relevant to the landings as well as the subsequent push into France. The War Room in which they worked received regular visits from luminaries that included King George VI, Winston Churchill, and Generals Eisenhower and Montgomery.

After a time in service, Boothroyd and Mountney applied for, and were granted, permission for duty on the continent. Because Mountney was not yet twenty-one years old, she was required to get signed permission from her parents before the Navy would post her outside of the United Kingdom. The two Wrens were to follow on the heels of advancing Allied troops from Caen, to Paris and onto Belgium where they continued to work with highly sensitive military communications by teletype and field telephones. Boothroyd said of her experiences,

> *I don't remember myself or my friends expressing any fear whatsoever. Our age, the job we had been called to do, and the excitement all played a part in our being completely confident. The thought of going into the unknown, or death never crossed our minds … we always thought we were on the winning side.*

Boothroyd also recalled hitchhiking throughout France and Belgium which, in her later years, she looked back upon as, 'amazing'. She said,

> *(W)e worked hard, played hard, and that was the order of the day. Discipline abroad was being in your cabin at the proper time, being on watch in good time, and being neat and tidy with hair off the collar.*[4]

Boothroyd left the service shortly after the war and was married at the end of 1945. Her wartime and lifetime friend, Laura Mountney, married Bernard Ashley in 1948 and became the world famous fashion designer, Laura Ashley.[5]

### 'I Was on Duty … and Feeling Very Sorry for Myself'
### One Wren's Christmas

One-time Wren Grace Goodfellow remembered her Christmas of 1942.

> *… I was stationed at RNAS Sandbanks, Dorset and billeted in the Red House, a lovely property, and was lucky enough to occupy the largest bedroom with five other girls. We had the luxury of an en suite bathroom, very rare in those days. The ceiling of the bedroom was decorated with a moon and stars, and we would shine our torches on it after lights out looking for imaginary aeroplanes.*

*I was on duty over the Christmas period and feeling very sorry for myself as it was the first time away from my parents and home. We had our Christmas lunch and a party of us who were off duty in the afternoon had been invited to an ENSA* (Entertainments National Service Association, established in 1939 to entertain service personnel during WWII) *concert on Brownsea Island. It was a most beautiful day and we donned our best blues and did not need our greatcoats. We were ferried to the island in a motorboat, but as we approached the shore, we saw to our horror, a line of soldiers, all obviously well-fed, watered, and full of 'Dutch Courage,' and clutching sprigs of mistletoe, waiting to greet us. 'We'll run for it,' we said, and we did. Not very sporting of us, but we were young and rather shy in those far off days. We were given very good seats for the concert about which I remember very little except for the lady who sang 'The Lights of Home,' a song made famous by* (Canadian-American singer-actress of the 1930s–1940s) *Deanna Durbin. I sobbed noisily and uncontrollably all the way through. What a wimp! … I could relate sad and tragic tales of the war years, as all those who lived through that dreadful period could, service men and women and civilians alike. But I prefer to remember the friendships of the girls I served with who were from all walks of life; the 'old salts' who at first resented us and then accepted us and were kind, the young ones who dated us, and, sometimes, married us. Please, God there will never, ever be such a world-wide conflict again.*[6]

## 'Joining the Wrens Was a Liberation'
## Six Wrens Look Back

A group of six women known as the 'Dundee Wrens' recalled their wartime thoughts and experiences. Helen Dunn enlisted in 1941 after her brother was killed in action at sea. Like her brother, she became a stoker and, hoping to be allowed to stay near home, was fortunate to be posted to Dundee.[7]

Babs Rickman remembered being given warnings and advice by members of her family about the possibility of forward behavior by the many navy men she was sure to encounter. She claimed that it was unnecessary when none of the men ever really looked at her. Her main motivations for joining the WRNS, she claimed, were '… because they had the best uniform and my mum was a lousy cook. I had to get away!' A popular saying among the Wrens during World War II was, 'I joined for the hat.' Rickman became a coding specialist who worked on highly classified electronic direction-finding equipment.[8]

Muriel Thompson said, 'Joining the Wrens was a liberation – the chance to see places and meet people that you would never have otherwise.' Thompson's rank was leading hand, the equivalent of a leading seaman. The rank was one above that of able seaman and one below petty officer. Thompson did not elaborate on her particular job, but as her rank was not that of a specialist she might have worked at clerical duties in an office or been assigned to work under the supervision of a specialist that could have included any naval job. She, like a good many other Wrens, met and married her husband while in uniform.[9]

Margaret Kennedy spent much of her time at the windswept and barren base at Scapa Flow. Her chief memory of the place was, 'They always said Scapa had too many Wrens and not enough men!' Like Muriel Thompson, Kennedy did not mention her specific job at Scapa. She could have done anything: office work, ship repair, storekeeping, communications, medical work or any of the other jobs assigned to base support personnel.[10]

Dorothy Garland was responsible for operating and maintaining the antisubmarine netting placed at harbor entrances. She did not mention being in any particular danger except for once having her bath interrupted by a German air raid. She said of her wartime service, 'They were really happy days. We were green as grass, we'd never been anywhere before and my main memory is of meeting so many lovely people.' Norma Abel agreed with Garland that friendships made in wartime were the most enduring aspect of her time as a Wren.[11]

### 'A Lot of People Would Have Done Exactly the Same'
### A Wren's Citation

If many of the men who served in the Royal Navy from 1939 to 1945 were recalcitrant to speak about their wartime experiences, so it was also for Beth Hutchinson, a Wren who had been decorated for heroism. In November 1943, Hutchinson was driving on patrol in a remote part of Scotland when a Swordfish torpedo bomber crashed nearby. Her subsequent actions were recognized in

1944 when King George VI presented her with British Empire Medal for bravery. The citation accompanying Hutchinson's award read,

> *An aircraft crashed in flames at Crossing Bombing Range. Wren Booth* (her maiden name) *drove with an officer to the scene of the accident, and, with complete disregard for her own safety, assisted in dragging the observer clear of the main wreckage while explosions inside the aircraft scattered burning debris and petrol all around them.*[12]

Hutchinson managed to extinguish the flames on the flier with her bare hands, put him into her vehicle, then drive him to the nearest medical facility. He died of his injuries. Hutchinson never told the story to any of her children or grandchildren. Her family was also unaware that she had been awarded the BEM. When she finally spoke about it some seventy years later, she said,

> *It was very dark and the weather wasn't very good. I can remember seeing a plane swoop down, but I didn't see it come back up. I drove over to the wreckage, where I jumped out of the vehicle. The pilot was already dead, but the co-pilot had been thrown clear and was on fire. I had to stamp out the flames with my hands. I was very upset that I couldn't save him, but he was so badly injured that it was a miracle that he had survived so long after the crash. You don't think about the danger at the time. If you are going to do it, you are going to do it. I am sure that an awful lot of people would have done exactly the same.*[13]

Hutchinson's daughter who was sixty-four by the time she became aware of her mother's deeds, said,

> *This is the first time I have ever heard her talk about it. She was so shy, and she did not want to cause any fuss. She just said that she did what she had to do.*[14]

ENDNOTES

1. Naval bases were named as if they were ships.

2. WAAF – Women's Auxiliary Air Force, ATS – Auxiliary Territorial Service (Women's branch of the Army).

3. Wrye Forest Volunteer Bureau (Contributor). 'One Wren's War.' BBC WW2 *People's War.* Article ID A3429209. 2004.

4. Wyedale (contributor). 'In The WRNS With Laura Ashley.' BBC WW2 *People's War.* Article ID A 2939646. 2004.

5. Wyedale.

6. Wildern School (contributor). 'A WREN's Christmas Memories.' BBC WW2 *People's War.* Article ID A 2907722. 2004.

7. Ross, Stewart. 'Dundee Wrens: Wonder Women of the Second World War.' eveningtelegrph.co.uk. 28 November 2013. Web. Accessed November 2014.

8. Ross.

9. Ross.

10. Ross.

11. Ross.

12. Hills, Suzannah and Watson, Leon. 'Former Wren, 92, Breaks 70 Years of Silence …' dailymail. co.uk. 7 November 2013. Web. Accessed November 2014.

13. Hills and Watson.

14. Hills and Watson.

# SIXTEEN
# HOSTILITIES CEASE

### 'An End to Six Years of War'

On 16 August 1945 Vice-Admiral Bernard Rawlings, second in command of the British Pacific Fleet, issued an important message from his flagship, HMS *King George V*. The same message was broadcast to all British and American ships of the BPF and US Navy Third Fleet.

*The surrender of the Japanese Empire brings to an end six years of achievement in war unsurpassed in the long history and high tradition of the Royal Navy. The phase of naval warfare that came to an end three months ago enriched the record of British sea power by such epic actions and campaigns as the Battle of the Atlantic, the domination of the Mediterranean, the maintenance of the Russian supply lines, and the great combined operations of 1943 and 1944. The worldwide story is completed by the inspired work by sea and air of the British Pacific Fleet and the East Indies Fleet. The Board are deeply conscious of the difficulty and novelty of the problems facing the British Pacific Fleet, the patience and skill with which they were overcome, and the great contribution in offensive power made by the Task Force operating with our American Allies. No less memorable is the work of the East Indies Fleet in the protection of India and Ceylon and in operational support of the Burma campaign. At this moment our eyes are turned to the Far East and it is fitting to recall in remembrance those who gave their lives in the days of disaster of 1941 and 1942. To their relatives and to the relatives of all officers and men of the Royal Navy and the Royal Marines and of the Naval Forces of the Commonwealth and Empire and to all in Admiralty service who have paid the full price of victory, the Board extend their profound sympathy.*[1]

### 'The Crew Lined the Guardrails to Cheer the Prisoners of War'

*King George V* drops
anchor outside
Tokyo Bay

In the closing days of August, *KGV* and other British and American ships dropped anchor in Sagami Wan, the sheltered body of water just outside of Tokyo Bay. Final diplomatic and military preparations were being made for the formal surrender ceremony. All American and British aircraft carriers remaining at sea were prepared to launch attack aircraft in the event of any Japanese treachery. Shore parties from British ships landed in Japan in order to assist with just liberated POWs. Allied military personnel also entered the major Japanese naval base at nearby Yokosuka for the purpose of taking it over.

Able Seaman Hubert Hancox remembered the last days of the war aboard *KGV*.

> *Our ship provided a platoon ready for landing parties ... after several days on an American landing type ship we went ashore to occupy Yokosuka naval base, quite near Mount Fujiyama, a glorious sight from Tokyo Bay where KGV was then anchored for several weeks. The landing party*

*returned to the ship after a week or so and the crew often lined the guard*
*rails to cheer the (aircraft) carriers loaded with the released British and*
*Australian prisoners of war ...*[2]

Once it was clear that Japan had, indeed, surrendered, ship's cook Victor Stamp, formerly of HMS *Ramillies,* was present to assist with the care for recently released British prisoners at Hong Kong.

*I'll never, ever forget that sight; skin and bone, skin and bone. We had to*
*feed them with a teaspoon of consome soup, otherwise you would kill them*
*... it was made up of meat bones and vegetables and all it was strained*
*through a cloth. We didn't dare give them anything solid, just a teaspoon.*[3]

Following a report he had received about the Japanese POW camps in Indonesia, Lord Mountbatten, Supreme Allied Commander of the South East Asia Theatre, ordered the cruiser HMS *Cumberland* to steam from Singapore to Java. The ship carried key members of the Recovery of Allied Prisoners and Internees (RAWPI) staff. They arrived in Batavia in mid-September 1945. The RAWPI personnel were under instructions to find and meet with allied prisoners in the camps who might be able to work on the post-war administration of Indonesia. *Cumberland,* along with her officers and crew, were also made available to personnel of the South East Asia Command. The latter organization was expecting to disarm and evacuate Japanese military forces in Java, take care of Allied POWs, and prepare to re-establish Dutch colonial control to the area.

Some of *Cumberland's* crew were to assist in caring for thousands of prisoners who had been interred since the Japanese takeover of Java some three and a half years earlier. There were military and civilian camps throughout Java. By the war's end, there were several camps in or near Batavia that held a combined total of about 18,000 women and children along with about 20,000 men and boys. According to Marine Musician Gus Guthrie,

*At Batavia, (we were) relieving the prisoner of war camp. There were*
*two camps; female and male and mainly all the inmates were Dutch.*
*There were a number of crew, Australians, from HMAS* Sydney[4] *and ...*

*(there) was an Englishman ... that my brother knew. He had beriberi of the head[5] (and seeing that) was a rather un-nerving experience. The ladies didn't appear to be too bad and, apparently, they permitted a bit of liaison between the Dutch men and women ... so much so, that there were some very young babies in the camp. We went to entertain them and got all the children to march around with us ... They showed us (around the camp) and it was quite difficult to imagine how they could live under those circumstances. Food was obviously of major concern and, in the male area of the prison, a chap was showing us around and he said, 'Have you noticed that there's no vegetation here? Well, the first sign of vegetation at all and, pfft!, it's off' ... it would be eaten in a very short time; whether it was raw, or cooked, or fried, or boiled.[6]*

HMS *Cumberland*

Guthrie recalled meeting Lady Edwina Mountbatten as she toured the prison camps. He stated that she was very much interested in seeing every corner of the camps and that she asked endless questions. She was keenly interested to know what life had been like in them. What Guthrie did not know, was that

Lady Mountbatten would be instrumental in helping to expedite the relief of the liberated prisoners. She would also dine with a very important British officer and former prisoner who had just been liberated from one of the camps.

The officer with whom Lady Mountbatten dined aboard *Cumberland* was an old-school adventurer and British Army officer. He had intimate knowledge of the history, social climate, and political feelings in Indonesia. He told her that the Indonesians were not in the least bit interested in seeing European Colonial rule restored once the Japanese had been sent away. Lady Mountbatten reported the information to Lord Mountbatten in Singapore. Mountbatten was thus able to see that British support for their Dutch allies against the already risen tide of Indonesian nationalism would be contrary to Britain's long-term interests. Meetings aboard *Cumberland* between Japanese, British, and Dutch principals led to a flurry of messages to and from Singapore. Mountbatten arrived at the decision that the final missions remaining to Britain in Indonesia were those of disarming the remaining Japanese forces and the evacuation of Allied POWs and internees. All other matters pertinent to Indonesia were to be left to the Dutch. The British stance was communicated to the Dutch at the end of September. *Cumberland* weighed anchor soon afterward and she was home by November.[7]

### 'A Lot of People Were Drunk'
### A V-J Day Celebration

Kenneth Waterson was a telegraphist aboard the destroyer HMS *Relentless* anchored in Trincomalee Harbor when word was received that Japan had quit and the World War was finally and completely over.

*That night Trincomalee had its celebrations. There were rocket displays* (for which ships fired off what would normally be distress flares), *jumping jacks* (a type of pyrotechnic) *and concerts … Ships were dressed, every color of flag was flown. There were lots of nationalities. The alphabet went down the USA (America) and USSR (Russia), the latter flew the hammer and sickle. All the flags were hauled down at sunset but were then immediately re-hoisted. The dark night showed up illuminated 'V's (for 'Victory') made up of coloured light bulbs. Some of these were in many colours.*

*When the shadows had gone, the ship next to us let loose with her siren. It was a horrible noise, worse than a(n) air-raid siren. After an interval of about fifteen minutes every ship in the harbor was blowing off a different note. The result was an awful din. In time various 'V's could be distinguished on various sirens. Some put in a 'J' after the 'V' making 'VJ' in Morse Code. Rockets (distress flares) and Vary lights (bright light flares) were being fired freely now all over the harbor. Green, red, yellow and white ones ... Green and red lights shooting up into the air and then back down into the sea. Rustic 'VJ's on hooters and much cheering completed an unreal atmosphere. Blackout was abandoned.*

*By 9:00 pm, the fun increased in tempo. Many were drunk now; where they got the spirits and beer is a mystery ... Early an attempt had been made to mount a concert but the hooters drowned out any attempt to sing. Shooting pretty lights into the air got pretty tame after a while. Ships started firing rockets at each other. Then they all started firing at the aircraft lined up on the upper deck of an aircraft carrier. An urgent signal was sent round the harbor to stop firing rockets ... It says something about discipline that the rocket shooting soon stopped. How it started I know not as I thought that all rockets were kept under lock and key.*

*Instead jumping jacks were fired from rocket launchers. These were fearsome projectiles. They came in various colors and shot from left to right, from front to rear. Shooting down between deck awnings they scattered all and sundry. They were powerful, much stronger than bonfire night jumping jacks. They possibly were Chinese ones but who got them and from where is not known. The awnings* (rigged on Relentless) *were burnt in several places and a fire arose on one of the gun covers.*

*This led to hoses being turned on to put out all the small fires that had started. Generously, ships put out each other's fires by hose. After that the hoses were turned on other ships' crews. Everybody was wet through. Chaps coming back on board from shore leave were caught in this deluge.*

*After that things died down, various concert parties were got up impromptu. We were tied up beside the* Woolwich, *the destroyer parent ship. We got out a singing party and wheeled our piano out onto the quarter deck so that others could see and hear us. The quarter deck was beautifully decorated with bunting. Out came our players in their costumes and started to sing. The stokers on the* Woolwich *did not seem to appreciate our singing; they turned a hose pipe on us. The drums were soaked as was the piano; the bunting was all bedraggled. They did have the foresight to close the bulkhead that gave us access to their ship. Had we made contact, World War III would have broken out between us. By now, a lot of people were drunk ...*[8]

### 'I Was Only Married a Fortnight'
### War Brides

The crew of the carrier *Victorious* was extremely disappointed that they were not among those selected to go to Tokyo Bay for the official surrender ceremony. They felt slighted as theirs had been the only one of the four British Pacific Fleet carriers to have remained continuously 'on the line' during operations against the Japanese. They resignedly accepted the decision to head for Sydney and, as they reached the Bay of Brisbane, all of the aircraft on board were disposed of by pushing them over the side.[9] Sailors clambered into them to strip them of dials, clocks, instruments, and all manner of souvenirs even as they were being unceremoniously shoved towards the edge of the flight deck. After a brief stay in Australia, the ship steamed back home where she arrived in October. Just two weeks later, she was ordered back to Australia to help transport troops and former POWs, many in poor physical condition, back to Britain. Two weeks after disembarking the troops and former prisoners at home, *Victorious* was ordered to Sydney again, this time to transport Australian women who had married British servicemen during the war back to Britain. There were close to 700 war brides.[10]

The women, ranging in age from fifteen to forty-one, had met and married British or Dutch naval personnel who had either taken shore leave or been assigned duty in Australia during the war. The men, from far and wide in England or the Netherlands, had left their brides behind when they were transferred away from Australia by the demands of the war. By the war's end, practically all of the husbands had either been demobilized or stationed back in their home country.

British and Australian authorities lobbied for transport service and *Victorious* was the only warship ever used by England for such a purpose. By July 1946, the Royal Navy had made modifications to the carrier's internal spaces, notably the hangar deck, and sent her to Australia to give passage to the women. The ship and practically all of the brides arrived at Plymouth after a thirty-six-day voyage.

One of the ship's log entries for 2 July 1946 was, 'Commenced embarkation of wives of naval personnel for passage to UK,' and one of the passengers, Mrs Bill West, described the ship's departure,

> The mighty Victorious *drew away from Woolloomooloo wharf with the brides at many vantage points. (There were) bright streamers trailing from the ship's sides. Our families and friends, apprehensive and tearful, (were) waving goodbye from the wharf and the (Sydney) Harbour Bridge gradually receded into the distance.*[11]

Mrs. West's husband, Bill, had served on *Victorious'* fellow carrier *Indefatigable* as a Telegraphist/Air Gunner on an Avenger. During a rough shipboard landing in late April 1945, the TAG was pitched violently forward. He struck his face against one of the plane's hard surfaces. The injury could not be well tended to in the carrier's sick bay so the injured air crewman was sent to a military medical facility in Sydney. He was not so severely injured, however, that he could not take advantage of evening or weekend liberty passes which he used for visits to the British Service Club. The Club offered home-style meals and recreation. It was there that he met the woman, a volunteer hostess, with whom he would remain married for over 60 years. After a period of dating during which he met her family, he had to make a request through his ship's captain for permission to marry. The prospective bride was interviewed by the Royal Navy who was satisfactorily impressed with her background, education and employment history. The young couple was allowed to marry. TAG West's military duties took him back to England alone where he was demobilized to return to his pre-war job. His wife reunited with him in August 1946.[12]

While in transit to England on *Victorious,* the brides were kept busy with work as typists and clerks. They were entertained with movies, arts and crafts, a library, a beauty salon, sports, fashion shows, a dress ball, lectures on what to expect in England and the traditional 'crossing the line' ceremony at the Equator. As *Victorious* had been built with numerous narrow and dark passageways, compartments, and spaces; there were nightly 'chastity rounds' conducted by ship's officers. These patrols were described by the captain as, 'rounds of all-weather decks, galleries, and gun positions … carried out frequently and at irregular periods after dark. All women had to be in their bunks by 11 pm.'

Despite all precautions and preparations, there were some aspects to the trip from Australia that were not fully happy or well publicised. According to Raymond Barker of *Victorious,*

> *It was (quite) a trip because some of (the women) fell in love with sailors on board and some of them didn't want to get off the ship at Plymouth (because) they wanted to go home again. Some of them, their husbands refused to come and meet them at Plymouth, and so we were left with some of these girls crying on the quayside. It was a most stressful trip. I had one come to work for me in the (ship's) office, Veronica was her name. She'd knocked on the office door and said, 'Can I do anything?' … She said, 'I can type and do things like that,' so I said, 'I can find you one or two little bits and pieces to do just to keep you out of mischief.' Then she confessed to me that she didn't want to go to her husband who lived in (England); that she'd fallen in love with a chap on board … 'Well,' she said, 'I was only married a fortnight and then he went away and I haven't seen him since.' One disappeared in (an eastern Mediterranean port); they weren't allowed to go ashore unless they had two naval escorts with them, two men with them, but this one gave the two men the slip and we never saw her again. We think she might have tried to hitch hike back to Australia on a ship going through the Suez Canal; we don't know. We didn't hear any more about her. So, yes, it was an interesting naval voyage the like of which I never contemplated … we had to mount night patrols round the ship to stop any malarkey from going on but, in fact, there was some and when we got to Ceylon; Colombo … the captain had all the war brides up*

*on the flight deck and he addressed them and he said that if any more of this nonsense came to his notice he would put them off at the next port because this was a mission of mercy that we were carrying out taking them back to their husbands and their behavior was very unbecoming. He didn't mention the behaviour of his crew which was none too salubrious either.*[13]

As they left the ship at Plymouth at the end of their journey, the brides were greeted by the mayor and handed a card that read,

*As you step ashore I bid you welcome to Britain and this historic city. Our ties with you and your folk have always been very close, and during the war those ties have been strengthened. For five years squadrons of the RAAF (Royal Australian Air Force) were honoured guests of this City. Many of our girls have found happy homes in your country. May you have great happiness here in the Motherland, and may God's blessing lay upon you.*[14]

### 'If There's a Heaven For People, There Could Be for Ships'

Veteran battleship HMS *Warspite* was back at Portsmouth and paid off in February 1945. She was then sold for disposal in 1946. As the old ship was being towed to the breaker's yard in 1947 she ran hard aground. By then former infantryman Donald Delves, who had benefitted from the battleship's shelling of the Germans at Salerno, was back in England, out of the service, and employed as a metal worker. Delves remembered the battleship fondly.

*After being demobbed our paths (mine and* Warspite's*) would cross again. Me, back in civvy street ... On 23 April 1947, my friend HMS* Warspite, *'The Grand Old Lady,' broke her tow and came ashore at Crudden Point, Prussia Cove in Mounts Bay. I worked on her during her stay there and cut off her front turret which weighed some 700 tons. Each day that I did this I kept thinking, 'I'm cutting up my friend who helped me at Salerno Bay.' She seemed almost human to me. I can't explain it but it was heartbreaking to destroy this fine warship. At the end of July 1950 she was refloated to go to a breaker's yard in South Wales, but shortly sprang a leak in her boiler* *room and had to be towed to Marazion, quite close to St. Michael's Mount, and beached. She was taken away piece by piece and by the end of August 1956, HMS* Warspite *was no more. My friend at Salerno was finally gone and it left me very sad. There was no warship like her. If there is a heaven for people, there could be for ships. I know the Lord will take her into His midst.*[15]

The plight of *Warspite* in Prussia Cove

Economic necessity held no sentiment and soon after the war numerous other Royal Navy ships, many of which, like *Warspite*, had been home to countless young men in their formative years were scrapped. The destroyer *Eskimo*, veteran of Narvik and the Pedestal convoy, was dismantled in 1949. Battleships *Rodney* and *King George V*, *Bismarck's* vanquishers, were broken up in 1948 and 1959 respectively. Light Cruiser *Ajax*, once entirely painted in pink and victor of the Battle of the River Plate, was almost sold to Chile. Prime Minister Churchill, unwilling to have the renowned ship be so ingloriously removed from the Royal Navy roster, blocked the transaction. The ship was sent under her own name and her own flag to the breaker's yard in 1950. Battleship *Royal Sovereign* was loaned to the Russians in 1944, renamed *Archangelsk,* and used by the Red Navy as an Arctic convoy escort. She was returned to Britain after the war to be scrapped.[16]

A few of the sturdiest wartime ships were retained in service. Light cruiser *Belfast* served in the Korean War and was later made suitable for the nuclear age through the addition of atomic, biological, and chemical warfare upgrades. She served until her final decommissioning in 1963. Aircraft carrier *Victorious* also stayed active after the war. She was thoroughly modernized in 1957. Equipped with the latest jet aircraft, she served as a front-line ship until suffering a catastrophic fire in 1967. Deemed too costly to repair, the ship was dismantled in 1969.

Only half dozen World War II navy ships remain in England. All are museum craft or memorials. Light cruiser *Belfast*, operated by the Imperial War Museum and open daily to visitors, lies calmly at anchor in the Thames River. The other ships are the destroyer *Cavalier*, the World War I-era monitor HMS *M-33*, and three submarines. Canada retains two ships from the Second World War. The Tribal class destroyer HMCS *Haida* is a National Historic Site at Hamilton, Ontario. The world's sole surviving Flower class corvette, HMCS *Sackville*, designated as a Canadian Naval Memorial, is at Halifax. Australia maintains a River class corvette, HMAS *Diamantina*, as a museum ship at Brisbane.

### 'I Came Off the Ship … And I Was Lost'

While post-war demobilization quickly thinned the Royal Navy's personnel rosters, a core of experienced and talented men remained in uniform. Among those who stayed were several who would rise to prominence. Captain Eric Brown, who demonstrated merchant ship launched aircraft for Winston Churchill and who later survived the sinking of HMS *Audacity*, went on to become one of the world's premiere test pilots. At the time of his passing in 2016, he held the record for the most carrier landings made by any single pilot. Over his career, Captain Brown test flew over 480 different types of aircraft. RAF pilot Kenneth Cross who survived the sinking of HMS *Glorious*, went on to head Britain's nuclear armed bomber command and ultimately became Air Marshal Sir Kenneth Cross. Albert Pitman who started out as teen-aged artificer aboard *Hood* earned an officer's commission and stayed in the Navy until 1968. In his very active civilian life, he worked as a theater manager and became the owner of, first, a pub and, later, an antique shop. Victor Stamp, the cook who 'did it all' while aboard *Ramillies*, remained in the Navy as a cook and cook instructor until 1960. Gus Guthrie, the Marine Musician and downhill skier at Murmansk, stayed with the Navy until forced to retire for medical reasons in 1953. Guthrie went on to a long and satisfying civilian career as a music instructor.

Raymond Barker of HMS *Victorious* decided to decline the Navy's offer of an officer's commission. When asked to at least think it over, he did not hesitate to say, no. Although he had no clear idea about what his post-war future would hold, he was certain that it would be as a civilian.

> I came off the ship … after almost five years (and) I was lost. It had been the crucible of my manhood, really. I had gone on when I was 19 and I came off when I was twenty-four … all my adult formative years had been on board that ship. It had been my security, my home, the place where I made friendships; some very good ones, as well … companionship, joys, sorrows; all kinds of emotions that had all been experienced on board that ship. I actually shed a few tears when I stood on the jetty at Devonport and looked at her. She was rusting and the guardrails were all chipped and battered; she was in a right old battered state … of course she had been neglected; she had been pushed too hard like a lot of the other ships and then she was seeing the end to her useful life and I felt deeply, deeply sad. Once I left the ship, she had been MY Navy, Victorious had been the Navy then … that was the end of my naval service, really.[17]

After some thought about it, Barker decided that he could not bear to return to his pre-war job as a newspaper reporter. He could no longer tolerate the profession's 'darker side' of unbridled alcohol abuse. Instead, admitting that his years in the Navy had encouraged him to enjoy travel, he went on to a lifetime career in the travel industry.

Frederick Jewett, a former boy seaman at HMS *Ganges*, had not completed the full term of his compulsory service when he requested to be discharged at the end of the war. He was required to show that he would be either employed in the mining industry, heavy manufacturing, or law enforcement. When he secured the promise of a job as a police officer in Newcastle, he was then asked by the Navy for a sum of 36 pounds for his release. Jewett gladly paid and was given his discharge. Jewett laughingly recalled that he was formally let go from the Navy one full day prior to what became his officially scheduled discharge date. In doing this, the Navy would retain the right to recall him for 'time in service owed' and then retain him for whatever length of time it deemed suitable.

Gunner Thomas Adams expressed that the most significant thing that he took from his time in the Navy was having learned to be tolerant of others. Adams' experiences as a Japanese prisoner of war led him to work with one of Britain's non-government Far Eastern Prisoner of War (FEPOW) Associations that were established to assist former POWs or their widows. The work of men like Adams has been taken up by members of COFEPOW, the Children of Far Eastern Prisoners of War, founded in 1997. The latter organization is a registered charity and one of its chief goals is to perpetuate the memory of those who, in service to Britain, were taken prisoner by the Japanese.

Gordon Richmond who had once met Mary Churchill aboard the battlecruiser *Renown*, was granted his discharge soon after the war's conclusion. He went on to a career in the merchant marine.

> *I got my* (Navy discharge) *notice to say, 'Thanks very much … that's the end of the line, mate … the boot.' So I was transferred (off my ship) to Sheerness to await my discharge. … We were all issued with what we called 'Demob Uniforms.' The Government had decided … we had a gratuity, fifty pounds, a lot of money then, so armed with my fifty pounds we went into the clothing store and were issued with suits. Well, the suits fitted where they touched. I think they had barbed wire knitted into them … I think they must have had contracts for the cheapest material that they could get for these suits … The hat looked like (what) an American gangster (would wear), with a narrow brim. I am sure it was cardboard … Well, of course, I got rid of that … didn't I? So that was the end of that … End of the line.*[18]

Nicholas Monsarrat, writing about what the Royal Navy's wartime sailors thought and spoke about noted that,

> *Their plans for the future all seem to center, not round jobs or a steady income, but on a house, a family, a private world which, no matter how cramped or poor it may be, will give them peace against all comers. That is*

*what they (were) fighting for – the sure welcome, the bride, the old woman,
the sprogs: their daydreams are the least ambitious and the gentlest of any
I know.*[19]

After the war, and to the present day, although in ever dwindling numbers,
Royal Navy veterans get together and reminisce. They often talk about things
to one another that they would prefer not to share with anyone else; not even
wives or children. Hubert Hancox who served aboard the battleship *King George
V* offered his view of it.

*A strong bond was formed by shipmates through shared experiences,
particularly so among old messmates … Our ship, a battleship, had a crew
of around 2,000 and one didn't know everyone, but your own messmates
became close … after all you lived, ate, relaxed in off duty hours, and slept
in the (same) confined space … (we) worked together, too … the ship's
company was your constant companions … at sea. It's good to meet up
with your old mates, and to an extent relive the days of our youth. We had
and still enjoy a good laugh … most of us did come home and, as in life
generally, one tends to remember the good times.*[20]

Of his own post-war sentiments, novelist Monsarrat wrote,

*I used to talk about the war at sea for a year or so afterward, and then it
became a bore, and peacetime grew exciting and much more important. I
wrote about it twenty years ago (in his 1951 novel,* The Cruel Sea*), but never
again. Yet even now, a great wheeling quarter century later (1970), it is still
vivid, still awful, still a scar of sorts, however handsomely healed …*[21]

ENDNOTES

1.  Mason, Geoffrey LCDR. 'HMS *King George V* – King George Class 14-inch Gun Battleship.' naval_
    history.net. Web. Accessed July 2014.

2.  historycentre (contributor). 'HMS *King George V* – My Experiences.' BBC WW2 *People's War.*
    Article ID A3186416. 2004.

3.   Imperial War Museum. Sound recording archive. 27307. Stamp, Victor. 2004.

4.   HMAS *Sydney* was a Leander class light cruiser of the Australian navy that had been sunk in August 1942 along with three US Navy heavy cruisers in the Battle of Savo Island during the first week of the Guadalcanal campaign.

5.   The prisoner, likely suffering from a severe Vitamin B1 deficiency, would be exhibiting symptoms of dementia.

6.   Imperial War Museum. Sound recording archive. 31437. Guthrie, Gus. 2008.

7.   Drooglever, P.J. 'SEAC in Indonesia, Voices From the Past?' *International Association of Historians of Asia.* 1998. The Indonesian declaration of independence was made on 17 August 1945. The Dutch resisted the movement and fought against it until December 1949 when the United Nations mediated a peace settlement and full independence for Indonesia from the Netherlands.

8.   Waterson, Kenneth. 'HMS *Relentless* (Chapter 1): The End of the Japanese War, 1945.' BBC WW2 *People's War.* Article ID A 2237591. 2004.

9.   This may be only partially true as other crewmen have mentioned that at least some of Victorious' planes were flown off.

10.   Imperial War Museum. Sound recording archive. 25209. Barker, Raymond. 2003.

11.   Plymouth City Council. 'Australian War Brides.' plymouth.gov.uk. Web. Accessed February 2014.

12.   Wartime Heritage Association. 'Bill West – World War II.' wartimeheritage.com. Web. Accessed February 2014.

13.   Imperial War Museum. 25209 (Barker).

14.   Plymouth City Council.

15.   Cornwallcsv (contributor). 'Donald Delves' War, Part 10: Postscript, Home, and HMS *Warspite* – The Grand Old Lady.' BBC WW2 *People's War.* Article ID A 4464399. 2005.

16.   After Italy surrendered, Stalin asked for one of the Regia Marina's new battleships as spoils of war. Neither Churchill nor Roosevelt agreed to the request, nor did they like Stalin's alternate demand for one of the Royal Navy's King George V class battleships.

17.   Imperial War Museum. 25209. (Barker).

18.   Guernseymuseum (contributor). 'Demob From HMS *Nigella*, Flower Class Corvette K-19.' BBC WW2 *People's War.* Article ID A 5079594. 2005.

19.   Monsarrat, Nicholas. *Three Corvettes.* Cassell Military Paperbacks. 1975. p. 123. This excerpt is from a chapter titled, 'East Coast Corvette,' that was originally published in serialized form in several journals between 1943 and 1944.

20.   historycentre (contributor). 'HMS *King George V* – My Expriences.' BBC WW2 *People's War.* Article ID A3186416. 2004.

21.   Monsarrat, Nicholas. p. 273.